HANDS-ON MATH PROJECTS
with REAL-LIFE APPLICATIONS

Ready-to-Use Lessons and Materials for Grades 6-12

GARY ROBERT MUSCHLA ♦ JUDITH A. MUSCHLA

Illustrations by Collen Duffey Shoup

**THE CENTER FOR APPLIED
RESEARCH IN EDUCATION**
West Nyack, New York 10994

Library of Congress Cataloging-in-Publication Data

Muschla, Judith A.
    Hands-on math projects with real-life applications / by Judith Muschla
and Gary Robert Muschla : illustrations by Collen Duffey Shoup.
      p.   cm.
    ISBN 0-87628-384-9 (paper)
    1. Mathematics—Study and teaching.   2. Activity programs in education.
I. Muschla, Gary Robert. II. Title.
QA11.M764 1996   96-24597
510 ' .71 ' 2—dc20   CIP

Printed in the United States of America

10 9 8 7 6 5 4 3

ISBN 0-87628-384-9

ATTENTION: CORPORATIONS AND SCHOOLS

The Center for Applied Research in Education books are available at quantity discounts with
bulk purchase for educational, business, or sales promotional use. For information, please
write to: Prentice Hall Career & Personal Development Special Sales, 113 Sylvan Avenue,
Englewood Cliffs, NJ 07632. Please supply: title of book, ISBN number, quantity, how the
book will be used, date needed.

**THE CENTER FOR APPLIED RESEARCH
IN EDUCATION**
West Nyack, NY 10994
A Simon & Schuster Company

On the World Wide Web at http://www.phdirect.com

Prentice Hall International (UK) Limited, *London*
Prentice Hall of Australia Pty. Limited, *Sydney*
Prentice Hall Canada, Inc., *Toronto*
Prentice Hall Hispanoamericana, S.A., *Mexico*
Prentice Hall of India Private Limited, *New Delhi*
Prentice Hall of Japan, Inc., *Tokyo*
Simon & Schuster Asia Pte. Ltd., *Singapore*
Editora Prentice Hall do Brasil, Ltda., *Rio de Janeiro*

For Erin

ABOUT THE AUTHORS

Gary Robert Muschla received his B.A. and M.A.T. from Trenton State College, and teaches at Appleby School in Spotswood, New Jersey. He has spent many of his 21 years in the classroom teaching mathematics at the elementary level. He has also taught reading and writing, and has been a successful freelance writer, editor, and ghostwriter. A member of the Authors Guild and the National Writers Association, he has conducted writing workshops for teachers and students.

Mr. Muschla has also authored four other resources for teachers: *Writing Resource Activities Kit* (The Center for Applied Research in Education, 1989), *The Writing Teacher's Book of Lists* (Prentice Hall, 1991), *Writing Workshop Survival Kit* (The Center for Applied Research in Education, 1993), and *English Teacher's Great Books Activities Kit* (The Center for Applied Research in Education, 1994).

Judith Muschla received her B.A. in Mathematics from Douglass College at Rutgers University and is certified K–12. She has taught mathematics at both the middle school and high school in South River, New Jersey for the last 21 years. She was a recipient of the 1990–91 Governor's Teacher Recognition Program Award in New Jersey.

While serving as a Team Leader at the South River Middle School, she helped revise the mathematics curriculum to reflect the standards of the NCTM, coordinated interdisciplinary units, and conducted mathematics workshops for teachers and parents.

Hands-on Math Projects with Real-Life Applications is the second book Gary and Judith Muschla have co-authored. Their first was *The Math Teacher's Book of Lists* (Prentice Hall, 1995).

ACKNOWLEDGMENTS

We'd like to thank James Pope, principal at South River High School, William Skowronski, principal at Appleby School, our supervisors, and colleagues for their support and encouragement of our efforts.

Special thanks to Caroline Fitzgerald and Geri Priest, who took the time to read our manuscript and offer helpful suggestions. Thanks also to Jamie Egan for helping us to better understand the mathematical aspects of music.

We are indebted to Sonia Helton, Professor of Education at the University of South Florida, for her insightful comments and recommendations for the projects in this book.

We greatly appreciate the help of Susan Kolwicz, our editor, who was always ready to answer our questions and offer advice that enabled us to make this a better book. Our appreciation also to Zsuzsa Neff, our production editor, who managed the task of turning our manuscript into a book.

Thanks to Colleen Duffey Shoup, whose illustrations have enlivened these pages.

And finally, we'd like to thank our students. In the end, they are why all of us are in this business.

ABOUT MATHEMATICS INSTRUCTION

Math is everywhere in our society, and its importance is increasing. As we move into the 21st century, it's becoming clear that most of the quality jobs being created require mathematical knowledge and skills. To compete in today's information-based world economy, students will need to analyze data, think logically, make decisions, and solve real problems. Knowing just the basics isn't good enough any more.

To prepare our students for the workplace demands they will face, we must revise our math curriculums so that students learn the skills that will enable them to compete. Math classes must offer students the opportunity to learn how to work individually and in groups. Students need a classroom environment where they are challenged to solve real-life problems, where they may collaborate and share ideas, where they express their thoughts in writing, where they utilize calculators and computers, and where they recognize that mathematics is not an isolated subject, but that it is connected to other disciplines. Math truly is all around us.

These are exciting days in mathematics. As we approach the new century, the needs for math skills will be greater than ever. As a math teacher, it is your task to provide your students with meaningful activities that will stimulate their minds, and help them to master the skills with which they may build successful and rewarding lives.

We trust that you will find this book to be a helpful resource as you encourage and support your students in their efforts to learn math. Our best wishes to you.

Judith and Gary Muschla

HOW TO USE THIS RESOURCE

Hands-on Math Projects with Real-Life Applications, for grades 6–12, is divided into two parts. Part I, "Implementing Projects in the Math Class," contains three chapters that are devoted to management. Part II, "The Projects," contains 60 math projects you may use to enhance your curriculum.

Read through Part I in its entirety. The information will help you to successfully implement project activities in your class. After reading Part I, you may select those projects from Part II that best support your programs and the needs of your students.

In Part I, Chapter 1 provides an overview of how to incorporate math projects in your class, Chapter 2 offers a variety of specific classroom management techniques and suggestions, and Chapter 3 shares several methods for evaluating the work your students do on projects. Each of the chapters includes several lists for teachers. The lists summarize information for various topics, making it easy for you to find the information you need. For example, "The Teacher's Role During Math Projects" outlines the many tasks you may assume when your students are engaged in project work. You'll find that your role expands when projects become a part of your class.

Each chapter also includes several reproducibles for students. The reproducibles can be quite helpful in establishing the routines necessary for successful project work. For example, when you divide your class into teams of 4 to 5 students for the first time, it's possible that many students may not have had much experience in working cooperatively to solve a complex problem. Distributing copies of "Rules for Working in Math Teams" highlights the behaviors that characterize effective teams. Knowing what is expected of them helps many students to behave appropriately.

Part II contains 60 projects that are divided into six major sections:

Section 1, "Math and Science"

Section 2, "Math and Social Studies"

Section 3, "Math and Language"

Section 4, "Math and Art and Music"

Section 5, "Math and Sports and Recreation"

Section 6, "Math and Life Skills"

Although the breakdown is useful for planning interdisciplinary units or finding a project that ties in to another subject, there is much overlap and all of the projects stand alone. Each project may be used to introduce, enhance, or conclude a unit or topic. Projects may also be used as challenges, enrichment, or extra credit. Some projects may be utilized as ongoing activities; for example, Project 31, "Keeping a Math Journal," or Project 32, "Math Portfolios." Project 24, "The Mathematics Publishing Company," shows students how to create and produce a mathematics magazine, which you may decide to publish regularly throughout the year.

Each project follows the same format. First comes information for the teacher, including background, goals of the project, math skills that are covered, special materials and equipment that are needed, and development. Next, for students, is the Student Guide, which provides strategies and suggestions on how they may solve the problem the project presents. Data Sheets and/or Worksheets provide students with additional information or a specialized workspace. The Student Guides, Data Sheets, and Worksheets, which are numbered according to each project, are reproducible for your convenience.

We suggest that you use this book as a resource, selecting projects you need to enhance your curriculum. The 60 projects contained in this book offer a variety of real-life situations that will help your students to realize the relevance math has in their lives, while at the same time reinforcing specific mathematics skills. The projects will help to prepare your students for the years to come.

CONTENTS

Part II The Projects—35

SECTION 1
MATH AND SCIENCE—37

SECTION 2
MATH AND SOCIAL STUDIES—99

SECTION 3
MATH AND LANGUAGE—151

SECTION 4
MATH AND ART AND MUSIC—211

SECTION 5
MATH AND SPORTS AND RECREATION—263

SECTION 6
MATH AND LIFE SKILLS—319

Skills List

Various skills are interwoven throughout the projects of this book. This list highlights what we feel are some of the most important ones. Each skill below is followed by the numbers of the projects in which that skill appears.

Writing to communicate ideas about math: 1, 3, 4, 9, 10, 24, 25, 26, 27, 29, 30, 31, 38

Using math to communicate ideas: 1, 3, 4, 18, 22, 33, 34, 40

Conducting a poll: 9

Classifying: 9

Writing a questionnaire: 12

Constructing frequency tables: 12

Collecting or researching data: 3, 4, 9, 10, 12, 17, 18, 19, 21, 23, 38, 45, 54, 57

Organizing data: 3, 4, 18, 19, 21, 23, 34

Reading charts, tables, labels: 3, 8, 9

Creating graphs, tables, charts: 1, 2, 10, 17, 19, 45

Determining the mean (average): 3, 4, 45

Interpreting or analyzing data: 2, 3, 10, 17, 18, 45

Making decisions: 1, 7, 8, 9, 17, 43, 44, 48, 50, 51, 52, 54, 57

Drawing conclusions: 2, 3, 17, 43, 44, 45, 48, 50

Making predictions based on math: 2, 12

Using statistics: 18, 45, 46

Estimating: 3, 4, 9, 43, 44, 48, 50, 51, 52, 54, 55, 57

Rounding: 14, 47, 50, 51

Using percents: 12, 19, 47, 57

Using measurements: 7, 11, 14, 50, 51, 53

Using scale: 7, 14, 53

Making a model: 11

Measuring distance: 14, 51

Measuring and dividing line segments: 13

Locating points on a grid: 13

Creating a timeline: 15

Visualizing spatial relationships: 11, 36

Using protractors to measure angles: 35, 42

Identifying types of angles: 41, 42

Recognizing parallel and perpendicular lines: 41

Recognizing geometric shapes: 7

Identifying two- and three-dimensional shapes: 6, 41

Recognizing polygons: 35, 42

Identifying congruent figures: 42

Understanding properties of equilateral triangles: 39, 42

Finding the sum of interior angles of triangles: 42

Finding the sum of interior angles of quadrilaterals: 42

Finding the measure of interior angles of regular polygons: 35

Using tessellations: 35

Identifying types of symmetry: 6, 13, 41, 42

Using transformations: 35

Identifying regular octahedrons: 39

Understanding Euler's formula: 39

Determining volume: 11

Using a compass: 39

Identifying the parts of circles: 39

Using decimal computation: 3, 4

Calculating with units of time: 4

Calculating with money: 7, 8, 9, 17, 43, 44, 48, 50, 51, 52, 54, 55, 57, 59

Estimating and planning a budget: 7, 44, 51, 52

Determining cost per person: 9, 48, 50

Comparing prices: 17, 50

Calculating miles per gallon: 51

Completing an order form: 55

Using a formula to find the finance charge on a loan: 57

Maintaining a checkbook balance: 59

Understanding the use of numbers as indicators: 56

Recognizing math's changing role in society: 16

Part I

IMPLEMENTING PROJECTS
in the
MATH CLASS

chapter 1

PROJECTS IN THE MATH CLASS—OVERVIEW

In a well-run math class, computation, problem-solving, and critical thinking are all taught. Instead of learning skills in isolation, students learn math in context where they can see how it is applied in real situations. In this way they come to recognize the importance of math in their own lives. The connection between math and the real world is a strong one. This is especially true of math classes in which projects are an important part of the curriculum.

Filled with activity and enthusiasm, a successful project-oriented math class is a center of individual learning, collaboration, cooperation, and sharing. Students work alone, together, and with the teacher. As fundamental skills are taught, practiced, and mastered, they are incorporated in problems that arise out of real-life situations. Students thus utilize the skills they are learning in meaningful ways.

YOUR ROLE

Your role changes when your students work on math projects. Along with your traditional responsibilities of introducing concepts, demonstrating skills via example problems, and grading the work of your students, you will become a facilitator and promoter. The horizons of your teaching will expand. More of your time will be spent working directly with individuals and groups. As students work on solving problems, you will circulate around the room, offering advice and suggestions, asking questions that lead to insights or direction, and giving encouragement and praise. Sometimes you may simply monitor a group's efforts, or model appropriate behavior. Occasionally you may need to pull a group back on task. See "The Teacher's Role During Math Projects.

There are many ways you can incorporate projects into your curriculum. While following your text, you can easily provide regular project activities. You may build time for projects into your schedule; for example, a day or two each week, or do units on projects a few times a year. Some teachers introduce a multi-step project and then give students time to work on it at the end of class over the next few days. No matter how you provide the time, however, you should be consistent. Students not only need sufficient time for working on projects, they also need to know when they will be working on them. This enables students to come to class prepared and ready to work.

The Teacher's Role During Math Projects

Since discovery is such an important part of any project, you must encourage your students to assume much of the responsibility for their learning and progress. Your role changes. Along with your traditional duties, you will be spending some of your class time doing many of the following:

- Presenting multi-step, critical-thinking projects based on real-life situations.
- Organizing and monitoring groups so that members work effectively together.
- Modeling appropriate behavior and problem-solving skills.
- Demonstrating to students what it is to be an enthusiastic problem-solver by showing them how you are willing to tackle those seemingly "impossible" projects.
- Brainstorming with groups.
- Guiding students in their research efforts.
- Showing students that process is crucial to finding solutions.
- Offering suggestions to solve problems.
- Offering encouragement and applauding efforts.
- Explaining that mistakes are merely steppingstones to finding solutions, and to learning.
- Answering questions.
- Helping students to sort through their thoughts as they consider problem-solving strategies.
- Showing students that various strategies may be used to solve the same problem.
- Providing sufficient time for working on projects.
- Monitoring student behavior and ensuring that classroom procedures are followed.
- Keeping students on task.
- Evaluating and assessing student progress.
- Providing time for sharing results.

PROBLEM-SOLVING STRATEGIES

Most of the math projects your students will be doing will require the use of computation, problem-solving and critical-thinking skills, and decision making. Since the type and nature of problems vary, there can be no set plan or step-by-step process that can be used all the time. You should familiarize your students with various strategies they can use as needed. Emphasize that strategies are methods or procedures that can be used alone or with other strategies. If a student should ask what strategy is best for solving a particular problem, a good answer is "the one that works best for you." You will likely find that different students will use different strategies to solve the same problem.

While some students may be quite adept at problem-solving, many will need guidance, and you may wish to distribute copies of "Problem-Solving Strategies." It is a guide that can help students get started in solving problems and keep them moving along.

There's also much you can do in regular lessons to help students acquire sound problem-solving skills that will be useful to them throughout their lives. See "Helping Students Develop Problem-Solving Skills" for a list of suggestions.

A vital part of any project is the sharing of solutions and results at the end of the activity. When results are shared, students have the opportunity to hear other viewpoints, learn about other methods that might have been used to solve problems, and realize that others may have experienced some of the same stumbling blocks they did. Not only does this help reduce an individual's feelings that he or she is the only one having trouble, it also helps build a sense of class community and problem-solving camaraderie.

Sharing may be oral, through discussions or presentations, or written in the form of logs or reports. Thus, speaking and writing become essential components of your math class.

Perhaps the biggest factor that holds many students back from becoming good problem-solvers is lack of confidence. Many students doubt they can solve complex problems and give up with little effort. Explain to your students that problem-solving skills come with practice. Just like anything else—learning a musical instrument, excelling at gymnastics, or playing chess—the more they work at solving problems, the better they will become. Distribute copies of "What It Takes to Become a Top Problem-Solver" to highlight some of the characteristics that successful problem-solvers share. The list can serve as a guide, detailing traits and attitudes your students should strive to acquire throughout the year.

CREATING YOUR OWN PROJECTS

While this book provides projects that require various steps and strategies, you may eventually wish to create projects of your own, designed specifically for the needs of your students. Material for math projects is all around you. As you develop projects, keep in mind the following points that will help ensure your projects are stimulating and exciting to your students:

1. Base your projects on real-life situations that are meaningful to your students.
2. Design projects that capture the interest of your students.

3. Make sure your students possess the mathematical skills to solve the problems they will encounter in your projects.

4. Develop projects that require critical thinking and decision making.

5. Create projects that require students to formulate a plan to find a solution.

For suggestions where you can find material from which to create projects for your students, see "Sources for Developing Math Projects."

Without question, math projects offer many benefits to students. Perhaps most important, when students work on authentic problems, they see how the math skills they are learning may be applied to the real world. Math projects open the door to bringing other subjects and disciplines into the math class, and students quickly recognize that math is interwoven through many parts of their lives. Math projects also give students the opportunity to work together cooperatively, share their experiences, and celebrate the solving of problems that might be overwhelming for one person to manage. Furthermore, when students collaborate on a project, students of all abilities have the chance to contribute to the solution. Everybody has a part to play, a role to fill. Everyone can be a contributor to and a sharer in success.

Problem-Solving Strategies

There are many ways to solve multi-step problems. If you believe there can be only one or two, you limit your options and reduce your chances of finding a solution. Following are some suggestions and strategies.

BEFORE YOU BEGIN SEEKING THE SOLUTION:

- Make sure you understand the problem. This may involve rereading it several times or discussing it with your group.
- Be sure you understand the question and what answers you are seeking.
- Look for "hidden" questions.
- Find the important information the problem provides, and eliminate information that is not essential. (Sometimes problems contain facts that you don't need.)
- Supply any missing information. You may need to do research, collect, and analyze data.
- Make sure you understand any special facts, data, or units of measurement.

AS YOU SEEK A SOLUTION, CONSIDER ALL OF THESE STRATEGIES:

- Look for patterns, relationships, connections, sequences, or causes and effects.
- Use guess and check (also called trial and error). Choose a place to start, try a solution, and see if it works. If it doesn't, try another.
- Write a list, organizing your facts and information. Sometimes this can show relationships that otherwise might be overlooked.
- Construct a table or chart. This is another way of identifying relationships.
- Think logically. Look for sequence and order.
- Rely on common sense. Some answers simply aren't possible. Don't waste time pursuing them.
- Sketch or draw a model to help you visualize the problem.
- Break down the problem into manageable steps, making it simpler. Solve a sub-problem that leads to the solution of a bigger problem.
- Look at the problem from different angles.
- Estimate. Rounding numbers off can make it easier to find a solution. Using whole numbers rather than fractions may help you to see operations more clearly.
- Act out the problem.
- Keep notes of your attempted solutions. This will reduce the chances that you'll repeat steps that don't move you forward.
- Review your notes and attempts at solutions periodically. By rechecking what you've done, you might see something you overlooked.
- Don't give up. The persistent problem-solver finds solutions.

WHEN YOU BELIEVE YOU HAVE FOUND THE ANSWER:

- Double-check your work.
- Be certain you used all the important information.
- Recheck your calculations.
- Be sure your answer is logical.

Helping Students Develop Problem-Solving Skills

You can help your students learn critical-thinking and problem-solving skills by doing the following:

- Present students with real-life problems to which they can relate.

- Offer problems that have multiple solutions and can be solved through several strategies.

- Encourage your students to try various strategies in solving problems.

- Organize students into cooperative teams.

- Encourage students to brainstorm for ideas that might lead to solutions.

- Give problems that have missing information or too much information. Such problems will require students to supply or eliminate data.

- Give problems that tie in to other subjects.

- Encourage students to keep logs or notes of their efforts at solving difficult problems.

- Require students to write explanations of how they solved problems.

- Remind students to always check answers for logic and accuracy.

- Encourage discussion and the sharing of solutions.

What It Takes to Become a Top Problem-Solver

Top problem-solvers share many of the same traits. You can become a good problem-solver. All it takes is practice. The more problems you solve, the more skilled you'll become. Try to make the following traits a part of your personality.

GOOD PROBLEM-SOLVERS ARE:

- Confident they can solve just about any problem.

- Persistent in solving problems.

- Willing to try different strategies to solve problems.

- Able to find important information and eliminate unimportant facts.

- Able to recognize patterns, relationships, and connections.

- Able to look at a problem from various viewpoints.

- Open to new ideas.

- Willing to make notes to keep track of their attempts at solutions.

- Able to draw upon other experiences in the solving of problems.

- Able to use logic and common sense.

Sources for Developing Math Projects

Good material for creating your own math projects is all around you. We find the following sources particularly useful.

- Your math text (especially the newer texts) likely contains sections such as "Challenges" that offer interesting facts or situations you can easily turn into fine projects. Some texts have sections of databanks that provide information that can serve as the basis for projects.

- National and local newspapers contain an assortment of valuable information. Charts and tables can be especially helpful.

- Regional and national magazines can be good sources of information for projects.

- Almanacs and other reference books can provide unusual and interesting data on countless topics.

- Major events at school can be your springboard for creating projects. Use homecoming, the Valentine's Day dance, or the prom to capture the interest of your students.

- Books of math puzzles and games frequently offer a wealth of ideas for projects.

- Consult with your colleagues and develop projects that include two or more subject areas. Science and social studies, in particular, share many topics with mathematics.

chapter 2

MANAGING PROJECTS IN YOUR MATH CLASS

A successful math class, where projects are an important part of the course of study, is the result of effective planning and management. Along with teaching required material, you must provide meaningful projects that have real-life applications. These are not easy charges. As students work on projects, they will be engaged in various tasks: they will need to consider different strategies, gather and analyze information, confer with each other, manipulate models, perform calculations, and test possible solutions. All this requires an environment that promotes vigorous inquiry, encourages students to assume the responsibility for their learning, and supports both individual and group activities.

STRUCTURING YOUR CLASS

Math projects offer students a chance to utilize various skills in solving authentic problems. Since projects often reach beyond the math class, they offer you an excellent way to broaden the scope of your curriculum and introduce exciting new activities to your teaching. There are many ways you can incorporate projects into your classes.

Perhaps the easiest is to select projects that support the unit you are teaching. For example, if you are studying a unit in geometry, Project 7, "Designing a Flowerbed," in which students work with rectangles, squares, circles, and scale, will be useful. If you are teaching a unit on data analysis, Project 12, "An Election Poll," will supplement your instruction.

Projects used to enhance a unit can be built into your daily schedule. We suggest you take a class period to introduce and begin the project. Explain the project, distribute any materials students might need, organize teams, and give students 20 minutes or so to plan, brainstorm potential strategies, and get started.

After this introductory period, resume your regular lessons, reserving about 20 minutes at the end of each period for students to continue working on the project. Providing students with time at the end of class eliminates the need for them to arrange to meet outside of class (although sometimes students become so involved with a project that they will meet on their own). This also allows you to assign their ordinary amount of homework, and continue moving forward with the unit. Since not all teams will finish at the same time, groups that finish early may work on extensions of the project, write in math journals, or simply do homework. When every team is done, you should schedule a period for sharing results.

Another way to incorporate projects into your classes is to periodically set aside time for them. After you complete a unit, take three or four days to work on a project. Some teachers prefer this method because it gives students a break from the routines of the class, but doesn't interfere with the general curriculum.

Perhaps you'll decide to build projects into your schedule. You might reserve every Tuesday and Friday for working on projects. This plan has the advantage of establishing a regular schedule that ensures time for project work. Since the projects of this book stand alone, each can be used at any time during the year and still provide the benefits of using a variety of skills in meaningful contexts.

Some projects, especially those for individuals, may be completed at home. You might give students a choice of these projects either as assignments or bonus activities. Even though the projects are completed on the student's time, you should provide class time for sharing. Responses to their results are important to students.

When selecting projects for your students, be sure to consider their needs and abilities. Never assign projects that require skills your students haven't yet mastered. Students will find such projects to be a frustrating struggle, and any new skills they acquire will be offset by the negative emotions they come to feel for math.

Without question, math projects offer students several benefits. They permit students to utilize many skills in solving various problems, give students a chance to take ownership of their mathematics learning, and help students to see the relevance between math and real life.

CREATING AND MAINTAINING A POSITIVE ENVIRONMENT

Problem-solving thrives in an environment in which people work on problems that have valid applications to life, feel free to risk making mistakes, and are encouraged to share their ideas. The best problem-solving occurs in classes where students enjoy the freedom to pursue learning in their own way. The tone you set in your classroom, your expectations, and the procedures you maintain are the foundation for such an environment.

Since students usually rise, or fall, to a teacher's expectations, always discuss your goals for the class with your students at the beginning of the year. Share with them how you intend to conduct the class, how the class will be organized, and what will be covered. Note what you expect from them.

For students to work efficiently on math projects, they need a classroom that is logistically comfortable for problem-solving. Tables are ideal; however, if you don't have tables, you can push desks together. Either way, you should provide enough room among teams so that they can function as single entities without distractions from other groups. Along with enough space among teams, there should be enough work area for students to discuss possible strategies with each other, confer about data, manipulate and examine models, and work on calculations.

Support problem-solving in whatever ways you can. Bulletin boards, corridor display cases, media center exhibits, and math fairs are just some ways you can draw attention to your program. Always look for ways to highlight lists of problem-solving strategies, interesting articles about math, and the work of your students.

While there is much you can do to promote success in your classes, students, too, must strive to make the class beneficial. This is particularly true during group activities.

Your students must be willing to accept more responsibility than is demanded by the traditional class. During project activities, they must remain focused on the tasks. Group work is not a time to talk about who might be named homecoming king or queen. Distributing copies of "The Responsibilities of the Math Student" to your students is an excellent way to share basic expectations for student behavior.

Unquestionably, student learning flourishes in the "right environment." One of your most important tasks as a teacher is to create a classroom filled with enthusiasm, the spirit of inquiry, and the desire to learn. The best classes are founded on the spirit of cooperation and energetic intellectual pursuit, in which it is believed that math can be learned (and enjoyed!) by everyone. For a summary of characteristics of math classes that have a positive atmosphere, see "The Right Environment."

TEACHING SUGGESTIONS

While every teacher has his or her individual techniques and methods, we've found the following plan is helpful in presenting projects and problem-solving. It can be broken down into three parts: (1) Introduction, (2) Work Time, and (3) Wrapping Up.

Introduction

Begin a math project by presenting the situation and problems to be solved. Offer examples, review any concepts or specific skills students will need to solve the problems they will confront, and relate the project to real-life scenarios as much as possible. Encourage students to ask questions. Having a student paraphrase the project and what needs to be solved can be helpful in clarifying what everyone is to do.

Once students understand the project, distribute copies of student guide sheets and discuss the information presented there. Data sheets and additional materials, if any, should also be distributed. Having everything they need to begin helps students to see the full scope of the project.

Work Time

As students work in teams, your task is to circulate around the room, offering help, encouragement, or simply observing. This is also a time to monitor and model student behavior.

Pay close attention that a team doesn't range off the topic. If you see this happening, you might point out their mistake, or nudge them in the right direction. However, avoid giving answers to any problems. If students feel you will provide answers, they will be less inclined to do the hard thinking that will result in finding answers themselves. To encourage students to find their own answers, some teachers insist that they (the teachers) may be asked a question only after the question has been presented to the team and no one else is able to answer it.

As you observe students, you may find that a team has trouble starting. Sometimes this is caused by students not being able to focus the problem. Have students restate the problem and break it down into parts, concentrating their efforts to identify the most important facts. Teams may also have trouble finding viable strategies that will lead to solutions. In this case, suggest that teams brainstorm various strategies and examine each one to see if it leads to a possible solution.

As you move around the room, be aware of the interactions of the members of each team. You'll likely see that some groups work well together with everyone sharing ideas, others are dominated by one or two members, and some are just unmotivated. When a team is working well, leave it alone. Merely offering a comment might disrupt its momentum. Remember, a project activity is a time for students to discover solutions. If, however, a group is not working well, you should sit in on it and model appropriate behavior. Make sure everyone is participating, and encourage team members to help one another. If necessary, for a time, assume the role of team leader to get things going, then gradually fade into the background as students begin to assume ownership of the project. In some teams you may need to remind students of the proper procedures and behavior often, especially during the first few weeks of class.

Wrapping Up

Sharing is essential to the successful culmination of a math project. Discussing methods and results helps students to realize that some problems have multiple solutions, which may be discovered through various strategies. This is an important lesson of authentic problem-solving. In the real world, many problems have several solutions and can be solved in many ways. For more information on sharing, see the section "The Importance of Sharing" presented later in this chapter.

INDIVIDUAL AND TEAM CONFERENCES

As students work on projects, you will monitor the progress of the teams. In many cases, teams will have questions, or you will need to discuss procedures, rules, or behavior. You will undoubtedly be conducting conferences with individuals or the entire team.

A conference doesn't have to be long; in fact, it may last only a minute or two. In most cases it will be conducted at the student's work area. The purpose of any conference is to help students better understand the project they are working on, as well as help them to improve their understanding of mathematics. Often you may find that students need you only to answer a simple question. In such instances, provide guidance and let them get back to work. However, if an individual or team seems stuck, use this as your starting point for the conference.

Focus any conference on a particular problem or skill. If you try to do too much, you'll only confuse students, or provide them with too much information. Either way, you'll end their efforts to solve the problem. During the conference be sure to keep your tone positive and offer specifics. You may need to point a team in the direction for finding more information, offer encouragement to the team that is about to give up, or assure a team that its efforts are worthwhile.

When you give praise, it should be genuine, because students can tell when it's not. Always avoid negative or sarcastic remarks, for these will only discourage students. The conference should be a time of help and support.

The Responsibilities of the Math Student

A successful math class results from several people working together to learn math. Accepting the following responsibilities is the first step to making your class worthwhile.

- Each day report to class on time and ready to work.

- Remember to bring your text, notebooks, pencils, calculators, and other materials to class.

- Pay attention in class; ask questions when you don't understand something.

- Work hard. *Everyone can learn math.* Finish your classwork and home-work.

- Work cooperatively with other students in groups. Share your ideas and be willing to listen to the ideas of others.

- Try various strategies in solving problems.

- Remember that solving complicated, multi-step problems takes time. Be persistent.

- Follow the classroom rules and procedures.

- Behave properly.

- Recognize the importance of math in your life.

The Right Environment

The following characteristics are found in math classes described as having a positive atmosphere.

- The goals of the class are high enough so that students have to work hard, but not so high that they feel frustrated with math and its applications.
- The classroom is built on openness, fresh ideas, and sharing.
- It is believed that everyone—regardless of gender and ethnicity—can learn math.
- Students' work is prominently displayed.
- The classroom is designed to support inquiry and problem-solving.
- The classroom is bright and cheerful.
- The classroom adheres to orderly procedures. Students maintain appropriate behavior and follow the classroom rules.
- Goals and objectives are clear to students.
- Classroom rules are fair and consistent.
- The grading system is reasonable and equitable.
- The teacher interacts with students, and is a guide, nurturer, cheerleader, and provider of information.
- Teachers model problem-solving behavior and share with students their own enthusiasm for finding solutions.
- Math is connected to real-life problems and situations.
- Cooperation is encouraged.
- Enough time is provided for problem-solving.
- Students are encouraged to consider and explain their reasoning during problem-solving.
- Students are encouraged to use various strategies in solving problems. They come to recognize that the same problem may have many solutions.
- Sharing is encouraged, especially how students worked out solutions to problems.
- Calculators and computers are used whenever technology is appropriate.
- Math is related to other subjects as much as possible.
- Manipulative materials are used whenever possible to show students relationships.
- Students learn the value of mathematics in their lives.
- Students and teachers become partners in learning mathematics.

THE VALUE OF COOPERATIVE PROBLEM-SOLVING

In many jobs people work in teams, and the experience your students gain now working together on math projects will serve them not only in your class but in the future as well. Teamwork fosters inquiry and discussion, and students often learn more when working together than they do trying to solve a complicated problem alone. Cooperative learning also provides students with the opportunity to acquire valuable social skills.

When students work in teams, they are more likely to take an active role. It is easier to get involved because the team provides support to individuals. Seeing other team members struggling with the same problems helps students feel less intimidated about offering their thoughts, and many students who wouldn't risk sharing ideas with the whole class usually will share with their team. Furthermore, when they offer suggestions toward the solution of a problem, they receive immediate feedback. This sharing frequently results in a free-wheeling give-and-take of mathematics that is as stimulating as it is useful.

As a team works on a math project, it becomes involved in various activities. Team members need to discuss and assign tasks, reflect on how to approach the problem, test strategies, gather and analyze data, reach solutions, and determine how to justify and share results. Teamwork helps build student confidence, promotes critical thinking, and results in a sense of ownership of the problem.

ORGANIZING YOUR TEAMS

Random groups tend to make the best math teams, although you should reserve the right to make adjustments. Groups of four to six generally work well for complex projects. With less than four, it's sometimes hard to generate enough ideas, especially if one of the students is absent or is shy or quiet.

An easy way to make random pairings is to simply count down your roster in sets of five, assigning the numbers 1 to 5 to students, as in this example:

Jim–1

Alicia–2

Tara–3

Rosa–4

Justine–5

Peter–1

Chris–2

Manuel–3

Dane–4

Erin–5

etc.

All of the 1's in the class would be on Team 1, all of the 2's would be on Team 2, and so on. This provides a good general breakdown. Before announcing the teams to the students, review them and make sure you have a mix of high and low abilities, as well as a mix of gender and ethnicity. Make any final changes before informing students about the groups.

You should also change your teams periodically. Rearranging groups allows students to interact with various personalities and see different viewpoints. In the real world, individuals are often required to work with people of varying outlooks and abilities. When making new teams, you can easily switch two members from each of the existing teams. Switching only one member keeps too much of the original team together.

After you have arranged your teams, explain to your students the purpose of working together. Suggest that a team may work most efficiently when tasks are divided. You may also suggest that students assume various roles that will help define responsibilities. For example, one student might serve as team leader. Her purpose is to keep the group on task and guide it toward the solution of the problem. Another might be the recorder, whose responsibility includes writing down the team's ideas, strategies, and conclusions. The list "How to Set Up Project Teams" provides many suggestions for organizing groups.

Unless your students have worked in teams before, they will probably need training in the procedures of teamwork. You should focus much of your attention on team interaction during the first project. You'll likely need to model behavior and remind students of procedures often, especially in the beginning of the year. Sit in on the various groups and show them how to act and behave. Acquiring the skills necessary for effective group work may take students a few weeks, and distributing copies of "Rules for Working in Math Teams" can be helpful in discussing expected behavior.

THE IMPORTANCE OF SHARING

Sharing is crucial to projects and problem-solving. Becoming aware of other strategies and solutions can broaden students' understanding of math. Sharing may take the form of an oral presentation or discussion, or be a written log or report.

At the end of a project, you should provide time for teams to share their methods and findings. For oral sharing, the student designated as presenter shares the team's results with the class. Encourage students to discuss successful strategies, as well as earlier strategies that they attempted but that didn't work. It's possible that other teams tried the same strategies, but got different results or experienced different problems. The more math is discussed, the more opportunities students have to gain new insights.

After the presentation, encourage questions from the class. Don't permit questions during sharing, because the presenter might become distracted and may not cover all of the essential points. During questioning, other members of the team may help the presenter, but only one student should speak at a time. This is also the time for members of other teams to offer comments or observations. Emphasize that any discussion should be positive, and don't allow sarcastic or negative statements.

How to Set Up Project Teams

Working together in teams offers students an excellent way to learn math. The following guidelines can help you to organize your math teams.

- For complex projects, groups of four to six work best for middle and high school students.

- Organize your teams randomly; however, be sure to mix abilities, genders, ethnicity, and personalities.

- To build team spirit suggest that teams select a name and design a team logo.

- Rearrange your teams periodically. This gives students the chance to interact with others and experience new working relationships.

- Always explain the purpose of group work, and your expected behaviors. Some students may have little experience working in teams.

- Since teams often benefit from a division of labor, consider having students assume specific roles, including:

  —*Leader*, who guides the team toward its goal and makes sure everyone stays on task.

  —*Recorder*, who keeps notes of the team's ideas, strategies, and solutions.

  —*Time monitor*, who keeps track of time and helps the Leader keep the team moving.

  —*Checker*, who reviews the work of the team.

  —*Materials monitor*, who assumes responsibility for any materials the team uses.

  —*Presenter*, who shares the team's findings with others.

Note: In small groups, students may assume more than one role.

© 1996 by The Center for Applied Research in Education

Rules for Working in Math Teams

The effectiveness of a math team depends on the ability of its members to work together. Keeping the following suggestions in mind can help you and your team work more efficiently.

Each member of the team:

- Is responsible for his or her own behavior.

- Should work with other team members.

- Should help other members.

- Should share his or her ideas.

- Should carefully consider his or her ideas before speaking.

- Should give the floor to others after speaking.

- Should listen carefully and politely when others are speaking.

- Should ask questions when he or she doesn't understand something.

- Should strive to keep the discussion on the project, and keep comments constructive.

- Should keep his or her emotions in check. When disagreements arise, they should be discussed calmly.

- Should carry out his or her role in the group the best he or she can.

Sometimes you will find that presenters may need help to cover all the issues. Guide students to report the strategies they used, their methods, procedures, and solutions. If a student becomes blocked, a helpful question from you can get him or her started again. Consider asking questions like the following:

How did you divide tasks in your group?

What was your initial plan?

What strategies did you consider?

What problems, or obstacles, did you run into?

What kinds of data did you need to gather?

How do you know your solution is valid?

Are there other possible solutions? If yes, what made you select one over the others?

At the end of sharing, summarize the project and the results obtained by the various teams. Highlight any unusual strategies or problems encountered, and be sure to discuss how the mathematics employed applies to life.

WRITING IN MATH CLASS

During the last few years, the benefits of writing in math class have become well documented. Writing provides students with a method through which they can examine and share their thoughts about mathematics in a formalized manner. Through writing students can connect concepts they've already learned with new ideas, summarize their understanding of math for themselves, and communicate their thoughts to others. Few will dispute that only when we truly understand something can we explain it and put it clearly into words.

Many types of writing can be done in math class. Some of the most common include:

- Writing about specific problems
- Formal papers
- Biographies of famous mathematicians
- Word problems for other students
- Publication of a mathematics magazine (see Project 24)
- Keeping a math journal (see Project 31)
- Maintaining a math portfolio (see Project 32)

Whenever your students write in math class, encourage them to share their thoughts and information about mathematical concepts, methods, and applications. Avoid allowing students to write about math in ways that show little thought, purpose, or insight. Students should select meaningful topics on which they can share information and their ideas.

In recent years, an extensive amount of research has been done on how people write. It has been found that authors write according to a process that has been aptly named the Writing Process. It's likely that the English teachers in your school are familiar with it. You might consult with your students' English teacher, and if he or she suggests that students use the Writing Process, you should too. You may wish to distribute copies of "The Writing Process," and discuss its stages with your students.

The Writing Process

When you are writing articles in math, it will be helpful to follow the stages of the *Writing Process.* You've probably learned about this in your English classes. Writing can be broken down into various stages, or steps. Authors go through these steps when they write, moving back and forth through the various stages as necessary. Understanding this process can help you with your writing. Following are the stages of the Writing Process.

STAGE 1: PREWRITING

- Thinking of a purpose
- Generating ideas
- Brainstorming
- Researching and gathering facts
- Analyzing ideas
- Organizing ideas
- Focusing ideas

STAGE 2: DRAFTING

- Writing
- Rearranging information and ideas as needed
- Expanding ideas

STAGE 3: REVISING

- Rewriting
- Rethinking, rearranging, deleting, adding
- Clarifying ideas
- Checking ideas
- Conducting more research
- Redrafting

STAGE 4: EDITING

- Proofreading
- Making any final corrections

STAGE 5: PUBLISHING OR SHARING

- Sharing your written work with others
- Producing copies of your work
- Displaying your work

USING CALCULATORS AND COMPUTERS

Skill in using technology is a necessity for many jobs, and will only become more important in the future. Technology should be considered a tool that enables students to focus their efforts on the higher-level skills of problem-solving. If students are more concerned about performing basic calculations with pencil and paper, they will be less concerned with exploring possible solutions to a problem. Rather, they will be more interested in simply "getting the job done," and will be glad to be finished with the tedious task of computation. Imagine a carpenter using only a handsaw instead of a power saw in the building of a house. (Craftsmanship has its limits.)

If you have access to computers, incorporate them as much as possible in your classes. Along with word processing for writing math magazines, reports, and articles, computers can be used to organize and analyze data, perform calculations, create spreadsheets, and draw graphs. If your school has a computer room, perhaps you can reserve time for students to work there.

By seventh grade many students are comfortable using computers (most students work on them at home and at school), and they are able to master new software easily. If you have the opportunity to take your class to a computer room, you might run a computer seminar for two or three days to familiarize students with the software they may use. (Preview any software to make sure it is appropriate and you understand how to run it.) After your initial introduction, ask those students who are most familiar with computers to help those who aren't. You'll find that students will pick up useful technology quickly, and it probably won't be long before they start showing you shortcuts.

A variety of software is available. If you are unfamiliar with computer software, check with the person responsible for ordering software for your school. Many software companies offer numerous titles and regularly send their catalogs to schools. Local software stores and many mail-order companies allow teachers to preview titles. Before buying software, however, be sure to check its specifications and its compatibility with your computers.

Technology can help your students go beyond mere solutions to true insights. Utilize technology in your math classes as much as you can.

A FINAL WORD

A math class in which students are actively engaged in working on projects appears, on the surface, to be quite different from a traditional math class. However, a close look shows these seemingly different models have much in common. In both, students are learning math, discipline is necessary, and motivation is crucial. In the traditional math class, however, students sometimes fail to recognize the far-reaching importance mathematics has in our lives. They don't realize that math is just about everywhere. Math projects demonstrate to students that it is. Math projects not only show the connections of math to other subjects, but also offer students the chance to incorporate various skills, strategies, and methods in finding solutions to meaningful problems.

chapter 3

ASSESSING MATH PROJECTS

As the objectives and methods of math teaching change, forms of assessment must change, too. It is through assessment that we, as teachers, can validate the effectiveness of our instruction and evaluate our students' understanding of mathematics. Assessment should always be viewed as an essential part of the learning process, and should involve both you and your students.

You may choose from a variety of tools when assessing your students' work on projects, including: observation logs, checklists, and point systems. Because these assessment methods are flexible, you can tailor them to meet your needs. Combining the assessments of projects with the tests and quizzes of the general curriculum can give you a detailed profile of your students' overall achievement in your class.

OBSERVATION LOGS

As you move around the classroom during project work, you may observe students working individually or in groups. Writing down your observations will provide you with a permanent record of their progress. A practical way to do this is to use either the "Individual Observation Log" or the "Group Observation Log," each of which is provided.

To reduce your workload to a manageable level, plan to observe only five to ten students per day in each class. Attach individual log sheets to a clipboard and carry it with you around the room, focusing your attention on the students you wish to observe that day.

When completing the logs, you may record items that indicate mathematical thinking, understanding of concepts, insights, or reflections. You might also note behavior. Selecting two or three skills or behaviors to concentrate on reduces the chances you'll feel overwhelmed with things to look for. It's helpful to develop your own system of shorthand using abbreviations, codes, and phrases. For example:

- Identify names with initials. "John" becomes "J."
- Abbreviate frequently used words. "Excellent" is "ex", "good" is "g," "fair" is "f," "well" is "w," "strategy" is "strat," "work" is "wk," "process" is "proc," "question" is "quest," "group" is "gp," "illustrate" is "il," "problem" is "prob."
- Use phrases whenever possible.

Here's a sample entry on an individual log: "Wked w with gp. Offered sketch to il prob."

INDIVIDUAL OBSERVATION LOG

Name _____   Section _____

Project _____

Date	Comments

GROUP OBSERVATION LOG

Names _____

_____

_____ Section _____

Project _____

Date	Comments

Conferences provide a fine opportunity to gain an understanding of your students' growth in mathematics. Simply talking to students about the project they are working on can give you insight to their thoughts and feelings about math.

While you can learn much about your students when they ask you questions, you can also pose specific questions to your students that will help show their understanding of math. Such questions may focus on comprehension of problems, formulation of strategies, procedures, calculations, justification of solutions, relationships between ideas, or group cooperation. Having a list of questions prepared ahead of time can help you zero in on points you wish to address. Since many of the students in a class frequently share the same problems and concerns, asking a few students the same questions will often provide information about the class's general thinking. See "Possible Assessment Questions" for a list of questions that you can ask during observations and conferences.

CHECKLISTS

Checklists are another useful tool for observation. Unlike an observation log in which you write notes detailing the progress of students, a checklist is an assortment of predetermined skills and behaviors. As you observe one of the skills or behaviors on your list for a particular student, you simply check it off. As with the observation log, it's more practical to select five to ten students per day in each class on whom to focus your attention. While a checklist may include numerous skills, you may decide to concentrate on only a few, selecting those that apply best to particular projects.

A sample "Skills Checklist" is included for your use. You may utilize it in its current form or as a reference for designing your own. The checklist presented here is set up for five days. It also provides space for comments should you wish to record something in more detail.

POINT SYSTEMS FOR PROJECT ASSESSMENT

Some teachers prefer, and many schools require, numerical scores or grades for the work students do. Since most projects are long-term, complex activities, it's not easy, or usually fair, to give students a grade based simply on completion. A system where points are assigned to specific parts of the project is an alternative.

While you can break down point totals to fit your personal grading criteria, the point system that is included in this section—see "Grading Projects via a Point System"—works well for most projects. It is based on a total of 100 points, which can be easily translated to percentages.

Possible Assessment Questions

Asking students questions about their work can provide you with valuable insight about their progress. The following questions are just some you may decide to use.

- What is this problem asking? How would you explain it to a friend?

- What must you find before you can come up with a solution?

- How are the facts of this problem connected? How does one fact relate to another?

- Is there any information in this problem that you don't need? What is it and why isn't it needed?

- Is there any information missing in this problem that is necessary to solving it? How would you go about finding it?

- What strategies might you try to solve this problem? Which do you think is the best one? Why?

- Can the information or facts presented in this problem be arranged in a pattern? In what way? How might that pattern help you solve the problem?

- Would drawing or sketching help you to solve the problem? If yes, how?

- How might you share your understanding of the problem with your group?

- How might your group divide tasks in solving this problem?

- How might your group work more effectively?

- What is the best solution to the problem?

- How can you justify your solution?

SKILLS CHECKLIST

Name _____   Section _____

Project _____

E=Exceptional   S=Satisfactory   N=Needs Improvement

Skill	Date						
Defines problem							
Identifies useful strategies							
Implements strategies							
Eliminates unnecessary data							
Collects needed data							
Organizes data							
Analyzes and interprets data							
Finds relationships							
Uses models							
Tests strategies							
Demonstrates solutions							
Explains results orally							
Explains results in writing							
Uses logic in arguments							
Makes estimates							
Makes accurate calculations							
Uses technology							
Cooperates with group							
Supports group members							
Shares ideas with others							
Listens to others' ideas							
Remains on task							
Is persistent							
Demonstrates creativity							
Shows enthusiasm							
Tries new ideas							
Takes risks							
Is confident							
Comments:							

Grading Projects via a Point System

The following is an example of how a project's parts can be broken down and quantified. The total number of points is 100. You may use this system, or design one of your own.

Outcome/Action/Behavior	Points
Satisfactory Solution	25

The solution is valid and practical.

Justification of Results	15

Students justified results through an oral presentation, written report, or discussion. They backed up the results with sound arguments.

Methods	15

Students eliminated impractical procedures and focused their efforts on the most useful. If necessary, the students eliminated and found data. They were able to analyze and organize information, and use technology where applicable.

Accuracy	15

Reasoning and computation were logical and accurate.

Creativity	10

Students showed original or insightful thinking.

Persistence	10

Students did not give up.

Cooperation with group	10

Students worked well together, shared ideas, and listened to the ideas of one another. They showed a willingness to help one another.

© 1996 by The Center for Applied Research in Education

EVALUATING WRITING

Many math teachers feel uncomfortable evaluating the writing of their students. However, with the growing realization that writing should be an integral part of a math curriculum, and that it often has a major role in math projects, more and more math teachers will be reading and commenting on the writing of their students. When your students write about mathematics, they share with you much of their understanding of and attitudes toward math.

You may evaluate various types of student writing, including articles, essays, reports, biographies of mathematicians, written logs of problem-solving, or simple ponderings over those "tough" problems. The exception here is math journals; we recommend that you don't grade journals. Journals (see Project 31) are storehouses of a student's thoughts, reflections, and impressions about math. Once you start grading them, many students will begin writing what they think you want to see—translated to "I'll get a better grade this way." Once that happens you'll no longer find the honesty that can be so valuable and refreshing in journals.

When you do grade the writing of your students, select a few points or criteria to focus on. This will make it easier to keep your objectivity. Also, rather than taking a pile of papers home each night to read, take only a workable number. If you try to do too much, you'll become frustrated and probably lose perspective. Concentrate your evaluative efforts on content. Since writers enjoy responses from readers, offer comments to your students, addressing mathematical ideas and issues. Keep your comments upbeat and positive. When criticism is necessary, be sure it contains suggestions for improvement. For more information about grading writing, see "Suggestions for Grading Writing in Math Class."

SELF-ASSESSMENT

A successful math class in which learning is vigorously pursued is a place of continuous assessment on the parts of both teachers and students. While virtually all students expect their learning to be evaluated by their teachers, few have ever been asked to assess themselves. Self-assessment is perhaps the most valuable of any form of evaluation.

Encourage your students to assess themselves. A good place to record thoughts about personal growth in math is in math journals. At the end of a project, ask your students to write a journal entry about the project. Suggest that they include the strategies they used, problems they encountered, and what they learned from the project.

If you prefer, you may distribute copies of the "Student Self-Assessment." Having students answer these questions will help them to evaluate their own work and learning. See Project 60 for a comprehensive assessment that may be applied to the entire year.

While we, as teachers, continuously evaluate the efforts of our students, it's helpful for us to step back occasionally and assess ourselves. This is particularly true for teachers who are implementing projects for the first time. At the very least, you should assess yourself by considering what went well and what you would do differently next time. Asking yourself the questions contained in the "Teacher Self-Assessment" can be most helpful.

Assessment clearly is an essential part of the program of any classroom. It should be continuous and effective, its overall purpose to promote and assist learning.

Suggestions for Grading Writing in Math Class

Grading the writing of students in math can be new territory for many teachers. The following ideas can help.

- Focus evaluation on content rather than mechanics.

- Offer comments and responses directly on student papers whenever possible.

- Keep comments positive. Offer specific suggestions for improvement.

- Comment only on one or two points. Mentioning more may only confuse or discourage students.

- Encourage students to edit each other's writing and revise their work before handing it in.

- Work with your students' English teacher in promoting effective writing techniques.

- Discuss with your students what you will be looking for during evaluation.

Grading Writing by the Numbers

Following is a model for scoring student writing, based on percentages.

Focus: The topic is clearly defined. All ideas support the topic. **20%**

Content: The student uses fresh, insightful, or original ideas. The topic is developed and supported with details. Mathematical reasoning is sound, and shows an understanding of concepts. **25%**

Organization: The piece progresses logically from beginning to end. An introduction, body, and conclusion can be identified. **25%**

Style: The writing is appropriate for the topic and audience. Ideas are communicated effectively. There is a distinct voice. **15%**

Mechanics: The writer uses correct punctuation, grammar, and spelling. **15%**

STUDENT SELF-ASSESSMENT

Name _____   Date _____   Section _____

Project _____

To evaluate your work and what you've learned during this project, answer the following questions.

1.   What did I like about this project? _____

_____

2.   What didn't I like about it?_____

_____

3.   What strategies did I use to solve the problem?_____

_____

_____

4.   Could I have used other strategies? If yes, which ones? _____

_____

_____

5.   Did I justify my solution sufficiently? Could I have provided more proof? How?

_____

_____

_____

6.   What did I learn during this project? _____

_____

_____

Teacher Self-Assessment

Honest answers to the following questions can help ensure that your next project will be even more successful.

- Did I present the project clearly? If not, how might I make it more clear?

- Did the students understand what they were supposed to do? How might I help them understand better?

- Did I arrange the classroom appropriately? What could I change?

- Were the students organized in effective groups? Whom would I change?

- Did I monitor students effectively? Do I know what each student learned?

- Did I ask appropriate questions that provided guidance without "giving away" answers? What was my best question? What was my least effective?

- Did I provide enough time for sharing and discussion upon conclusion? If not, how might I arrange more time in my schedule?

- What would I do differently to improve this project?

Part II

THE
PROJECTS

Section 1

...

MATH AND SCIENCE

THE BENEFITS OF RECYCLING

Most communities across the country have recycling programs. In many, newspapers, glass, aluminum cans, and plastic bottles are collected and transported to recycling centers where they can be processed and used again in some form or another. While recycling has been supported from the beginning by environmentalists, only in recent years have the true benefits of recycling been realized.

GOAL: Working in groups of 4 or 5, students will research recycling to determine who or what benefits from recycling programs. Each group will write a one-page summary of its conclusion and present its findings to the class. *Suggested time*—4 to 5 class periods over 2 weeks.

MATH SKILLS TO HIGHLIGHT:

1. Using data as a basis for making decisions about recycling
2. Analyzing and simplifying numbers to choose an appropriate scale for a graph
3. Reading and creating graphs, tables, and/or charts
4. Using math and writing as a means to communicate ideas

SPECIAL MATERIALS/EQUIPMENT: Reference books and articles about recycling; markers; felt-tipped pens; oaktag; poster paper; rulers; compasses; protractors; scissors; paste; tape. *Optional*—Computers and printers to produce spreadsheets, graphs, and tables.

DEVELOPMENT: Before beginning this project, talk about recycling with your students. If your community is like most throughout the country, it has recycling programs and your students will be familiar with them. Most people assume that recycling is beneficial. But who actually benefits and in what ways? At the very least, recycling programs reduce stress on the environment by cutting the demand for natural resources. In addition, recycling programs create jobs (recycling companies have become thriving businesses), save money, and spur the development of new technologies.

- For this project, focus your groups on the main areas of recycling—newspapers, glass, aluminum cans, and plastic bottles. While some communities also recycle things like grass clippings and used motor oil, information on the first four will be easier to find.

- Distribute copies of Student Guide 1–1, and review it with your students. Be sure they understand what they are to do. Point out that students should concentrate their research efforts not only on the benefits recycling offers people, but also its benefits for the environment.

- Mention that this project is quite broad, and that groups may come to different conclusions. Findings should be supported with facts.

- Hand out copies of Data Sheet 1–2, "Some Facts About Recycling." The purpose of this sheet is to provide students with interesting information about recycling. It may help them to get started with their research.

- Since students will need to conduct research, you should plan to spend at least two class periods in the library. A week or so ahead of time, inform your school's librarian about your project and ask her or him to reserve books on recycling.

- Encourage students to spend some of their own time researching.

- Remind students to keep an accurate list of their sources. This will make it easier to verify facts.

- Reserve at least one class period for students to meet in groups to analyze and organize their data. They should work toward a consensus regarding the benefits of recycling. To support their findings, suggest that they create posters, charts, graphs, tables, or transparencies for the overhead projector. You may set aside additional class time for them to work on their presentations.

- If students have access to computers, they may wish to use them to create spreadsheets, graphs, or tables to illustrate their results. Many word processing programs possess spreadsheet capabilities.

- Set aside at least one class period for the presentations.

WRAP-UP: Students present their findings to the class.

EXTENSIONS: Visit a recycling center for a class trip. Invite a recycling expert to discuss recycling with the class, or explore other areas of waste management such as nuclear waste.

Name _____   Project Due Date _____

THE BENEFITS OF RECYCLING

Situation/Problem:

Most communities across the country maintain recycling programs in which newspapers, aluminum cans, glass bottles, and plastic bottles are recycled. Most people assume recycling is beneficial. But who actually benefits? For example, does recycling reduce stress on the environment? Does it improve the quality of life for people? Does it create new jobs, save money, or promote the development of new technology?

For this project, your group will attempt to answer the question: What are the benefits of recycling? You will write a one-page summary of your conclusions, and then present your findings to the class.

Possible Strategies:

1. Divide the tasks of this project among group members. Tasks will include researching, analyzing and organizing information, creating materials such as graphs, posters, and other displays to support your conclusions, and presenting your conclusions to the class.

2. After gathering research, analyze your information and draw conclusions.

Special Considerations:

- When organizing tasks, divide them equally. For example, one member may research newspaper recycling, another may research aluminum cans, and still others may research glass and plastic bottles. Some members may be responsible for creating posters to support your conclusions, while others may do the actual presentation.

- During research, look for the benefits recycling offers to people, companies, and the environment. Support your findings with facts.

- Keep an accurate list of your sources by using a standard bibliographical format. Specific page numbers where information was found should also be noted. Your English text or a writer's stylebook has information on bibliographies.

- After you have gathered all your information, analyze it and make conclusions about the benefits of recycling. Explain your conclusions in a one-page summary. Your summary should contain three parts—an opening in which you provide your results, a body which offers details supporting your results, and a closing in which you reemphasize the main point of your summary.

- Illustrate your results with graphs, charts, tables, or posters.

- If you have access to computers, consider using them to create graphs and tables from spreadsheets.

- Consider how you will present your findings to the class. Will one group member act as spokesperson, or will each member take a part in the presentation? Rehearse your presentation so that you are able to conduct it smoothly. Be ready to answer questions from the class.

To Be Submitted:

1. Project summary
2. Notes and sources
3. Supplementary materials such as graphs, tables, charts, etc.

© 1996 by The Center for Applied Research in Education

(Data Sheet 1–2)

Name _____

SOME FACTS ABOUT RECYCLING

- Between 1988 and 1992, the number of curbside recycling programs throughout the United States increased from about 1,500 to 5,400.

- In a typical year, about 4 million tons of plastic and 40 million tons of newspaper are thrown out in this country.

- On average, paper makes up about one-third of the municipal waste throughout the country.

- Between 1990 and 1994, nearly 85 new paper mills using recycling technology were built in the U.S. Since 1993, the cost such mills pay for old newspapers has increased over 1,000 percent.

- One ton of paper made from recycled paper saves about 15 trees and 7,000 gallons of water.

- It takes close to a half million trees each week to supply Americans with their Sunday newspapers.

- If each American recycled just 10 percent of the newspapers he or she reads, about 25 million trees would be saved each year.

- Every ton of paper that is recycled saves about 17 trees.

- Recycling glass reduces energy costs for making new glass by close to 30 percent.

- Aluminum cans made from recycled aluminum save up to 95 percent of the energy costs for making cans from new aluminum.

- 65 billion (that's right!) aluminum soda cans are used every year.

- 2.5 million plastic bottles are used in the U.S. every hour.

ENDANGERED SPECIES—CAN THEY BE SAVED?

In 1973 Congress passed the Endangered Species Act to protect plant and animal species that were facing extinction. Any individual or organization may petition the Fish and Wildlife Service/the National Marine Fisheries Service to add a species to the endangered species list. Depending upon its risk of extinction, a species may be listed as endangered or threatened. In either case, the species becomes protected by law. It is illegal to hunt, buy, or sell endangered species, their body parts, or products. Another aspect of the Endangered Species Act is to preserve ecosystems on which endangered plants and animals depend.

Saving endangered species is a complex issue. In recent years it has become controversial as well. Some people feel the costs don't justify the results. This is especially true when preserving the habitats of endangered plants and animals comes into conflict with the loss of jobs or the curtailment of development. Other critics point out that for every success there are many more failures. As they work through this project, your students will confront these and other issues that force a person to wonder: When a species stands in the way of human development, can it be saved?

GOAL: Working in groups of 4 to 5, students will select an endangered species and try to determine its long-term chances for survival. After researching and drawing conclusions, each group will report its findings to the class, supporting its views with posters, graphs, tables, or charts. *Suggested time*—4 to 5 class periods over 2 to 3 weeks.

MATH SKILLS TO HIGHLIGHT:

1. Researching, reading, and interpreting data
2. Using data to draw conclusions and make predictions
3. Creating graphs, tables, or charts

SPECIAL MATERIALS/EQUIPMENT: Reference books and articles about endangered species; markers; felt-tipped pens; oaktag; poster paper; rulers; protractors; compasses; scissors; paste; tape. *Optional*—Computers and printers to produce spreadsheets, graphs, and tables.

DEVELOPMENT: You might consider collaborating with your students' science teacher on this project because of its focus on endangered plants and animals. Before introducing the project, discuss endangered species with your students. Ask them if they can name some endangered plants or animals. Ask if they know of species that were on the endangered species list once, but have sufficiently recovered in population that they are no longer considered endangered. For example, the American bison, the American alligator, and the gray whale have all made significant comebacks.

Unfortunately, despite protection, many species show slow improvement, or even decline in number. Some examples include the California condor, whooping crane, and black-footed ferret.

- Begin this project by explaining to your students that each group will select a plant or animal currently on the endangered species list. They will research their subject, finding out why it is in danger of becoming extinct, as well as what is being done to save it. (Data Sheet 2–2, "Examples of Endangered Animals," contains several animals that face extinction.) Based upon their research, students will formulate a conclusion and make a prediction as to the chances of the species being saved.

- Distribute copies of Student Guide 2–1, and discuss its points with your students. In particular, note how they should concentrate their research under "Special Considerations."

- Remind your students that any conclusions they draw should be made in the light of the evidence they uncover.

- You may wish to hand out copies of Data Sheet 2–2, "Examples of Endangered Animals." This is only a partial list, but it is good for starting the project. Students can easily find comprehensive lists of endangered animals and plants in encyclopedias and other references.

- Distribute copies of Data Sheet 2–3, "Some Facts about Endangered Species." The information on the sheet can provide students with important background information as they begin their research.

- If available, encourage students to use computers for creating graphs, tables, and charts. Computers may also be used for research in accessing on-line services or CD databases.

- Plan on spending at least one class period in the library for research. Inform your school librarian a week or so in advance so that she or he can reserve materials on endangered species and be ready to help your students. Suggest to your students that they meet out of class if they need more time for research.

- Reserve at least one class period for groups to meet, analyze information, formulate conclusions, and begin to create materials to support their findings.

- At least one class period will be necessary for the presentations of the groups.

WRAP-UP: Each group presents its conclusions to the class.

EXTENSION: Have students write articles based on their research, and submit the articles to school, district, or PTA publications.

Name _____   Project Due Date _____

ENDANGERED SPECIES—CAN THEY BE SAVED?

Situation/Problem:

It has been estimated that plants and animals are becoming extinct around the world at the rate of one species each hour. For this project, your group is to select an endangered species, research why it is in danger of becoming extinct, and what is being done to save it. Based upon the information you find, you are to predict its chances for long-term survival. You will present your findings to the class.

Possible Strategies:

1. Review a list of endangered species and decide which animal or plant your group would like to research. (You will be able to find lists of endangered species in encyclopedias and similar references.) To narrow your choices, do some preliminary research on several species.

2. Divide the tasks for this project among group members. You'll need to be concerned with research, analysis of the facts, drawing conclusions, creating materials to support conclusions, and making your presentation.

Special Considerations:

- In researching your species, concentrate your efforts on questions such as the following:

  —Why is it in danger of becoming extinct?

  —Where is its habitat?

  —Who or what is responsible for it being in danger?

  —When have the greatest numbers of the species' population been lost?

  —What is being done to save the species?

  —What is the cost of the preservation efforts?

  —Who is involved in trying to save the species?

  —What are the chances of the species' long-term survival?

- Maintain an accurate list of your sources. Use a standard bibliographical format. Check your English book or a writer's stylebook for standard forms.

- After gathering your information, analyze your facts and draw conclusions from it. Include a prediction of the species' long-term chances for survival. Be sure to back up your predictions with facts.

- Support your conclusions with materials such as graphs, charts, and tables. For example, some graphs you may create include:

  —stem-and-leaf plots

  —pictographs

  —bar graphs

  —line graphs

  —circle (or pie) graphs

- If possible, use computers for research as well as to help you create support materials.

- Plan your presentation. You may appoint one group member to share your findings and prediction, or each member may play a part. Rehearse your presentation so that it is smooth.

To Be Submitted:

1. Notes and sources
2. Supplementary materials including any graphs, tables, and charts

Name _____

EXAMPLES OF ENDANGERED ANIMALS

The following animals have been identified as being endangered. This means they are perilously close to extinction. Note that this is only a partial list. For a complete, updated list of endangered species, check current references in your library.

Endangered Animal	Primary Habitat
American Manatee	Coastal waters of the Atlantic from Florida to South America
Bald Eagle	North America
Black-Footed Ferret	Western Canada to Texas
Blue Whale	Oceans around the world
California Condor	California
Cheetah	Africa, eastern Iran, India
Chimpanzee	Africa
Gorilla	Central and western Africa
Gray Wolf	Eastern Europe, Russia, Canada, U.S., Mexico
Humpback Whale	Oceans around the world
Ivory-Billed Woodpecker	Southeastern U.S., Cuba
Jaguar	Southwestern U.S., northern Mexico, Central and South America
Ocelot	Southwestern U.S., Mexico, Central and South America
Peregrine Falcon	Central Alaska, northcentral Canada to central Mexico
Whooping Crane	North America

Name _____

SOME FACTS ABOUT ENDANGERED SPECIES

- Endangered species are animals and plants that are in danger of dying out very soon unless they are protected.

- Passed in 1973, the United States Endangered Species Act makes it illegal to hunt, buy, or sell endangered species and their body parts or products. Another purpose of the Act is to save ecosystems on which endangered plants and animals depend.

- In 1970, the rate of extinction was estimated to be one species per day. By 1990, the rate of extinction around the world was estimated to be one per hour.

- In the United States, close to 500 plants and animals are listed as threatened or endangered.

- There are many natural causes of extinction, including floods, fires, diseases, volcanic eruptions, changes in climate, a loss of habitat or food required by the species, and calamities such as the catastrophic meteor hit that is believed to have caused the destruction of dinosaurs.

- Humans are the major cause of extinctions today through overhunting, overfishing, destruction of habitats, the overuse of pesticides, and the releasing of pollutants into the environment.

- Up to 20 million acres of rain forest are cleared each year for farming. Such destruction of habitats threatens countless plants and animals.

- By the year 2025, if present trends continue, it has been estimated that at least 2 million species will become extinct because of rain forest destruction.

CHARTING YOUR CALORIES

Our bodies burn the calories obtained from food for energy. Since our bodies store extra calories as fat, calorie "counting" often becomes a major activity for people trying to lose or gain weight. In your class, for example, you might have a dancer trying to lose a few pounds, a football player trying to gain, and a wrestler concerned about maintaining his weight so that he may compete in a particular weight category. For many people, becoming aware of their caloric intake is an important part of understanding the body's overall nutritional needs. This project offers students the chance to trace the calories they consume. As they do, they will undoubtedly learn quite a bit about nutrition.

Note: You might like to follow this project with Project 4, "How Many Calories Do You Burn Each Day?" Together, the two projects will help students realize the important role calories play in a healthy diet. Project 9, "The School's New Lunch Program," also focuses on nutrition.

GOAL: Working individually, students will maintain records of the caloric content of foods they eat over a seven-day period. Upon completion of this period, they will average the calories they have consumed and write a brief report describing their daily caloric intake. *Suggested time*—1 to 2 class periods. Much of the work for this project will be completed out of class.

MATH SKILLS TO HIGHLIGHT:

1. Reading charts and labels to find information
2. Collecting and organizing data
3. Using estimation and decimal computation
4. Determining the mean
5. Analyzing data to draw conclusions
6. Using writing and math as a way to share ideas

SPECIAL MATERIALS/EQUIPMENT: Reference books and articles that contain the number of calories found in specific foods; assorted boxes and cans to show examples of food labels, which you may collect in advance. Students will also need to check the labels on the packages, cans, and bottles of the foods they eat to find the number of calories contained in the food.

DEVELOPMENT: Consider working with your students' health instructor or the school nurse for this project. Such people can offer valuable insights on nutrition. Introduce the project and explain that a calorie is a unit of energy a food supplies. Since for most people excess calories are stored as fat, balancing caloric intake with the body's caloric needs is a good way for an individual to attain his or her ideal weight.

- Start this project by telling students they will chart the amount of calories they eat each day for a period of seven days. Not only will this help them realize their caloric needs, but it will also make them aware of the caloric payload of many foods.

- Distribute copies of Student Guide 3–1 and review it with your students. Make sure your students understand where they can find the number of calories in the foods they eat. Also be sure they understand that the calories listed on package labels refer to serving amounts. A 16-ounce package of pasta, for example, might contain eight servings. Point out the recommended calorie consumption averages for young people noted on the Student Guide.

- Obtain labels from various food packages ahead of time, bring them to class, and show students how to read them. In particular, focus their attention on the calories contained in the food or beverage, and the serving size.

- Since students will be eating many foods for which they won't be able to check labels—for example, unpackaged foods at restaurants and the school lunch—they will need to consult reference books and articles to find estimates of the calories these foods contain. Emphasize, however, that the best way to maintain an accurate account of calories is to refer to the label that comes with food. (For school lunches, you may wish to check with your cafeteria service, and find out if they can provide caloric information on the foods they serve to your students.)

- If you wish, you may hand out copies of Worksheet 3–2. Students may use this sheet to keep track of the calories in the foods they eat at each meal and snacks. You'll need to photocopy seven sheets per student. Stapling them together helps prevent individual sheets from getting lost. Of course, you may instruct students to design their own sheets.

- Remind students to keep track of all the foods they eat for seven days. While it is best to record the foods for seven days in succession, if students miss a day, they may simply continue with the next. When you assign the project, consider giving them some leeway on the deadline. Making the project due in ten days gives students extra time if they need it.

- Encourage your students to consult references on the caloric content of foods on their own. We suggest that you also plan to spend a period in the library for students who will require extra time or help. Inform your librarian of this project so that she or he may reserve materials in advance.

- After charting their caloric intake for seven days, students are to find their daily average of caloric consumption. If necessary, review the steps for finding an average (mean). Students are to write a brief summary of their findings.

WRAP-UP: Students should share their summaries. You may display the summaries.

EXTENSION: Have students reconsider their charts, and make recommendations on how they might improve their diets.

Name _____   Project Due Date _____

CHARTING YOUR CALORIES

Situation/Problem:

Many people pay close attention to the number of calories they consume each day. Some may be concerned with losing or gaining weight, while others simply wish to keep track of what they eat. For this project, you will record the number of calories you consume over a one-week period (seven days). At the end of the period, you will find your average caloric consumption and write a brief summary of your findings.

Possible Strategies:

1. Use a chart to record the calories you eat each day.
2. Be as accurate as possible in your recordkeeping. Although in some cases you may need to estimate calories, the more exact you are, the more your final totals will reflect your actual caloric intake.

Special Considerations:

- Record the number of calories contained in each food you eat at every meal.
- If possible, record the calories at the end of the meal. If you wait too long afterward, you might forget. If you can't keep a chart with you at meals, use a small notepad.

- Record the calories of all snacks.

- Water has no caloric content; virtually all other beverages do.

- Check the labels on packages, cans, or bottles for the number of calories a food or drink contains. This number usually appears as the number of calories "per serving." Be careful here because most packages contain several servings. You need to multiply the calories by the number of servings you actually eat.

- Be sure to include the extras such as butter, salad dressings, and mayonnaise. Adding butter to a slice of toast increases the total number of calories.

- If you eat at a restaurant, politely ask the server if he or she can tell you the number of calories in the food you have ordered. Some restaurants have such information and gladly provide it to their patrons. If not, simply record the foods you eat and consult a reference book for the caloric values later.

- After recording the calories you consumed each day, find your average daily caloric intake over the seven-day period.

- Compare your average to the following Recommended Average Calorie Intake Amounts:

  —Females, ages 11–14, 2,200 calories per day

  —Females, ages 15–18, 2,100 calories per day

  —Males, ages 11–14, 2,700 calories per day

  —Males, ages 15–18, 2,800 calories per day

- For your summary report, share your findings and thoughts. Remember to use an opening, body with supporting details, and a closing.

To Be Submitted:

1. Chart of caloric intake
2. Summary report

© 1996 by The Center for Applied Research in Education

(Worksheet 3–2)

Name _____

A DAILY CALORIE CHART

Day Number _____   Date _____

Type of Food	# of Servings	×	# of calories per serving =
B r e a k f a s t			
	Total breakfast calories =		
L u n c h			
	Total lunch calories=		
D i n n e r			
	Total dinner calories=		
S n a c k s			
	Total snack calories=		
	Total for Day =		

HOW MANY CALORIES DO YOU BURN EACH DAY?

The calories our bodies obtain from food are either stored as fat or burned for energy. The more physically active a person is, the more calories he or she will utilize. You can expect to use far more calories running a marathon than watching a marathon on TV while stretched out on the couch. This project will help your students to understand the relationship between calories and physical activity.

Note: Consider using this project as a follow-up for Project 3, "Charting Your Calories."

GOAL: Working individually, students will record their physical activities throughout the day for a seven-day period. They will tally their daily caloric expenditures, and also find their average caloric expenditure. They will then summarize their results in a short written report. *Suggested time*—2 to 3 class periods.

MATH SKILLS TO HIGHLIGHT:

1. Collecting and organizing data
2. Using estimation and decimal computation
3. Calculating with units of time
4. Finding the mean
5. Using writing and math as a way to share ideas

SPECIAL MATERIALS/EQUIPMENT: Reference books that contain the amount of calories used during specific physical activities; calculators. *Optional*—A scale for students to weigh themselves.

DEVELOPMENT: Consider working with your students' physical education or health teacher for this project. They will undoubtedly be able to offer advice, suggestions, and information. Before beginning the project, explain to your students that our bodies use the calories in food for fuel. Our bodies burn (or utilize through chemical change) calories for energy. Excess calories are stored as fat.

- Start the project by telling your students they will be required to maintain records of their physical activities for the next seven days. They will then find a caloric value for each activity. Multiplying this by their weight and the time they spend at the activity will give them the approximate total number of calories they used.

- Hand out copies of Student Guide 4–1 and go over it with your students. Emphasize that they are to maintain a record of all the physical activities they do each day for seven days.

- Distribute copies of Data Sheet 4–2, "Caloric Expenditures and Physical Activities." Review it with your students. Make sure they understand how to use the formula for finding the total number of calories burned for specific activities. To use the formula, students will need to know their weight. You might provide a scale in class, or ask students to weigh themselves at home or in gym. *A word of caution here:* Be sympathetic to the feelings of students who might be sensitive about their weight.

- Point out that the caloric values on the Data Sheet are approximations. Although various books will give slightly different values, most fall within the same range.

- Emphasize that while the Data Sheet provides a variety of activities, it's likely that some activities will not be listed. In such cases students should consult exercise or physical activity books in the school or public library. Since the Data Sheet provides so many activities, research time with reference books should be minimal. Encourage students to consult references on their own time.

- If you wish, you may distribute copies of Worksheet 4–3, which students can use to chart their activities and caloric expenditures. If you decide to use this worksheet, you'll need to photocopy at least seven pages per student. Stapling them together reduces the chances that individual pages will be lost. Make additional sheets available for students who need more. If you prefer, suggest that students design their own charts.

- Although students will monitor their activities for seven days, you might want to give a nine- or ten-day deadline for completion of the charts. If students miss a day, they can simply make it up the next day.

- Upon completion of their charts, students are to find their total caloric expenditures for each day and their daily average caloric expenditures.

- When they are done, students are to write a brief report, summarizing their findings.

WRAP-UP: Discuss the relationship between calories and physical activities. You may also display their reports.

EXTENSION: Invite a personal fitness trainer to speak to your class about the importance of exercise.

Name _____   Project Due Date _____

HOW MANY CALORIES DO YOU BURN EACH DAY?

Situation/Problem:

Physical activity burns calories. But do you know how many calories you burn each day? This project will help you to find out. You will keep track of your activities for seven days. Based upon the time of each activity and your weight, you will calculate the total number of calories you used for specific activities. You will then find the total number of calories you expended each day.

Possible Strategies:

1. Use a chart to record the activities you perform each day.
2. Be as accurate as you can in recording activities and times.

Special Considerations:

- Record every activity you do from the time you wake up in the morning to the time you go to sleep. Also be sure to record your sleep time.

- Along with each activity, record the length of time you were involved with it. Convert times to decimal equivalents based on one hour. For example, a half-hour would be 0.5, 15 minutes would be 0.25 or 15/60.

- Try to record activities as you do them. If this is impossible, at the end of the day, review all the things you did and write them down on your chart. It's important to record each activity.

- Use Data Sheet 4–2 to find values for caloric expenditures. For activities not on this sheet, you should consult reference books in the library. Even then, you may need to estimate some activities.

- If you must estimate the calories used during some activities, select similar activities and base your estimations on them.

- To use the formula on Data Sheet 4–2, you'll need to know your weight. If you are not sure and don't have access to a scale, use an estimate.

- Use a calculator to find the total number of calories used during specific activities.

- Total all the calories spent on all the activities for each day.

© 1996 by The Center for Applied Research in Education

- Analyze your results and consider the following questions:

    —Are you more active during the week or on weekends?

    —What activities do you expend the most calories on? The least?

    —Do you think your average caloric expenditure will be about the same throughout the year? Or do you think it will vary? Why or why not?

    —Did your results surprise you in any way? Explain.

- Write a brief report summarizing your findings. Be sure to write clearly, use an opening, body with supporting details, and conclusion.

To Be Submitted:

1. Chart of physical activities and caloric expenditure
2. Summary report

Name _____

CALORIC EXPENDITURE AND PHYSICAL ACTIVITIES

Below are various activities and estimates of the amount of calories you would burn each hour for each pound you weigh while taking part in them. You can find an estimate of your caloric expenditure by using this formula:

Your Weight × Cal. per hr. per lb. × Time = Total Calories

Let's say you weigh 120 pounds and mow the lawn for your mother for an hour and a half. You'd multiply 120 × 2.7 × 1.5, which equals 486 calories. By mowing the lawn for an hour and a half, you'd have used 486 calories, roughly equal to that hamburger and French fries you gulped down for dinner.

Note: The number following the activity is the calories per hour per pound (Cal. per hr. per lb.) you'd burn during the activity.

Badminton–2.7	Keyboarding–0.8
Baseball–2.9	Lying at ease–0.6
Basketball–4.5	Mowing the lawn–2.7
Boxing–4.5	Marching (rapid)–3.9
Canoeing (leisure)–1.2	Playing drums–1.8
Card playing–0.7	Playing flute–1.0
Chopping Wood (ax)–2.3	Playing piano–1.1
Cleaning (house)–1.6	Playing trumpet–0.9
Cooking–1.3	Playing violin–1.3
Cycling–2.5	Racquetball–4.0
Dancing (ballroom)–1.6	Raking leaves–2.3
Dancing (rock & roll)–2.8	Rowing machine–3.1
Eating–0.8	Shoveling snow–3.9
Fishing–1.7	Sitting–0.6
Football–4.4	Skating–2.8
Gardening–2.1	Skiing (cross-country)–3.7
Golf (walking)–2.3	Skiing (downhill)–2.5
Gymnastics–3.7	Sleeping–0.4
Hiking–3.6	Soccer–3.7
Horseback riding–2.7	Swimming–3.8
Ironing–0.9	Tennis–2.5
Jogging (distance)–4.2	Walking–2.2
Judo (vigorous) 4.3	Weight training–1.9
Jumping rope–3.8	Writing–0.8

(Worksheet 4-3)

Name _____

A DAILY ACTIVITY CHART

Day Number _____   Date _____

Starting Time	Ending Time	Length of time	Activity	Cal. per hr. per lb.	Weight	Total Calories
					Total Calories for Day	

A MATHEMATICAL SCAVENGER HUNT THROUGH THE HUMAN BODY

Students enjoy scavenger hunts. They're fun, challenging, and exciting. This one has a twist, though. Students are to look for numbers associated with the human body.

GOAL: Working in pairs, students will consult texts and reference books to match numbers with organs and parts of the human body. They will complete a list of 1 through 15, matching organs and/or body parts to the corresponding number. (For example, 1 would correspond to 1 head, 1 nose, 1 heart, etc.) Should students complete all 15, they may search for other organs and body parts associated with numbers. (For example, there are 206 bones in the average person's body.) Students will also be required to state the function of any organs or body parts they use in their lists. *Suggested time*—2 class periods.

MATH SKILLS TO HIGHLIGHT:

1. Developing a "sense" of small and large numbers
2. Thinking creatively about numbers

SPECIAL MATERIALS/EQUIPMENT: Reference books and texts on the human body; at least 15 3 × 5 note cards for each pair of students.

DEVELOPMENT: This project requires that students skim books and reference materials about the human body and focus on numbers. Consider turning the project into a contest. You might award a prize, such as a homework pass, to the pair of students who finds the most numbers associated with the body. If your students are studying the body in health or science, you may wish to coordinate this project with the teacher(s) of those subjects.

- Begin the project by asking your students if they know what a scavenger hunt is. Probably most have taken part in one. Explain that for this scavenger hunt, they will search for parts of the human body that correspond to numbers. For example, we have 1 nose and 2 eyes (or ears, or arms, or legs). So far it sounds easy, but the hunt gets progressively harder. For example, what part of the human body corresponds to 13? Don't tell them, but the average person's face has 13 bones. Such facts require some diligent hunting.

- Hand out and review Student Guide 5–1 with your students. Make sure they understand what they are to do. They are to find corresponding body parts for the numbers 1 through 15. Once they have tried to find all 15, they may extend their list to other numbers. Mention that some numbers, for example the average number of red blood cells in an adult's body, might be quite big.

- Explain that for some numbers they will find more than one answer; however, they will need to list only one. Instruct them to cite the source in which they find their information. This is important for verification.

- Emphasize that students are to know the function of the body organs they use. For example, if they say that we have 2 kidneys, they should know what function the kidneys perform in the body. They may write the function on their note cards.

- The following answer key provides some of the more common answers for numbers 1 through 15. Accept any answer students can justify.

  1 nose; head; trunk; heart; liver
  2 eyes; ears; lungs; kidneys; legs; arms; hands; feet
  3 types of muscles; major parts of the brain
  4 chambers of the heart
  5 lobes in the lungs (three in the right lung and two in the left)
  6 types of joints
  7 pairs of upper ribs (called true ribs)
  8 carpal bones in the wrist
  9 segments into which each lung is divided internally
  10 toes
  11 the ordinal number of the next to last pair of ribs
  12 pairs of ribs
  13 bones in the face
  14 phalangeal bones that shape the five digits (in one hand)
  15 true ribs and sternum

WRAP-UP: Conduct a class discussion and go over the answers. Students will be surprised at the various answers for some numbers.

EXTENSION: Compile the class's answers and make a class poster or chart of your Mathematical Scavenger Hunt.

Name _____   Project Due Date _____

A MATHEMATICAL SCAVENGER HUNT
THROUGH THE HUMAN BODY

Situation/Problem:

You and a partner will take part in a math scavenger hunt. As with all scavenger hunts, some items are easy to find, while others require some looking. For this hunt you must find parts of the human body that correspond to the numbers 1 through 15. For example, we each have one head, and that corresponds to 1. Sounds easy? What can you come up with for 13? While you must try to find corresponding body parts up through 15, you may wish to do more research and find examples that correspond to higher numbers. Simply extend your list and add numbers and body parts as you find them. You will also need to know the function of the body parts or organs you list.

Possible Strategies:

1. Use 3 × 5 note cards to list body parts for specific numbers. Use only one card per number.
2. Consult reference books for information about the human body. Skim the information for numbers.

Special Considerations:

- There are many answers for some numbers. Humans have one head, one nose, one heart, one gallbladder, one liver. . . . We (usually) have two hands, two feet, two eyes. . . .

- For some numbers it will be easier to find corresponding body parts than others. You may look for groups of muscles or bones that work together.

- Write the function of the body part or organ on your note card.

- Because answers vary, include the source where you found specific information. Write the author's last name, the title of the book, the publication date, and the page number. Put this information on the note card for the number.

- If you can't find body parts for all the numbers 1 to 15, skip the ones you can't find and try to find others. For example, there are 206 bones in the average person's skeleton. There are about 700 million alveoli in the lungs. (For such large numbers, approximations are acceptable.) List as many additional numbers and body parts or organs as you can.

To Be Submitted:

Your completed note cards

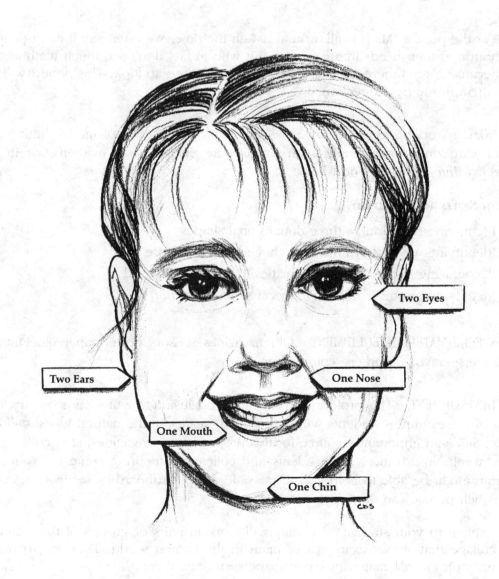

Two Eyes

Two Ears

One Nose

One Mouth

One Chin

IT'S ONLY NATURAL

We hear the phrase "Math is all around us" all the time. We often say it to students, most of whom nod their heads in agreement, but who in fact don't see much math at all. This isn't because it's not there; they simply don't know where to look. This project will at least point them in the right direction.

GOAL: Working in groups of 2 or 3, students will make a collage by cutting pictures out of magazines or drawing them to illustrate examples of mathematics in nature. *Suggested time*—2 class periods.

MATH SKILLS TO HIGHLIGHT:

1. Identifying two- and/or three-dimensional shapes
2. Identifying types of symmetry as they appear in nature
3. Recognizing instances of mathematics in the natural world
4. Identifying instances of the Fibonacci series (*optional*)

SPECIAL MATERIALS/EQUIPMENT: Old magazines; scissors; poster paper; glue; transparent tape; rulers; crayons; markers; colored pencils.

DEVELOPMENT: This project is an excellent conclusion to a unit on geometry, because many of the examples students will find of mathematics in the natural world will be geometric. Since an important resource for this project is old magazines, start collecting them a few weeks in advance. Ask students and colleagues to bring some in. Your school's librarian might be able to help, too. If possible, keep cardboard boxes in your classroom into which people can drop magazines.

- Explain to your students that they will work in pairs or groups of three to create a collage that shows examples of math in the natural world. They are to find these examples in old magazines, newspapers, or draw them.

- Show students some examples of math in nature. Your textbook, as well as reference books in the library, probably contain several examples. A snowflake, which has six sides, is a hexagon. The sun, moon, and planets are spheres. Our galaxy, the Milky Way, is a spiral, as are some kinds of snail shells.

- If you have already studied symmetry with your class, ask your students to identify symmetry in some of the things they find.

- Distribute copies of Student Guide 6–1 and review it with your students. Make sure they understand what they are to do.

- Hand out copies of Data Sheet 6–2, "Math in Nature." This sheet offers several examples in nature where math is apparent and easy to find. It will help your students in their search for material for their collages.

- Depending upon the level of your class, you may wish to discuss the Fibonacci series.

- Suggest to students that they try to develop a theme for their collages, based on Data Sheet 6–2. Of course, they may combine several themes or even create a collage that sweeps across all of nature. Encourage them to be creative.

- In creating their collages, have students cut and paste or draw examples of math in nature. They should number each picture; then, on a separate sheet of paper, identify the math it represents. They should attach their identification sheet to the side or bottom of their collages when they are done.

WRAP-UP: Display the collages in the class or hallway. Discuss the many examples students found of math in nature.

EXTENSION: Suggest that students find examples of math in the artificial world, such as in architecture.

Name _____   Project Due Date _____

IT'S ONLY NATURAL

Situation/Problem:

You and your partner(s) will make a collage of examples of mathematics found in nature. You will cut out pictures from old magazines or newspapers, or draw pictures of your own to create your collage.

Possible Strategies:

1. Brainstorm with your partner(s) to identify geometric shapes and properties you already know about. For example, if you think about it, you know that the earth is a sphere.
2. Try to develop your collage using a variety of items that illustrate different shapes and properties in math.

Special Considerations:

- Scan old magazines and newspapers for pictures you can cut out to use on your collage. Cut out pictures carefully and neatly.
- Consider drawing some pictures.
- After collecting several pictures, place them on your poster paper and try to arrange them in a visually pleasing way.
- Select a title for your collage.
- Identify each picture on your collage by a number. List the numbers on a separate sheet of paper and explain the geometric shape or mathematical principle represented by the picture. Attach this sheet to your collage.
- Your collage should focus on the natural world. Avoid including any pictures of man-made objects.

To Be Submitted:

Your collage and list of mathematical shapes or principles

© 1996 by The Center for Applied Research in Education

Name _____

MATH IN NATURE

Following are some examples of mathematics in nature. There are many more.

pinecones—spirals and Fibonacci numbers
sunflowers—spirals and Fibonacci numbers
ponds and lakes—reflections
Borchan—crescent-shaped sand dunes
star sapphire—pentagon
Queen Anne's lace—symmetry
butterfly—symmetry
pineapple—spiral, Fibonacci numbers
fruits (cross-sections)—symmetry
fairy rings (mushrooms)—circles
ripples on water—circles
diatoms—circles
growth rings (trees)—concentric circles
Milky Way Galaxy—spiral
constellations—angles
spider webs—concentric polygons
planets, moons, stars—spheres
flower stalks—lines or arcs
salt—cubic crystals
tree trunks—lines or cylinders
earthworms—cylinders
orbits of planets—generally circular (with slight variations)
orbits of comets—elliptical or parabolic
snowflakes—hexagons
chambered nautilus (snail)—spiral
common starfish—pentagons
honeycombs—hexagons
many animals (including humans)—symmetry
morning glory buds—spirals
daisy heads—spirals

DESIGNING A FLOWERBED

The design of a flowerbed—whether for an office building, park, school, or backyard—requires many skills involving math. Measurement, geometry, scale drawing, estimation, and, of course, computation of total costs make this project both interesting and comprehensive. Upon completion of the project, students will no doubt gain a better understanding of plants and flowerbeds, and may even wish to design a flowerbed for their own homes.

GOAL: Given a budget and a list of plants from which to choose, groups are to design a flowerbed and calculate what the total costs will be. *Suggested time*—3 to 4 class periods.

MATH SKILLS TO HIGHLIGHT:

1. Using geometric shapes to design the flowerbed, either with pencil and paper or computer software
2. Using a scale to make a diagram
3. Estimating costs and planning within a budget
4. Calculating with money, and making an itemized tally of expenses

SPECIAL MATERIALS/EQUIPMENT: Rulers; reference books on plants; graph paper; measuring tapes; yardsticks or metersticks; crayons or colored pencils should students wish to color their designs. *Optional*—Computers and printers.

DEVELOPMENT: With its emphasis on plants, you might want to work with your students' science teacher on this project. Consider taking students outside to observe flowerbeds or gardens. This will sharpen their visual perception, stimulate their imaginations, and enhance their sense of relationships. You might also have students find the dimensions of a flowerbed with measuring tapes or yardsticks to give them an impression of size.

- To start the project, distribute copies of Student Guide 7–1 and discuss the information. Explain that each group will work independently to create a unique design for a flowerbed. Discuss the skills that students will likely use to complete the project, and encourage them to refer to this guide as often as needed.

- Hand out copies of Data Sheet 7–2, "Facts and Prices of Selected Plants." This sheet provides descriptions and costs of trees, shrubs, and flowers that students might use in their flowerbeds. The prices are general, and the plants on the sheet grow well in much of the continental United States. If you wish to provide a broader assortment of plants and prices, obtain and hand out the price lists and sales material from local nurseries and discount stores. If you do this, consider presenting the project in the spring. Spring is the time gardening centers bombard the public with sales material, which you can easily make available to your students, providing them with plenty of additional choices. Of course, you may also suggest that students consult reference books to learn about other plants they might use.

- Pass out copies of Worksheet 7–3, which is a grid on which students may sketch their design. Provide several sheets and suggest that students try various arrangements. (An option is for students to design their flowerbeds on computers. Various software packages—Logo™ as well as numerous drawing and art programs—enable students to create, arrange, and rearrange geometric shapes.) When working with designs on a grid, remind students of the importance of a scale. Perhaps each side of a block will be equal to two feet. Mention that students might wish to color their designs to obtain an accurate pictorial display of the plants they selected.

WRAP-UP: Make photocopies of the final designs of each group and share them with all the class members. A group spokesperson should be ready to explain and justify the group's selections.

EXTENSIONS: Design a real flowerbed for the school, or one for home. Invite a nursery representative to speak to the class about how flowerbeds are designed. Estimate the cost of maintaining the flowerbed throughout the year by including the costs of fertilizer, water, weed and bug killer, and possible replacement of plants.

Name _____   Project Due Date _____

DESIGNING A FLOWERBED

Situation/Problem:

Imagine that your school's PTA has donated $350.00 toward the design of a new flowerbed in the school courtyard. Your class has been chosen to provide the design and select the plants. The area for the flowerbed is 30 feet by 30 feet and enjoys full to moderate sunlight. Since the PTA would like to see several possible designs, your class will be divided into groups with each group responsible for coming up with its own design. You will be given a list of possible plants from which to choose, including prices. Your goal is to design an attractive flowerbed at the best cost.

Possible Strategies:

1. Study some actual flowerbeds to gain an impression of size, color, and arrangement of the plants.
2. Sketch designs of possible flowerbeds on graph paper. Set up a scale. Place plants on the sketch where you think they would look best in the actual flowerbed.

© 1996 by The Center for Applied Research in Education

Special Considerations:

- Visualize what your flowerbed will look like now and in the future.
- Consult references to find out more about possible plants you might use.
- Seek a balance between the plants you select and the overall cost of the flowerbed.
- Take into account the flowering periods of plants. Tulips, for example, bloom in the spring; marigolds bloom from summer to fall.
- Consider how much sunlight the plants you select need. Also consider the amount of water necessary.
- Consider whether trees and shrubs are deciduous or evergreen. Deciduous plants lose their leaves in the fall; evergreens remain green throughout the year.
- Consider upkeep. Daffodils are perennials; they return each spring. Impatiens are annuals; they do not return each year and will need to be replanted. This will require new funds and labor each year for planting.
- Ground-cover plants such as rug junipers do precisely what their name implies—they remain low and cover the ground. They are generally hardy and require little upkeep.
- Many plants, especially shrubs and trees, are sold in gallon containers that are related to the plants' size. A plant in a 3-gallon container, for example, is smaller than one in a 5-gallon container.
- Generally, the most attractive flowerbeds are those that have a mixture of plants—flowers, shrubs, and trees with pleasing colors.

To Be Submitted:

1. A final design of the flowerbed, including a scale
2. Itemized tally and final cost of expenses

Name _____

FACTS AND PRICES OF SELECTED PLANTS

TREES

Japanese Maple—red-leafed deciduous tree, 15–20 feet. Full sun to light shade. (4 ft. high, $19.95)

Dogwood—deciduous, white or pink flowers in late spring. 20–30 feet. Half sun to light shade. (Pink, 4 ft. high, $19.95; White, 5 ft. high, $24.95)

American Holly—slow-growing evergreen. 45–50 feet. Full sun to light shade. (4 ft. high, $29.95)

Canadian Hemlock—evergreen, graceful pyramidal shape. 40–70 feet. Full sun to light shade. (5 ft. high, $21.95)

SHRUBS

Azalea—variety of flower colors. Blooms in spring. Up to 4 feet. (3 gal., 12 in. high, $3.95)

Rhododendron—evergreen up to 12 feet. Red, purple, and white are typical flower colors. (3 gal., 18 in. high, $7.95; 5 gal., 24 in. high, $12.95)

Dwarf Burning Bush—deciduous, up to 6 feet. Brilliant red leaves in fall. (3 gal., 12 in. high, $8.95)

Forsythia—fast-growing. 8–10 feet, bright yellow flowers in early spring. (6 ft. high, $9.95)

Common Juniper—evergreen. 5–10 feet, spiny blue-green leaves. (5 gal., 8 in. high, $6.95)

Blue Rug Juniper—evergreen. Excellent ground cover with blue-green foliage. (3 gal., $2.95)

FLOWERS

Daffodils—hardy bulbs. 4–18 inches. Variety of colors. Spring blooming. (Pack of 10 bulbs, $2.95)

Tulips—hardy bulbs. 6–30 inches. Variety of colors. Spring blooming. (Pack of 10 bulbs, $2.95)

Common Petunias—10–18 inches. Variety of colors. Bloom from late spring to the first frost. Annuals except in the mildest of areas. ($.79 ea.)

Geraniums—12–24 inches. Variety of colors. Bloom from late spring to the first frost. Annuals. ($3.95 ea.)

Marigolds—6–18 inches. Variety of colors. Bloom from summer to first frost. Annuals. (6 for $1.59)

Impatiens—6–18 inches. Variety of colors. Bloom from summer to first frost. Excellent for shady areas. Annuals. (6 for $1.49)

Hyacinths—hardy bulbs. 12–15 inches. Mostly white, blue, or purple. Spring blooming. (Pack of 20 bulbs, $2.95)

Crocuses—hardy bulbs. 2–6 inches. Variety of colors. Late winter blooming. (Pack of 20 bulbs, $2.95)

Lilies—hardy bulbs. Up to 36 inches. Variety of colors. Summer to early fall blooming. (Pack of 12 bulbs, $3.95)

Chrysanthemums—1–4 feet. Variety of colors. Late summer and fall blooming. ($3.95 ea.)

Note: Unless stated as an annual, the plants above are perennials. The plants on the list generally tolerate varying amounts of sunlight and grow well in many different regions of the country. Heights given in the descriptions are adult sizes; heights given with prices are the size at the time of sale.

Mulch is available at a cost of $2.95 per 2-cubic-foot bag, which will cover 16 square feet at a depth of one and a half inches. Mulch is decorative and helps retain soil moisture.

(Worksheet 7-3)

Name _____

CENTIMETER GRID

project 8

BUYING A CLASS AQUARIUM

One of the major overall objectives of any math class is to prepare students for coping with the real world. At its simplest, this aim includes educating students so that they can evaluate and compare the features, benefits, and costs of items they wish to purchase. This project, which requires students to research and decide on equipment and materials necessary for setting up a class fresh-water aquarium, will help them to acquire important real-life skills.

GOALS: Working in groups of 3 to 4, students will assume they have been given $125.00 with which they may purchase a class aquarium. Their task is to buy the biggest tank, with its necessary accessories, and populate it with the greatest number of guppies or goldfish they can while staying within budget. *Suggested time—*2 to 3 class periods.

MATH SKILLS TO HIGHLIGHT:

1. Evaluating the features and benefits of items against their cost
2. Making decisions regarding price
3. Using charts and tables to obtain information
4. Tallying total costs

SPECIAL MATERIALS/EQUIPMENT: Calculators. *Optional*—Catalogs of aquarium equipment and supplies.

DEVELOPMENT: Explain to your students that aquariums are common in homes, businesses, and schools. People find aquariums to be interesting hobbies, and some researchers note that aquariums seem to provide people with a sense of relaxation and enjoyment.

• Start this project by telling students to imagine that the class has been given $125.00 by an anonymous donor (and obvious aquarium aficionado) to buy an aquarium for the class. Since many options are available in purchasing an aquarium, the class will be divided into groups and each group will develop a proposal for the size tank, accessories, and fish to buy. The proposals may not exceed the budget. Groups should attempt to select equipment and materials that use the money most wisely.

- Distribute copies of Student Guide 8–1, and review it with your students. Be sure to emphasize the many factors detailed on the Guide that must be considered in buying an aquarium.

- Hand out copies of Data Sheet 8–2, "Aquariums and Accessories." This sheet contains information on equipment, materials, and prices that students may use in developing their proposals. To keep the choices somewhat simple, we suggest that students select either guppies or goldfish for their tanks.

- If you wish to broaden the scope of the project, obtain and distribute copies of catalogs that contain information about aquarium equipment and accessories. Should you decide to do this, be sure to start accumulating the catalogs well in advance of the project so that you have enough for your students. Newspapers sometimes run advertisements regarding the sale of aquariums.

- If your state has a sales tax, you may instruct your students to figure in its cost on the items they would buy.

- Remind students to select a spokesperson to present their proposal to the class. Their selections should be supported.

WRAP-UP: Groups share their proposals with the class.

EXTENSIONS: If possible, obtain money and set up a class aquarium based on the class's suggestions. Assume that the anonymous donor provided $50.00 more for fish. Checking catalogs, what other types of fish would students buy for their aquariums? Remind them to keep the size of the tank in mind, and also the sensibilities of the fish. Some fish do not get along well with others.

Name _____   Project Due Date _____

BUYING A CLASS AQUARIUM

Situation/Problem:

An anonymous donor has given your class $125.00 to buy and set up a fresh-water aquarium for your classroom. Since there are many different sizes of tanks and accessories, your class has been divided into groups. Each group will research aquariums and make a proposal for the size tank, accessories, and fish to buy. While you should select the biggest tank and most accessories you can, you may not go over your budget.

Possible Strategies:

1. Round off prices to do quick estimates of costs.
2. Select the tank, hood, light, and filter first. These will be some of your biggest costs.

Special Considerations:

- Remember that fish need room to grow and thrive. Most aquarium supply shops suggest that you follow the rule of one inch for one gallon. For every gallon of water in your tank, you may have a fish one inch long. If you have a ten-gallon tank, for example, you may keep 10 one-inch fish, or 5 two-inch fish, etc.

- While much equipment and supplies for aquariums are necessary, some are mostly decorative.

  —Stones are colorful and provide a nice bottom, but are not required.

  —Seaweed offers realism, allows fish hiding places, and adds oxygen to water (supplementing the job of the air pump), but is not required.

  —Snails and algae-eaters (aquarium catfish) help clean the aquarium, but are not required.

- Use Data Sheet 8–2 for a list of items you may need and their prices.

- To reduce the chances you will run over your budget, keep a running tally of the items you are considering.

- Pay close attention to your costs. Some prices are given for tanks of a specific size.

- After you have decided on equipment, accessories, and fish, total your costs and subtract them from your budget. Next, write your proposal. Double-check your numbers, and be able to justify your decisions.

- Select a spokesperson to present your proposal to the class.

To Be Submitted:

A copy of your proposal, including the items you would buy and the total costs

Name _____

AQUARIUMS AND ACCESSORIES

Tank	Hood with Light	Filter
10 gal., $ 6.97	$13.95	$14.99
20 gal., $27.97	$17.95	$17.99
30 gal., $54.97	$19.95	$19.99

Air pump (suitable for all three tanks above), $9.65

Air line and air stone (suitable for all three tanks above), $2.50

Charcoal, per 10-gal. tank, $4.19

Stones, 5-lb. bag (about 1 lb. per gal. is needed), $2.50

Fish Food, 3.5 oz., $6.49

Guppies, 1 pair, $2.00

Common goldfish, $0.95 each

Snails, $0.85 each

Algae-eater (catfish), $1.95 each

Additional notes:

- Guppies are about two inches long.
- Goldfish may grow to be five to seven inches, but will remain three to four inches in tanks where there is much competition among fish for food.
- Algae-eaters are about three inches long.
- Filters are necessary to circulate and clean the aquarium's water.
- Charcoal is necessary for cleaning the water and reducing bacteria.
- Hoods act as a top for the aquarium (some fish try to "jump" out), and lights provide illumination.
- Heaters, needed for tropical fish, are not needed for tanks that contain guppies or goldfish.

project 9

THE SCHOOL'S NEW LUNCH PROGRAM

Just about everybody in every school everywhere has a gripe about his or her school's lunches. No matter what the menu offers, and no matter what efforts are taken in preparation, there are always some dissatisfied students (and teachers). Complaints range from the lack of choices to the lack of taste to high cost. While this project may not result in changing your school's lunch offerings, it will give students a chance to design potential menus that are tasty and nutritious.

GOAL: Working in groups of 4 to 5, students will design a five-day meal plan, based upon the National School Lunch Program Requirements. *Suggested time*—3 class periods.

MATH SKILLS TO HIGHLIGHT:

1. Classifying objects
2. Conducting a poll and using the results to make a decision
3. Obtaining information from food ads or labels
4. Estimating total costs
5. Determining cost per person

SPECIAL MATERIALS/EQUIPMENT: Cookbooks; books on nutrition; circulars and advertisements from supermarkets; felt-tipped pens; markers; rulers; drawing paper for the menus. *Optional*—Word processors or computers and printers to design menus.

DEVELOPMENT: Since it focuses on groups of food and making proper dietary selections, this project could be part of a science, nutrition, or health unit. Consider enlisting the aid of your school nurse or your students' science or health teachers.

- Start this project by explaining that students will have the opportunity to design a week's menu for the school's lunch program. While they will be free to make any selections they want, they must follow dietary guidelines and keep the cost reasonable—within the bounds the typical student would be willing to pay. For most schools, caviar's out!

- Distribute copies of Student Guide 9–1, and review it with your class. Discuss how a poll is an excellent method by which to find out people's thoughts and opinions about an issue. In this case, polling students about their thoughts about lunch might result in uncovering fine ideas.

- Distribute copies of Data Sheet 9–2, "The National School Lunch Program Requirements." Explain that this sheet is a guideline detailing some types of foods that school lunches should contain. Your students should refer to it when designing their menus. Note that the requirements are minimums. Groups may design menus that exceed the minimum requirements.

- Point out that students may wish to consult nutrition books for foods that aren't listed, but which may be substituted for foods on the list.

- Remind students that as they are designing their menus, they must also remain aware of the prices of the foods they are choosing. Suggest that they check the advertisements and circulars from supermarkets for current prices. They will need to calculate the total costs of each lunch for 30 people, then find the cost of an individual lunch for each person. They should price the lunches individually for each day.

- Hand out copies of Worksheet 9–3. Students may use this sheet for writing their menus and computing costs.

- After they have decided on and priced their meals, they should design an attractive menu that includes the cost of each lunch. Word processors or computers that have clip-art and multiple fonts will enable students to create attractive menus; however, if you don't have access to this equipment, students may simply use pens, markers, etc.

WRAP-UP: Each group shares its menu with the class. A spokesperson from each group explains the group's menu, detailing why certain foods were selected. After each group has shared its menu, conduct a discussion that examines the nutritional content of school lunches.

EXTENSIONS: Vote on the most popular menu. If students have access to a home-economics or home-living class, suggest that they prepare some of the foods on the menu.

Name _____   Project Due Date _____

THE SCHOOL'S NEW LUNCH PROGRAM

Situation/Problem:

Your group will create a five-day menu for your school's lunch program. Your menu should be both nutritious and popular with the students. You will be responsible for totaling the costs of the foods you select, and setting the prices students will pay for lunch. Plan the lunch program for 30 students.

Possible Strategies:

1. Poll your friends to find out what foods they would like the lunch program to offer.
2. Select foods from groups that comply with the National School Lunch Program Requirements.
3. Divide the tasks for this project.

Special Considerations:

- Divide responsibilities according to the interests of group members. For example, two students may like to design and conduct the poll, two others may create the menu, and another may enter the menu on a computer (if one is available). All members may work together to select the foods and find the prices.

- For a poll to be effective, the pollsters decide upon specific questions before contacting people. Try to think of three to five questions that you can ask others about school lunches. Avoid questions that may be answered with a simple "yes" or "no," and include questions about foods and also prices.

- Decide whom you will poll. You may limit your poll to your class, or ask students from other classes, too. Remember, the more people you poll, the more accurate your information will be.

- Refer to Data Sheet 9–2 which contains examples of food from each food group. You may consult reference books on foods and nutrition to find other types of foods to serve.

- In designing your menu, make sure you meet all of the nutritional requirements each day.

© 1996 by The Center for Applied Research in Education

- As you decide on foods for your menu, check advertisements and supermarket circulars for the prices of these foods. You may use Worksheet 9–3 to help you list foods and compute costs. Remember to buy enough food for 30 students.

- Do not calculate the costs of paper plates, napkins, or utensils.

- Make an attractive copy of your menu. Include the price you would charge for the lunch. If you have access to computers, consider using one to create and print your menu. You may also create an attractive menu using markers and pens.

To Be Submitted:

1. A copy of your menu
2. Your completed worksheet

Name _____

THE NATIONAL SCHOOL LUNCH PROGRAM REQUIREMENTS

Meat/Poultry/Fish/Bean Group—1 serving

Fruit/Vegetable Group—2 servings

Bread/Cereal Group—1 serving

Milk Group—1 serving

Following are some examples from each group:

MEAT/POULTRY/FISH/BEAN GROUP

Lunch meat

Hamburger

Hot dog

Tuna

Turkey

Chicken

Peanut butter

Eggs

Peanuts

FRUIT/VEGETABLE GROUP

Fresh fruits

Fruit juices

Salads

Corn

Potatoes

Tomatoes

Broccoli

Carrots

Peppers

BREAD/CEREAL GROUP

Slices of bread

Rolls

Cakes

Pasta

Pizza

Rice

Tortillas

Noodles

Muffins

Bagels

MILK GROUP

Milk

Yogurt

Cheese

Cream cheese

Butter

Cottage cheese

Ice cream

Name _____

A FIVE-DAY MENU

	Menu	Need to Buy	Price
DAY 1			
DAY 2			
DAY 3			
DAY 4			
DAY 5			

Total cost for Day 1 = _____ Cost per student _____

Total cost for Day 2 = _____ Cost per student _____

Total cost for Day 3 = _____ Cost per student _____

Total cost for Day 4 = _____ Cost per student _____

Total cost for Day 5 = _____ Cost per student _____

WHAT'S THE WEATHER?

Weather is something that affects virtually everybody. Because students have firsthand experience with it, the weather is a subject to which they can relate. It also provides an opportunity for students to practice their skills of observation, analysis, and interpretation.

GOAL: Working in pairs or teams of 3, students will observe and chart various weather conditions—including temperature, wind speed and direction, wind chill, barometric pressure, precipitation, and cloud cover—for seven days. At the end of this period they will organize and represent their observations via graphs, tables, or charts. They will also write a brief summary report of their observations. *Suggested time*—2 to 3 class periods.

MATH SKILLS TO HIGHLIGHT:

1. Using observation skills to collect data
2. Interpreting data
3. Expressing information in the forms of graphs, tables, or charts
4. Using writing as a means to express ideas in math

SPECIAL MATERIALS/EQUIPMENT: Oaktag or poster paper; rulers; felt-tipped pens; markers; colored pencils; daily newspapers (or access to TV and radio weather reports) for weather data. *Optional*—Computers and printers for creating graphs, tables, or charts, and writing summary reports.

DEVELOPMENT: Consider working with your students' science teacher for this project. Perhaps your students will be studying weather in science, and you may decide to assign the project to coincide with their science activities. To promote interest in the project, discuss with your students how weather plays a major role in our lives. Ask how the weather affects them. The softball game might be rained out, skiing might be poor because of the lack of snow, frigid weather forces people to wear heavy clothing, and hot humid weather makes us seek air conditioning.

- Start the project by explaining that students will work in groups of 2 or 3. They will observe and chart various weather factors for seven days.

- Hand out copies of Student Guide 10–1. Review it with your students. In particular, point out the weather factors under "Special Considerations" they are to observe and record.

- Emphasize that students are to record information about these weather factors for seven consecutive days. They may obtain their data from local newspapers, or TV or radio weather reports.

- Hand out copies of Data Sheet 10–2, "Weather Words." This sheet provides information about the weather. Suggest that students consult their science texts and other references for more information.

- After obtaining their information, students are to analyze and organize their data, then create posters that use graphs, tables, or charts to represent their data. They may represent their data in various ways. Give them some examples to avoid confusion. For example, bar graphs may be used to show the temperatures over the period. Double bar graphs may be used to show the daily high and low. Line graphs may be used to indicate wind chill. Some students may wish to simply display all of the data they find on a chart or table. You should provide suggestions based on the degree to which your students have studied and understand graphs. The groups are also required to write a summary of their observations. You may wish to set aside one or two class periods for this work.

WRAP-UP: Display posters and reports. Conduct a class discussion about the observations.

EXTENSIONS: Check a copy of *The Farmer's Almanac* and compare the actual weather with what was predicted. It should be interesting. You may invite a meteorologist in to talk to the class about how mathematics is important to weather forecasting.

Name _____   Project Due Date _____

WHAT'S THE WEATHER?

Situation/Problem:

Working with your partner(s), you will chart specific weather conditions in your town for seven days. After compiling your data, you will organize and display your data on poster paper. You will also write a brief summary report describing your observations.

Possible Strategies:

1. To maintain the accuracy of your data, try to obtain information from the same source each day.
2. Divide the responsibility for obtaining data with your partner(s). For example, you may collect the data on Monday, Wednesday, and Friday, while your partner(s) take the other days. Perhaps you will be responsible for finding the temperature and wind speed for all of the days, and your partner(s) will find the other factors.

Special Considerations:

- You are required to observe the weather noting the following factors:

    —Temperature (the high and low of the day)

    —Wind speed (average and gusts)

    —Wind chill

    —Barometric pressure

    —Degree of cloud cover (for example, partly sunny, mostly cloudy, sunny, etc.)

    —Precipitation

- In addition, you may record the following:

    —Time of sunrise and sunset

    —Normal high and normal low temperatures

    —Coldest and highest temperature on each day in the past

    —Severe weather (if any) through history on each day

- Accurately record your observations each day. Note your source. Consult local newspapers or watch TV and radio weather reports for information.

© 1996 by The Center for Applied Research in Education

- After recording your data, analyze and organize it. Use poster paper, and create charts, tables, or graphs to represent your information. Be creative, add color, and use symbols to show weather details. For instance, illustrate a cloudy day by drawing a sky with plenty of clouds. Show a sunny day by drawing the sun. A partly cloudy day may be shown by drawing the sun with a cloud partially blocking it. You may even wish to draw a weather map.

- If you have access to computers, consider using them to create graphs, tables, or charts, as well as to write your summary report.

- Your summary report should describe your observations and sources. You should also explain why you illustrated your observations the way you did. Why, for example, would you select one type of graph over another? Write clearly.

To Be Submitted:

1. Posters containing graphs, tables, or charts that represent your weather observations
2. Summary report

Name _____

WEATHER WORDS

Following are important words associated with weather and weather reporting.

atmosphere—The thin envelope of gases, water vapor, dust, and other airborne particles that surround the earth. Commonly referred to as the "air."

barometer—An instrument used to measure atmospheric pressure.

blizzard—Heavy snow or blowing snow accompanied by winds of at least 35 miles per hour.

climate—The average daily or seasonal weather of a particular place or region.

cloud—A mass of small liquid water droplets or ice crystals suspended in the air.

dew—Moisture that has condensed on objects near the ground.

dew point—The temperature at which water vapor condenses to a liquid.

drizzle—Precipitation consisting of very small droplets of water.

fair—Weather condition in which clouds cover less than 40% of the sky, there are no extremes in temperature or wind, and there is no precipitation.

fog—A cloud hovering close to the Earth's surface.

front—The area in which two air masses come into contact.

frost—A thin layer of ice crystals that form on the ground and other surfaces when water vapor condenses below 32 degrees Fahrenheit.

gust—A sudden, brief increase in wind speed.

hail—Precipitation consisting of pellets of ice.

high pressure—An air mass associated with fair weather.

humidity—The amount of water vapor in the air.

hurricane—An intense storm that generally forms over tropical regions. It brings heavy rain, strong winds, and powerful storm surges that can cause severe flooding.

lightning—The visible discharge of electricity associated with a thunderstorm.

low pressure—An air mass associated with storms.

meteorology—The science that studies the weather.

mostly cloudy—Condition when 70–90% of the sky is covered with clouds.

mostly sunny—Condition when 10–30% of the sky is covered with clouds.

overcast—Condition when 90% or more of the sky is covered with clouds.

partly cloudy (or partly sunny)—Condition when 30–70% of the sky is covered with clouds.

precipitation—Any form of water, including rain, drizzle, sleet, hail, or snow, that falls to the ground.

rain—Precipitation consisting of droplets of water.

sleet—Precipitation consisting of ice particles.

smog—Fog mixed with particles of pollution.

snow—Precipitation consisting of small ice crystals.

sunny (or clear)—Condition when less than 10% of the sky is covered with clouds.

temperature—Degree of hotness or coldness of the air.

thunder—The sound caused by lightning heating air and causing it to rapidly expand.

tornado—A violent whirlwind often accompanied by heavy rain, hail, thunder, and lightning.

variably cloudy—Condition when cloudiness of the sky varies between 20–90%.

weather—The condition of the atmosphere at a given time.

wind—Moving air.

A FLIGHT TO MARS

A human expedition to Mars has been the dream of space enthusiasts for years. Probably within the next 25 years, a human flight to Mars will be launched. As the baby boomers witnessed the moon landings, their children will see astronauts walking on Mars. Even today, long before that flight becomes a reality, we can speculate what it will be like. Your students can do some speculation, too, for this project.

GOAL: Working in groups of 3 to 5, students will assume that their group is part of the first human flight to Mars. They will further assume that the entire expedition will last about two and a half years. As crew members, their group shares a cubicle that is 2 feet by 2 feet by 2 feet ($2' \times 2' \times 2'$) in which they may store personal items on the trip. They are to decide which items or equipment they would bring, being sure that their materials will fit within the cubicle. At the end of the project, each group will need to share its list and explain why it selected the materials it did. *Suggested time*—2 to 3 class periods.

MATH SKILLS TO HIGHLIGHT:

1. Making a model
2. Visualizing spatial relationships
3. Using measurement to determine dimensions and volume

SPECIAL MATERIALS/EQUIPMENT: Rulers; tape measures; poster paper; graph paper; thin markers; crayons; colored pencils. *Optional*—Reference books about Mars.

DEVELOPMENT: Tell your students that within their lifetimes it's probable humans will journey to Mars in exploration. The trip will be long and dangerous, the conditions on board will be cramped and mostly uncomfortable, and there won't be any fast-food outlets along the way. Given those conditions, ask your students why they think people would go. (You might mention that the conditions were probably tougher for the early comers to the New World.)

- Start this project by explaining that each group is to assume it will be part of the crew of the first human expedition to Mars. They will share a cubicle, 2' × 2' × 2' in which they may store personal belongings. Materials for basic needs such as food, water, clothing, toothpaste and brushes, and exercise equipment are supplied for them. Personal items might include things like a Bible, books, small tape players, tapes, batteries, games, maybe even musical instruments.

- Hand out copies of Student Guide 11–1 and review it with your students. Make sure they understand that they do not need to bring along items or equipment that satisfy basic needs of food, shelter, clothing, exercise, or personal hygiene.

- Using poster paper, cardboard, or similar materials, construct a model of a 2-foot cube so that your students can visualize the size of the space they will be able to store items in. Use tape to secure the sides. You might have a group of students do this.

- Hand out rulers to students for measuring items. Encourage them to measure items at home, because it's unlikely they will have the items they'd like to take on such a flight in class. Tape measures are also useful. (Many students will probably have access to rulers and tape measures at home.)

- Emphasize that group members are to share the cubicle. They should agree as to what items or equipment to bring.

- Note that students may bring along as many items as they wish, provided they fit into the cubicle. Packing is an important consideration.

- Point out that the items they select should be practical. Items that provide benefits to several members of the group or crew should be given priority.

- Distribute copies of Data Sheet 11–2, "Information About the Red Planet." This sheet contains facts about Mars that will help students understand Mars's environment. Suggest that students consult other references for more information.

- After selecting the items they would bring, your groups are to draw what they think their cubicle would look like once it is packed. They should use graph paper for this. Graph paper will make it easier for students to create and use a scale. Suggest that they draw the cubicle from a front perspective, although they might like to draw other perspectives as well. They may illustrate their work with markers or colored pencils. They should list their items on the side of their illustration. Depending on the type of drawing, they may not be able to show all of the items inside their cubicle.

WRAP-UP: Each group will display its picture, and the group's spokesperson will explain why the group selected the items it did.

EXTENSION: Suggest that students consult additional sources on Mars to find out what a flight to the planet would entail. Have them report back to the class with their findings.

Name _____   Project Due Date _____

A FLIGHT TO MARS

Situation/Problem:

Your group will be among the crew of the first human expedition to the planet Mars. Leaving Earth when Mars and the Earth are making their closest approach to each other, the flight will last about six months. The crew will have to remain on Mars for 19 months until Mars and Earth approach each other again, then they will spend another six months on the flight returning home. The entire expedition will take about two and a half years. All of your group's basic needs—food, water, clothing, items for personal hygiene, and exercise equipment—will be provided. Because the space on board is limited, each group will be assigned a cubicle 2 feet high, 2 feet wide, and 2 feet deep in which members may store personal items. Your team must work together to agree on a list of items you would take to Mars. The items must be able to fit within the dimensions of the cubicle.

Possible Strategies:

1. Brainstorm a list of items and equipment. List as many things as you can, then go back and eliminate. Remember, your group must share the space in the cubicle.

2. Consider bringing items that everyone can use. For example, books may be read by everyone.

3. Try to avoid items that will take up a lot of space, unless they are extremely important to the group.

Special Considerations:

- Obtain the measurements of items you would like to bring. Divide the task of measuring among group members. If each of you measures five items, the overall task of measuring will not be so time-consuming.

- Although dimensions are important, weight is not. Your ship will be built in space where there is no gravity. The gravity on Mars is 38 percent of Earth's.

- Remember that your trip will last about two and a half years. Select items that will last.

- Refer to Data Sheet 11–2 for information about Mars. Consult other references for more information.

© 1996 by The Center for Applied Research in Education

- Sketch or draw your cubicle and then sketch the items inside. Work with a scale, something like two inches equals one foot. This will help you to visualize how items would fit in your cubicle.

- After you have selected the items your group would take, draw an example of your packed cubicle. Use graph paper for this and create a scale. Several lines on the paper might equal one foot. Depending on the perspective you use—whether you draw your cubicle from the front or side, for example—you may not be able to show all of the items inside. Color your picture, and list the items along the side.

- Pick a spokesperson to share your picture, and explain why you chose the items you did.

To Be Submitted:

Picture with list of selected items

(Data Sheet 11-2)

Name _____

INFORMATION ABOUT THE RED PLANET

Mean Distance From Sun: 141.3 million miles (227.9 million kilometers)

Length of Year (in Earth time): 687 days

Length of Day (in Earth time): 24 hours, 37 minutes

Diameter: 4,200 miles (6,800 kilometers)

Number of Moons: 2 (Phobos and Deimos)

Mean Surface Temperature: –9 degrees F (–23 degrees C)

Surface Gravity (compared with Earth): 0.38

Main Gases in Atmosphere: Carbon dioxide, with small amounts of nitrogen,
oxygen, and argon

Landscape: Reddish rock and dust, a result of iron oxide. This is where the name Red Planet comes from. The land is dry, dotted with towering volcanoes, and criss-crossed with "canals." Once thought to be real canals dug by Martians, most planetary scientists now believe the canals are dry riverbeds and streams. It is thought that Mars once had flowing water.

Potential Habitat for Humans: Living on Mars would mean existing in temperatures much like those found on Antarctica. Humans would also need pressurized suits and oxygen. The first human bases on Mars would probably be constructed underground.

Why Go to Mars? Mars is probably the most hospitable planet in our solar system, except for Earth. Many scientists believe that water is trapped beneath its surface. If this is true, that water can be used by future astronauts. Some scientists believe that varieties of Arctic plants may be able to grow on Mars. This could be a source of oxygen. Along with revealing information about the formation of our solar system, Mars could one day be a colony for humans.

Section 2

•••

MATH AND
SOCIAL STUDIES

AN ELECTION POLL

Polls, especially around election time, are a part of our lives. Polls show people's opinions about issues, how they feel about policies, and how they might vote. At their simplest, a poll might be little more than a few questions that a researcher asks randomly selected individuals. Sophisticated polls, however, consist of carefully designed questions targeted at specific groups. This project gives your students a chance to conduct an election poll.

GOAL: Working in groups of 4 to 5, students will write at least five questions on political issues, concerns, and candidates involved in an upcoming election. The class, as a whole, will select the best questions for inclusion on a questionnaire that will be distributed to potential respondents. After the questionnaires have been collected, students will work in their groups, construct frequency tables, and analyze the results. A class composite result will be expressed as a percent. *Suggested time*—2 to 3 class periods over two weeks.

MATH SKILLS TO HIGHLIGHT:

1. Writing a questionnaire, the results of which may be analyzed
2. Gathering data by means of a questionnaire
3. Constructing frequency tables and determining the frequency of responses
4. Using percents to show information
5. Making a prediction based on collected data

SPECIAL MATERIALS/EQUIPMENT: Calculators for tabulating results and finding percentages. *Optional*—Computer and printer for writing the questionnaires; a clipboard to use for conducting the survey.

DEVELOPMENT: Becoming involved with political polls is an excellent way for students to learn about issues that may influence the outcome of elections. The best time to assign this project is a few weeks before the November elections. You may focus the project on presidential, gubernatorial, state, or local elections, or a combination of the different races and the issues that accompany them. Since it is likely that students will be following the elections in their social studies class, you might wish to share this project with your students' social studies teacher. She or he might incorporate it into her or his plans, expanding the project and its benefits.

- Start the project by explaining to students that they will work in groups to develop questions for an election poll. Each group will contribute questions to a questionnaire.

- Note that there are many ways to conduct polls. They may be conducted over the phone, through the mail, or via a personal interview. Sometimes the questions in a poll are designed to be answered with a simple yes, no, or undecided; sometimes people are asked for explanations; and sometimes they are asked to rate, or prioritize, issues or concerns.

- If you are working with your students' social studies teacher, she or he might be able to discuss some of the issues of the upcoming election with your students before they begin this project. If you are working alone, spend some class time discussing the issues, and encourage students to read about the campaigns on their own.

- Hand out copies of Student Guide 12–1, and review it with your students. Make certain they understand that each group is to contribute to the class's overall efforts. (Each group will write questions for the poll, then the class as a whole will pick the best ones.) Especially note that students should consider using questions that may be answered with a yes, no, or undecided. These are easiest to interpret. While questions may ask respondents to rank issues, such questions are harder to interpret. Depending on your class, you may instruct students to avoid such questions.

- Distribute copies of Data Sheet 12–2, "Poll Points," and go over it with your students. The sheet offers information about polls, as well as some sample questions and suggestions on how to conduct the poll.

- We recommend that you review the drafts of each group's questions before it writes its final copy. This enables you to offer suggestions if necessary.

- After each group has written its questions, work together as a class to select the five to ten questions that will be included on your classroom questionnaire. Try to include at least one question from each group. A good way to select the questions is to show them on an overhead projector and discuss the merits of each. Some questions may ask similar information. In this case, discuss what makes one question better than the other.

- Once the questions have been selected, ask for a volunteer to type the questionnaire. Using a computer or word processor makes revision easier. A quality printer will allow you to produce an attractive questionnaire. (Polls often ask respondents information such as their age, sex, and political affiliations. If you wish to expand the scope of your questionnaire, ask the class if they wish to collect such data. If they do, include such questions on the questionnaire.)

- Photocopy enough questionnaires so that each student has 20 to distribute. The more respondents the class obtains, the more accurate the results of their poll will be. If your class has 25 students, and each one hands out 20 questionnaires, you should get enough back to have a large sample.

- Explain to students that they might ask friends, relatives, and neighbors to answer their questionnaire. They should not go door to door or ask strangers.

- Set a deadline for the completed questionnaires to be returned. Five to seven days is reasonable.

- After the questionnaires have been returned, students should work in their groups to tabulate the results of their questionnaires. (Each group works with the questionnaires its members distributed.) Suggest to students that they create a frequency table to record the results for each question.

- After each group has analyzed the results for their questionnaires, you should compile the results for the class. You might do this on an overhead projector. Have the class help you express the overall results as percentages, for example, "65% of respondents answered yes to question 1." (If the class gathered data about the respondents, you may wish to analyze the answers according to these different categories.)

WRAP-UP: Discuss the results of the poll with your class. Based on the results, make predictions for the upcoming election.

EXTENSION: Suggest that students continue to follow the election and pay close attention to how polls play a role in campaigns. Polls may even influence the outcome of the election.

Name _____   Project Due Date _____

© 1996 by The Center for Applied Research in Education

AN ELECTION POLL

Situation/Problem:

Your group is to develop at least five questions about the issues or candidates during an upcoming election. After writing your questions, you will work with the rest of your class to select five to ten questions that will be included in a class questionnaire that students will distribute. After gathering data, each group will take part in analyzing the results of your poll.

Possible Strategies:

1. Learn about the upcoming election by reading newspaper or magazine articles and watching news broadcasts.
2. Discuss campaign issues with your group.
3. Brainstorm possible survey questions with your group. See Data Sheet 12–2 for examples.
4. Choose what your group feels are your best questions.
5. Keep your questions simple. If they ask for too much information, you will have a hard time analyzing the answers.

Special Considerations:

- After each group has written its questions, you will meet with the entire class and select five to ten questions that the class agrees are the best. These questions will be compiled in the form of a questionnaire. Your teacher will provide class members with several copies of the questionnaire.

- Each student should distribute the questionnaire to 20 people. (Only survey friends, relatives, and neighbors. Do not go door-to-door or survey strangers.) When you hand out the questionnaire to people, ask them to complete it while you wait. If they want to do it later, they may forget or not have the time. Don't pressure them, though. If they need more time, pick the questionnaire up later. *Note:* Handing your questionnaire to people on a clipboard encourages them to answer the questions immediately. Have a pen or pencil handy.

- After obtaining your results, your group should make a frequency table to record your results. Here's how to make a frequency table for questions that require a yes, no, or undecided response:

  —Make a table with three columns.

  —List the possible answers along the left.

  —Provide a tally mark in the second column.

  —Total the frequencies in the last column.

Response	Tally	Frequency
Yes		
No		
Undecided		

- A frequency table for questions that asks respondents to rank issues may be done in a similar manner. For each ranking, a separate tally would be marked.

- After each group has analyzed its results, the entire class will compile the results and use percentages to express the data.

To Be Submitted:

1. A copy of your group's questions
2. A frequency table showing the results for each question on the questionnaire

Name _____

POLL POINTS

Following are some tips that will help you write and conduct an effective election poll.

1. The more respondents you have, the better your chances for accurate results. A poll that has 500 respondents, for example, will show more accurate results than a poll of 20.

2. Carefully consider the questions you will ask for your poll. Questions that can be answered with a "yes," "no," or "undecided" are easiest to interpret. Questions that ask respondents to rank issues or concerns in the order of importance provide more information, but are usually harder to analyze. Think about how to phrase the questions and the possible ways to construct the frequency table. Consider the use of "other" and "none" as responses.

   An example of a yes/no question: In the upcoming election, will you vote yes or no for the referendum on building a new school in town?

   Yes ___   No ___   Undecided ___

   An example of a question that asks respondents to rank issues: Rank the following in order of importance to you (1 being of most importance, 5 being of least).

   Crime ___   Job Security ___   Health Care ___   Taxes ___   Other ___

3. Many polls ask respondents to note their age, sex, political affiliation, etc. This helps the pollsters interpret the results according to specific groups. You may want to include such information on your poll.

4. Questionnaires should be printed clearly, and should be easy to read. Have a clipboard and pen handy to make it easier for people to answer your questionnaire.

5. When you distribute questionnaires to potential respondents, be polite. If someone is not interested, don't press him or her; simply thank the person anyhow.

6. When someone is filling out your questionnaire, give the person time. If a person doesn't have the time now, ask him or her to return the questionnaire to you by a specific day. Since you will have distributed questionnaires to people you know, you should plan to go to them to collect the questionnaires; this will speed results. Set a deadline a few days ahead of when you really need the questionnaire. Remember, everyone's time is valuable.

7. After people answer your questionnaire, be sure to thank them. After all, they are doing this for you.

Some Useful Vocabulary When Conducting a Poll

Data—Facts and figures we can use to obtain information.

Frequency—The number of times an event occurs.

Frequency Table—A table that organizes the results of a tally so that the frequency of each can be recorded.

Poll—A survey, often one asking people how they will vote in an election.

Pollster—An individual conducting a poll.

Sample—A small group used to provide information about a larger group. For example, it would be impractical (if not impossible) to ask every person in a particular state which candidate he or she will likely vote for in an upcoming election. By asking 1,000 random voters, however, pollsters can make a prediction how the election in the state may turn out.

Statistics—Data that is collected and arranged in a systematic manner.

Survey—A method of collecting data from a sample.

Tally—A count or total of specific responses to a question on a poll.

FLAGS

Depending upon the curriculum and grade level, various countries, or, in the case of the U.S., different states are studied in social studies. In this project, students will find and enlarge pictures of flags of a specific country or state. The enlarged pictures may be used for bulletin boards, hallway displays, as part of multicultural activities, or as pictorial displays of countries or states.

GOAL: Working individually, students will look in encyclopedias and other references to find a picture of the flag of a specific state or country. They will enlarge the flag proportionally. *Suggested time*—2 class periods.

MATH SKILLS TO HIGHLIGHT:

1. Measuring and dividing line segments
2. Locating points on a grid
3. Identifying lines of symmetry

SPECIAL MATERIALS/EQUIPMENT: Encyclopedias and other reference books that contain countries' flags; tracing paper; rulers; carbon paper; colored pencils; markers; white drawing paper. *Optional*—French curve.

DEVELOPMENT: You may wish to work with your students' social studies teacher on this project. If your school has a multicultural committee, its members might be interested in correlating this project with other activities. Before introducing the project to your students, consult their social studies teacher for countries or states they will be studying throughout the year. You may wish to compile a list from which students may choose, or you may open the project up a bit and let them select any country or state in which they are interested. Many students will choose countries of their ethnic origins. It is not necessary for every student to choose a different country.

- Begin this project by explaining to your students that they will select a specific country or state, obtain a picture of its flag, and then enlarge the flag in an exact proportion. The finished enlargements will be 6 × 9 inches.

- Distribute copies of Student Guide 13–1. Review it with your students.

- Distribute copies of Data Sheet 13–2, "Steps to Enlarging a Pattern." Carefully review with your students the instructions for increasing the size of the pictures of their flags. Depending on your class, you may feel you should demonstrate the process.

- If you have reference books in class, let students choose a country or state and its flag. If you don't have the necessary references in class, schedule a period in the library. As students are looking through books, hand out rulers, tracing paper, and colored pencils. Once students have selected their flag, they should trace it. Remind them to be as accurate as possible during tracing. (If you have access to a photocopier, consider copying their flags; however, be aware that some colors don't copy well.) If students conduct their research in the library and the rest of the project is to be completed in class, instruct them to lightly color (or label the colors of) their traced picture. Emphasize the need to color lightly because students will have to draw lines over the picture later.

- Discuss lines of symmetry with your students, and note that symmetrical lines make enlargements easier. Since one side of a symmetrical figure is a mirror image of the other side, a student has to locate points only on part of the figure to make an enlargement.

- Encourage students to use rulers for straight lines, and a French curve for irregular curves. However, some students, especially good artists, may wish to sketch the intricate details of their flags by hand.

- After enlarging their flags, students should color them according to the flag's actual colors.

WRAP-UP: Display the finished flags throughout the school, or in math or social studies rooms.

EXTENSIONS: Students may wish to enlarge other items such as maps, or they may wish to create their own patterns for enlargement.

Name _____   Project Due Date _____

FLAGS

Situation/Problem:

Flags are a symbol of a people's heritage. They adorn public buildings, fly on ships, are displayed at citizens' homes, and are carried during celebrations. Think of all the flags waving at the Olympic Games. Wherever the people of a country go, they carry their flag. American astronauts even planted the Stars and Stripes on the moon. In this project, you will select a country (or state), obtain a picture of its flag, and enlarge and color it.

Possible Strategies:

1. Choose a country (or state) in which you are interested, and obtain a picture of its flag.
2. Look for lines of symmetry to simplify your drawing. This will help you to make an enlargement that is proportional to the original picture by only enlarging part of the flag.

Special Considerations:

- Follow all directions on Data Sheet 13–2 carefully. In addition:

    —Do not choose a picture of a furled flag. Make sure that the lines of your flag are straight. Wavy lines (as if the flag is blowing in the breeze) will be hard to enlarge accurately.

    —Be sure your vertical and horizontal lines are straight.

    —Check the numbers you will use to enlarge your flag. Are they arranged consecutively?

    —Check the letters. Are they alphabetical?

    —Do your numbers and letters correspond to lines and not spaces?

    —Plot the points carefully. Estimate, if necessary.

    —Draw or sketch irregular lines.

- If the flag you chose has any lines of symmetry, use the lines of symmetry and carbon paper to trace part of your flag.

- Use colored pencils or markers to color your flag.

To Be Submitted:

1. Original picture or tracing
2. Enlarged drawing of your flag

© 1996 by The Center for Applied Research in Education

Name _____

STEPS TO ENLARGING A PATTERN

1. Trace the picture of the flag you wish to enlarge from a reference book. Lightly color or colorcode it. You can colorcode it by using a letter; for example, R for red, B for black, and Br for brown. This saves you the time needed for coloring, although coloring will give a more accurate representation.

2. Obtain a plain piece of 8-1/2 × 11-inch white paper on which you will draw your enlarged flag. Draw a 6 × 9-inch rectangle horizontally on the page. This will be the full-sized pattern of your enlarged flag.

3. Divide the full-sized pattern into one-inch squares. Draw these lines *lightly* in pencil. Be accurate.

4. Start at the lower left-hand corner of your full-sized pattern and number 1 to 10 across the bottom. Each number should be placed directly below a line, not between lines.

5. Start at the lower left-hand corner of your full-sized pattern and letter from A to G, moving upward. Each letter should be placed directly before a line, not between lines.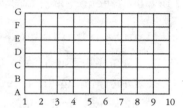

6. Now take the tracing of your flag. Divide the tracing into 9 equal sections, moving from left to right across the bottom, and numbering from 1 to 10 in the same way you labeled the full-sized pattern. Draw the vertical lines.

7. Divide the picture of the small flag into 6 sections vertically, and letter them from A to G, as in the full-sized pattern. Draw the horizontal lines.

8. Locate points on the small flag and transfer them to the large grid. Continue to do this by including all points in the intersections. Estimate the placement of several other points until a shape is outlined.

9. Fill in the other points by sketching or using a French curve. To use a French curve, do the following:

   —Locate 3 points on a section of the curve. This may require some trial and error.

   —Draw the curved section up to, but do not include the third point.

   —Move the curve and repeat this procedure until all irregular curves are sketched.

Note: If your flag has any lines of symmetry, you will only have to enlarge part of the pattern. Fold the paper along the line of symmetry and place a sheet of carbon paper inside so that the carbon side is down. Look carefully for the lines showing through the back of your folded sheet, and trace firmly over them. You should be making a mirror-image on the blank side of the sheet beneath the carbon paper.

© 1996 by The Center for Applied Research in Education

CREATING A SCALE MAP

The ability to read maps is a skill most people use throughout their lives. While students have many opportunities to copy and read maps, few ever create them. When they do, they realize that mathematics plays a major part in mapmaking.

GOAL: Working in pairs or groups of 3, students will create a scale map of their school, school grounds, or their yard at home. They will include landmarks, important details, legends, and an accurate scale. *Suggested time*—2 class periods.

MATH SKILLS TO HIGHLIGHT:

1. Measuring and rounding distances
2. Determining an appropriate scale
3. Making a scale drawing

SPECIAL•MATERIALS/EQUIPMENT: Measuring tapes; yardsticks; metersticks; or trundle wheels; compasses (for finding directions); rulers; crayons; colored pencils; markers; poster paper (approximately 22 × 28 inches).

DEVELOPMENT: Give students options regarding the maps they would like to draw. Students who have a large yard may wish to measure and create a map of that; students who live in apartments might prefer to measure and create a map of their school or school grounds. If students are to draw a map of their school, you might decide to limit the map to a section or wing.

- Begin this project by explaining that maps use a scale to ensure accurate distances. On a world map, one inch might equal 1,500 miles, while on the map of a small town, an inch might equal one-fourth of a mile. On a map of a yard or block, an inch might only equal several feet. Scales are created with mathematics.
- Distribute copies of Student Guide 14–1, and review it with your students.

- If you wish, you may simplify the project by instructing students to create a scale map of your school or school grounds. In this way, you may take your class to obtain the necessary measurements together.

- In measuring distances, remind students to be as accurate as possible. We suggest that distances be rounded to the nearest foot, nearest yard, or nearest meter.

- Suggest that students sketch a rough copy of their map first. This will help them to "see" relationships and estimate where things should be.

- Distribute copies of Data Sheet 14–2, "How to Make a Map." Go over it with your students, making sure they understand how to create a scale for their maps. You may want to check the scales students select before they start making the final copies of their maps.

- After students draw their maps, they should label and color them. Suggest that they provide legends, label the directions, and, of course, note the scale.

WRAP-UP: Display the maps of your students.

EXTENSION: Encourage students to pursue a study of an instrument called the architect's scale, and use it to make a scale drawing of their house. If their house has two stories, they may need to create more than one drawing.

Name _____   Project Due Date _____

CREATING A SCALE MAP

Situation/Problem:

You and your partner(s) are to create a scale map of a familiar place such as your school, school grounds, or the yard of your home.

Possible Strategies:

1. Accurately measure distances (rounding to the nearest foot, yard, or meter).
2. Note landmarks. In the case of a yard, this might include things like trees, woodpiles, sheds, etc. You might include such things in a legend on your map.
3. Create a rough sketch of your map before drawing a final copy. A "rough" will help you to visualize perspectives and landmarks.

Special Considerations:

- Use a measuring tape, yardstick, meterstick, or trundle wheel for measuring distances.
- Use a pad and pencil to record distances. Don't try to remember them; you won't.
- As you record distances, sketch your map, placing landmarks "about" where they would be. Record the distances in feet, yards, or meters. It's a good idea to locate landmarks using the measurements from two boundaries.
- Use a compass to find directions. Be sure to label the directions correctly on your map.
- Consult Data Sheet 14–2 for information about working with scale drawings.
- Be sure the final copy of your map is accurate. Label distances and landmarks, add color, include a legend and directions. You may want to compare your map to the original area and check it for accuracy.

To Be Submitted:

1. Your map
2. Your records of measurements and calculations

Name _____

HOW TO MAKE A MAP

1. Decide upon the boundaries of your map.

2. Make a sketch of the area you will include on your map. Note the approximate position of any landmarks. In a school, landmarks might include stairwells, display cases, or water fountains. Landmarks in a yard might include trees, flowerbeds, decks, sheds, or woodpiles.

3. Accurately measure the boundaries (length and width) of the area. Locate the position of landmarks by obtaining at least two measurements from boundaries.

4. Select the scale by considering your longest measurement, and how to "fit" it on the paper. Remember that the scale should be as long as possible so that your map will look good on the paper.

5. To choose the best scale, divide the longest length of your paper in inches (or centimeters) by the longest dimension of the boundary in feet (or meters).

   —Round your quotient down to the nearest quarter or eighth inch (or centimeter). Here's an example: The longest boundary on your map is 80 feet. The longest dimension of your paper is 28 inches. $\frac{28}{80}$ = .35. Since .35 is between .25 (one-fourth inch) and .375 (three-eighths inch), you must round down so that your scale will be $\frac{1}{4}$ inch = 1 foot.

   —Now take the other dimension of the boundary and the other dimension of the paper, and divide the length of the paper by the length of the boundary.

   —Round your quotient down to the nearest quarter or eighth inch (or centimeter).

   —Compare the scales. If they are the same, great! If they are different, use the smaller scale.

6. To place items on your map, use your measurements and the scale you have chosen. For example, suppose an apple tree is 21 feet from the fence on the eastern side of the yard, and 16 feet from the fence on the northern side. If your scale is $\frac{1}{4}$ inch = 1 foot, multiply the number of inches by the number of feet to determine the number of inches the actual distance would be on your map. Note the example of the math below.

$$\frac{1}{4} \times \frac{21}{1} = \frac{21}{4} = 5\frac{1}{4}$$
$$\frac{1}{4} \times \frac{16}{1} = 4$$

Place the tree 5 $\frac{1}{4}$ inches from the fence on the eastern side, and 4 inches from the northern side.

115

A GAME: WHAT DATE IS THAT?

When your students are learning about the ancient civilizations of the Egyptians, Greeks, and Romans in social studies, you may wish to incorporate a study of the number systems of these civilizations in your math class. Learning about ancient number systems can help students gain an understanding of the evolution of mathematics and appreciate the Hindu-Arabic system we use today.

GOAL: After learning about ancient number systems, students, working in pairs or groups of 3, will use these number systems to create a timeline of important dates in the history of the civilization they select. The timelines will include only dates and not the events that go with them. The timelines can then be photocopied and distributed to the class, whose task will be to convert the dates to the Hindu-Arabic number system we currently use and match the dates with their events. *Suggested time*—2 class periods.

MATH SKILLS TO HIGHLIGHT:

1. Writing numbers using other number systems
2. Comparing the Hindu-Arabic number system with ancient number systems
3. Determining units of a timeline
4. Creating a timeline of important dates in history (using an ancient number system)

SPECIAL MATERIALS/EQUIPMENT: Black felt-tipped pens; rulers; 8-$\frac{1}{2}$ × 11-inch white paper for drawing the timelines; history books and other reference books containing information about the ancient civilizations students will study.

DEVELOPMENT: Check with your students' social studies teacher in advance to find out when she or he will begin teaching ancient civilizations. Suggest to the other teacher that you would like to teach your students about the number systems of these civilizations. Of course, you may assign this project even if your students are not studying ancient civilizations. If that is the case, encourage your students to consult books in the library about the ancient Egyptians, Greeks, and Romans, particularly their number systems.

- Begin this project by explaining to your students that many ancient civilizations have contributed to the development of mathematics and the number system we use today.

- Note that we use the Hindu-Arabic number system, which was developed over 1,200 years ago in the Middle East and India. This number system was not introduced to Europe until the 1100s.

- You may discuss any or all of the three number systems included in this project—the ancient Egyptian, Greek, and Roman. If you wish to limit the project, select one or two. However, using all three will result in a greater variety of timelines, which will make the Wrap-up activity more interesting. (Since these ancient civilizations are often taught in succession in many history classes, a good time to assign this project might be as soon as all of the civilizations have been studied.)

- Distribute copies of Student Guide 15–1, and review it with your students.

- Distribute copies of Data Sheet 15–2, "Ancient Number Systems," which shows how people in the selected civilizations wrote numbers. Review the procedure for working with numbers for each civilization as outlined on the sheet. You might want to write a few dates using an overhead projector or the chalkboard, and have students convert them to the number systems of the ancient civilizations. This will be good practice.

- Explain that students should designate B.C. where necessary for dates. Although ancient civilizations did not use B.C. with their calendars, students will be converting the dates of the ancient civilizations to our modern Hindu-Arabic number system, so the B.C. notation is necessary.

- Instruct students, who will be working with partners, to pick one of the number systems, list at least five important dates in the history of that civilization, then express those dates using the ancient number system. If you wish to expand the project, suggest to students that they may do more than one number system. (Prior to this class, ask students to bring their history books to your math class. They'll probably need a reference to identify accurate dates. You may also consider obtaining additional references from the school library.)

- Instruct students to create a timeline using the dates they selected. They are to write the dates in the number system they chose. Remind them not to list the event next to the date, but instead leave a blank line. Their classmates will interpret the date and write the event on the line. Depending on your class, you may want to review how to construct a timeline so that the dates will correspond with points on the number line.

WRAP-UP: Photocopy the timelines and distribute them to the class. Students can then try to work out the dates and match them with the correct events. This can be an enjoyable activity.

EXTENSION: Encourage students to select a fictional civilization (from literature or their own imaginations), and create a number system for this civilization.

Name _____   Project Due Date _____

A GAME: WHAT DATE IS THAT?

Situation/Problem:

Imagine that you and your partner are students in ancient Egypt, Greece, or Rome. Like students today, you have assignments to do and facts to learn. You are to select *at least* five important dates in the history of your civilization, and create a timeline. You must write the dates using the number system of your civilization. (Don't label the events on your timeline. Simply leave a line next to the date for the event, and let your friends convert the dates to our number system. They should then try to match events to the dates.)

Possible Strategies:

1. Discuss with your partner which ancient civilization(s) you would like to work on for this project.

2. Use a reference book, your social studies text, or history book to select important dates in the history of your civilization(s).

Special Considerations:

- Be sure the dates you select are accurate.

- Refer to Data Sheet 15–2 to learn how to write numbers using ancient number systems.

- Carefully recheck your numbers when written in an ancient number system. Because the dates on your number line will be converted to the Hindu-Arabic system, use B.C. if necessary. (Of course, before the birth of Christ, there was no "B.C." designation for dates.)

- Before drawing your timeline, decide when it will begin and when it will end. Divide the timeline into equal units, and place dates as closely as you can to where they should appear on the timeline.

- Use black felt-tipped or heavy black ball-point pens to draw your timeline. The black will reproduce more clearly on a photocopier.

- When you draw your timeline, do not label the dates with their events. Be sure to write the answers on a separate sheet of paper.

To Be Submitted:

1. Your timeline with dates written in the ancient number system

2. A key that contains the dates in our number system and a list of events to which they refer

(Data Sheet 15-2)

Name _____

ANCIENT NUMBER SYSTEMS

We use the Hindu-Arabic number system today. It was developed in the lands of the Middle East and India before 800 A.D. and eventually spread throughout the Western World during the 1100s. As you'll see when you examine the ancient number systems below, the Hindu-Arabic system was a major improvement.

Egyptians (about 3000 B.C.): The ancient Egyptians wrote numbers the same way they wrote words—tediously—by carving or scratching pictures in stone or wood.

   | = one (picture of a finger)

   ∩ = ten (picture of a heel bone)

   𐦂 = one hundred (picture of a coiled rope)

   ⚲ = one thousand (picture of a lotus flower)

   ↶ = ten thousand (picture of a bent finger)

   𓆏 = one hundred thousand (picture of a tadpole)

   𓀀 = one million (picture of an astonished man)

To write their numbers, the Egyptians would repeat the symbols, with the largest number on the left and other numbers in descending order.

The date 1290 B.C. was the year Ramses II became pharaoh of Egypt. He ruled for 67 years during Egypt's Golden Age. In the ancient Egyptian number system, the date 1290 B.C. would be written:

    ⚲ ⫝⫝ ∩∩∩∩∩∩∩∩∩   B.C.

  one thousand   nine tens
         two hundreds

119

© 1996 by The Center for Applied Research in Education

Greeks (about 100 B.C.): The ancient Greeks were the first to use alphabetic symbols to stand for numbers. They were able to express large numbers by using 27 symbols. (They used their alphabet, which had 24 letters, and borrowed the other 3 letters from other alphabets.)

α = 1	ι = 10	ρ = 100	͵α = 1000
β = 2	κ = 20	σ = 200	͵β = 2000
γ = 3	λ = 30	τ = 300	͵γ = 3000
δ = 4	μ = 40	υ = 400	͵δ = 4000
ε = 5	ν = 50	φ = 500	͵ε = 5000
ς = 6	ξ = 60	χ = 600	͵ς = 6000
ζ = 7	ο = 70	ψ = 700	͵ζ = 7000
η = 8	π = 80	ω = 800	͵η = 8000
θ = 9	ϙ = 90	ϡ = 900	͵θ = 9000

The Greeks wrote numbers by placing the largest symbol on the left, and the corresponding symbols for the other numbers to the right, in descending order.

The year 429 B.C. saw the birth of Plato. The ancient Greeks would have written the date as:

υ κ θ B.C.
400 20 9

Romans (about 100 A.D.): The ancient Romans could express all numbers from 1 to 1,000,000 with a minimum of 7 symbols.

I = 1	C = 100
V = 5	D = 500
X = 10	M = 1,000
L = 50	

They built numbers by putting symbols together in the following way:

- A smaller number to the right of a larger one means to add.
- A smaller number to the left of a larger number means to subtract.
- A vinculum, written as a —, placed over a letter means to multiply that value by 1,000.

It was on March 15, 44 B.C. (known as the Ides of March) that Julius Caesar was assassinated. The Romans would have written the year like this:

X L I V B.C.
50 – 10 5 – 1
or or
40 4

AN INTERVIEW TO MATH'S PAST

One way to view mathematics is to see it as a tool, a means of expressing quantities and values. As such a tool, math is reflected in a society's economy, customs, and routines. For example, in the 1930s, the cost for spending an afternoon in a movie theater was about a dime (often to see a double feature). Today the cost is several bucks and counting, and we won't even mention the quality of the shows! The increase in ticket prices is an indication of change in our society. Change is frequently shown through a comparison of numbers. In this project, students will view the past through numbers, gaining an appreciation of how our society has changed over the years.

GOAL: Working alone, students will interview a senior citizen, preferably a relative. They will ask this person what life was like when he or she was young, and particularly what role mathematics played in his or her life. After completing the interview, students will present their findings to the class in an oral report. *Suggested time*—2 to 3 class periods over a two-week period.

MATH SKILL TO HIGHLIGHT:

Recognizing the changing role of mathematics as a society changes through time

SPECIAL MATERIALS/EQUIPMENT: Pads or a clipboard for notetaking; note cards for organizing oral presentations. *Optional*—Tape recorder for taping the interview.

DEVELOPMENT: Students are used to learning about the past through books. Seldom do they learn about it, however, by speaking with someone who has lived it.

- Begin by explaining that students are to interview a senior citizen about what life was like, especially in terms of mathematics, when he or she was young. Students should try to interview a grandfather, grandmother, great uncle, or great aunt. A great-grand-parent would be even better. If older relatives are unavailable, suggest that students interview older friends or neighbors of the family. Discourage them from interviewing people they don't know well.

- Distribute copies of Student Guide 16–1. Review it with your students and make certain they understand what they are to do. In particular, note the sample questions. Such questions are important because they will help keep the interview focused on math.

- Distribute copies of Data Sheet 16–2, "Tips for Conducting Effective Interviews." Remind students that since they are looking for mathematical facts of the past, they must ask questions that will elicit responses about math.

- Mention that during the interview students should look for ways that the use of math has changed. For example, today, clerks at cash registers seldom figure out how much change to give to a customer after a purchase. The register computes the change for them. Another example: electronic "money" is becoming the major means of transactions for some people. They do their banking via computer. Yet another example: computers today make mathematical calculations in seconds that would have taken hours or days just a generation ago.

- After completing their interviews, students should organize their notes to make an oral presentation of their findings to the class. They should use note cards for this.

- You may want to limit the length of time for the presentations; about three minutes is reasonable. Less time makes some students hard-pressed to finish sharing their information, while more time adds up to a significant amount of class time.

WRAP-UP: Students present their findings orally to the class.

EXTENSION: Working in groups, students brainstorm how the use of mathematics might change in the future. A spokesperson for each group shares the group's conclusions with the class.

Name _____   Project Due Date _____

AN INTERVIEW TO MATH'S PAST

Situation/Problem:

To find out the role mathematics played in the past, you are to interview a senior citizen. After your interview, you will present your findings to the class in a brief oral report.

Possible Strategies:

1. Decide whom you will interview. A grandfather, grandmother, great uncle, or great-aunt will have spent his or her youth at a time when life was quite different. If you are unable to interview a relative, consider interviewing an older close friend or neighbor. Do not interview anyone without your parent/guardian's permission.
2. Determine in advance the time period your interview will focus on. This will help you to ask questions that will provide you with information about the role math played in society at that time.

Special Considerations:

- Since the focus of your interview will be on mathematics, your questions should zero in on math. Following are some areas you might like to explore with your interviewee:

  —What was the pay per hour (or the salary) of your first job? What was your job, and what were your responsibilities?

  —What was the price of a gallon of gasoline?

  —What was the cost of a new car?

  —What was the price of a new house? What was the cost of renting an apartment?

  —What were the prices of clothing, shoes, and food?

  —What did people do for entertainment when you were young? How much did this cost? What was considered a "fun" activity?

  —What kind of math did you learn in school? How much math homework did you receive? What was your math class like? How did you figure out answers to long or difficult problems?

  —Did you ever need to use math on a job? If yes, in what way?

  —In what ways have you seen mathematics change during your life?

  —What surprises you about math's role in society now?

- Add your own questions to those listed above.

- Pay close attention to major events that might have influenced the life of your interviewee. The Great Depression and World War II, for example, affected countless people. If they did affect your interviewee, find out how.

- Refer to Data Sheet 16–2 for advice on how to conduct an effective interview.

- In organizing your notes, compare the math facts of the past with the uses of math today. Look for similarities and differences. Note any major changes.

- In preparing your oral presentation, use note cards to help you remember important facts. Be sure to number your cards.

- If your teacher puts a time limit on your presentation, make sure your talk fits into the allotted time. Rehearse your report; time yourself if necessary.

To Be Submitted:

Your note cards

(Data Sheet 16-2)

Name _____

TIPS FOR CONDUCTING EFFECTIVE INTERVIEWS

You can learn much valuable information about a topic during an interview. Following are some suggestions that will help you to get the most out of any interview you conduct.

- Think about who is best able to give you the information you are looking for.
- Learn as much about the subject in advance as you can. This will help you to formulate questions that will provide you with useful information.
- Think of questions before the interview. Write them down. Use questions that require explanations. Avoid questions that can be answered with a simple yes or no.
- Be ready to ask a follow-up question to clarify or expand an answer you receive.
- If you are not sure about an answer, ask for more explanation.
- Consider recording your interview on a tape recorder. Keep in mind that some people do not like to be recorded. Ask first. If they object, don't use it. If they don't mind, be sure you have a clean tape and fresh batteries. (Take along a pen and pad just in case.)
- If you are taking notes with a pen and pad, don't try to write down everything your interviewee says. Focus on the main points. Use your own personal shorthand of abbreviations. For example, *John* is *J*, *math* is *m, and* is +. Inventing your own codes will help you to take notes quickly.
- For important facts or statements, try to write down the person's exact words. You can quote the person after the interview. Whenever writing a person's exact words, be sure to use quotation marks.
- After you have asked your questions, end the interview by thanking the interviewee for his or her time. Don't keep the interview running after it's done. End by thanking the person. Writing a thank-you note a few days later is a nice gesture.

125

RATING CONSUMER PRODUCTS

We live in a society where we have a choice of purchasing countless consumer products. Just consider how many types of sneakers we can buy, or how many brands of potato chips we can choose from. To help us select the best product from among many, we can turn to articles and books that rate various products. Most rating systems rely on statistics, which in turn are built on mathematics.

GOAL: Working in pairs or groups of 3, students will select products to research. They will evaluate and compare the features and prices of each product, and try to determine which is best for their needs. They will illustrate their results via charts, and share their conclusions orally with the class. *Suggested time*—2 to 3 periods over two weeks.

MATH SKILLS TO HIGHLIGHT:

1. Gathering and analyzing data
2. Comparing prices and features of products
3. Making decisions based on collected data
4. Creating charts to illustrate conclusions

SPECIAL MATERIALS/EQUIPMENT: White poster paper; rulers; markers; and felt-tipped pens for making charts. Students will need to obtain samples of the products they select to research; however, in most cases, the products will be inexpensive and easy to obtain and research. Copies of articles or samples of magazines such as *Consumer Reports*, in which products are rated, will give students an idea of how products may be compared.

DEVELOPMENT: Ask your students what rationale they use to buy products. For example, why did they buy the sneakers they are wearing? Most likely they tried on various styles, were impressed with the sneaker through advertising, or heard about it from a friend. They might have seen somebody else wearing the sneaker and decided they liked it. Explain that people usually have reasons for buying one product instead of another.

- Begin the project by explaining that students will work with a partner(s). They will select a type of product—see Data Sheet 17–2 for some examples—and rate samples of the product produced by different companies. Ultimately, they are to determine which brand is best.

- Note that this project may require meeting outside of class. Since students who are friends usually find it easier to work together at home, try to allow friends to be partners.

- Distribute copies of Student Guide 17–1 and review it with your students. Emphasize that they should compare at least three brands of the same product, although encourage them to compare as many brands as they can.

- Distribute copies of Data Sheet 17–2, "Tips for Comparing Some Everyday Products," and go over it closely with your class. Mention that the products listed on this sheet are just some examples of the types of products they might decide to compare. There are many others. You might wish to brainstorm examples of more potential products with your class; list them on the board or use an overhead projector. This will give students more choices.

- Explain that since the features of different products vary, students should select features or categories for comparison based upon their specific product. Video games would be compared differently from brands of pretzels.

- Suggest that students may compare products by using them, tasting them (in the case of food), reading their specifications or ingredients, and asking others about them.

- After students have finished their research, they should write their findings and reasons. They will present their conclusions to the class.

- Remind students to create a rough chart on scrap paper before attempting to draw their final copy. Encourage them to design a chart that will be informative as well as easy to read.

WRAP-UP: Present oral presentations using charts to support findings. You may also wish to display the charts.

EXTENSION: Suggest that students select a product they like, and encourage them to consult *Consumer Reports* or other publications to find out if the brand they use is the one recommended in terms of price and quality. Frequently, students are surprised that the brand they use is overpriced or of lesser quality than competing brands.

Name _____/_____   Project Due Date _____

RATING CONSUMER PRODUCTS

Situation/Problem:

You and your partner(s) are to select a product, and compare at least three brands of it. You are to compare its features and price, and try to determine which is the best choice for a consumer's hard-earned dollars. After you have reached your conclusions, design a chart to support your findings and present your data to the class through an oral report.

Possible Strategies:

1. Consult examples of articles that compare or rate products. The magazine *Consumer Reports* is a good source. Copies may be in your school or public library.

2. Brainstorm with your partner(s) which types of products you might like to research. Consult Data Sheet 17–2 for some ideas.

3. Divide the tasks for the project. While you will work together on much of this, you may find it helpful if one of you interviews people for research, while the other compares product specifications. If your partner(s) is more artistic than you, he or she may draw the chart and you handle the oral presentation.

Special Considerations:

- After selecting your product, decide which features or qualities you will compare. Write these categories on a sheet of paper, then compare the products.

- Consider developing a rating scale. You might use something like 1—Superior, 2—Fair, 3—Poor. Compare each brand according to your scale.

- Along with their physical features, products may also be compared according to their specifications or ingredients.

- You may find it helpful to ask friends and acquaintances about specific products. To ensure accurate results, always ask the same questions in the same manner. Write the questions you intend to ask ahead of time. Focus your questions on features or qualities.

- After obtaining your data, analyze it and make decisions comparing qualities to price.

- Create a chart illustrating your results. Sketch a rough copy of your chart first. This enables you to revise the chart before starting the final copy. Arrange the design so that it presents the data clearly. List your products by brand name, and your categories for comparison. If there is room on your chart, you may wish to provide a brief summary of your results.

- Before presenting your findings to the class, write notes so that you don't forget to mention any important information. Rehearse your presentation.

To Be Submitted:

1. Research notes
2. Chart

Name _____

TIPS FOR COMPARING SOME EVERYDAY PRODUCTS

Popular products are compared and rated regularly in magazine articles and books. Many educated consumers rely on such articles to help them buy the products that fit their needs and budgets.

SOME WAYS PRODUCTS ARE COMPARED:

- Special Features
- Simple Directions
- Texture
- Price
- Power
- Resale Value

- Ease of Use
- Taste
- Ingredients
- Comfort
- Durability
- Attractiveness

SOME PRODUCTS TO CONSIDER COMPARING:

Video games

Potato chips

Pizzas

Ice cream

Pretzels

Clothes

Video game systems

Sodas

Fast food restaurants

On-line systems

Sneakers

Computers

EXAMPLES OF PRODUCTS AND FEATURES/QUALITIES YOU MIGHT COMPARE:

Video games (action, color, graphics, realism, sound, excitement, ease of use, easy-to-read manual, price)

Pretzels (type, taste, saltiness, crispness, fat content, natural versus artificial flavoring, ingredients, cholesterol, price)

Sneakers (purpose, comfort, durability, style, color, price, non-marking soles, technology)

Jeans (comfort, style, price, texture)

LANDS OF ETHNIC ORIGIN—A STATISTICAL POTPOURRI

If your class is like most, you probably have students who come from various backgrounds. Exploring the countries of students' ethnic origins can be an interesting activity. Asking students to investigate countries of origin from a mathematical perspective can impress them with the value of math, as well as help them to learn about the countries from where their families came.

GOAL: Working individually, students will research a country of their ethnic origin, and use mathematics to describe it. Upon completion of their research, students will create a mathematical Fact Sheet, a "statistical potpourri," highlighting information about their country. *Suggested time*—2 class periods over two weeks.

MATH SKILLS TO HIGHLIGHT:

1. Researching statistical information about selected countries
2. Analyzing and organizing data
3. Using mathematics to communicate ideas

SPECIAL MATERIALS/EQUIPMENT: Reference books, including almanacs and atlases to research countries; white paper for the Fact Sheet; colored pencils; rulers; crayons; markers; felt-tipped pens; correction fluid. *Optional*—Computers and printers to design the Fact Sheets.

DEVELOPMENT: Discuss with your students that the United States is a country of immigrants. All of our families have roots elsewhere. Even the ancestors of Native Americans came to North America across a land bridge between Asia and Alaska during the Ice Ages.

- Begin this project by explaining that students will work alone and research a country of their ethnic origins. If students have several backgrounds in their family, they should pick one, or, if they are ambitious, two or more. (If a student is unsure of his or her background, give the student the option of simply selecting a country that interests him or her.)

- Note that students are to base their research on mathematics, their purpose to create a Fact Sheet of statistics.

- Distribute copies of Student Guide 18–1, and review it with your class. Be certain they understand what they are to do.

- Hand out copies of Data Sheet 18–2, "Tips for Creating a Country's Fact Profile Sheet." Review it with your students, and point out that the categories listed are some types of facts they should look for during research. It's likely that some students will be able to find more; and some students will have trouble finding information about all the categories on this list. Obviously, it depends on the country.

- To help students with their research, you may wish to take the class to the school library for one period. Inform the librarian in advance that you'll need books about various countries. It would help if you could poll your students and write the countries they'll be researching; particularly note any obscure ones.

- After completing their research, students are to create a statistical Fact Sheet about their country. Remind them to arrange their data in a clear and logical manner. Suggest that they do a rough draft first. (If students have access to computers and printers, they may wish to design their Fact Sheets on this equipment. Warn them, however, that they will need to contend with tabs and spacing.) They should include their sources on the bottom of their Fact Sheet.

WRAP-UP: Display the Fact Sheets.

EXTENSION: Suggest that students research and compare the statistical data they found on their country with the state they live in or one of the big states of the U.S. California, Texas, New York, and Michigan are good examples; these states will be larger, have bigger populations, and greater economies than many countries around the world. Discuss this with your class.

Name _____   Project Due Date _____

LANDS OF ETHNIC ORIGINS—A STATISTICAL POTPOURRI

Situation/Problem:

You are to research the country of your ethnic origin from a mathematical perspective. When you are done with your research, you are to create a Fact Sheet, highlighting the information you found.

Possible Strategies:

1. If you are from several ethnic backgrounds, select the country you would most like to learn about.
2. Consult books that contain information about your country, and focus on information that is expressed in numbers. See Data Sheet 18–2 for examples.

Special Considerations:

- Take accurate notes. List your sources on your notes. This is helpful should you need to recheck some facts. (It's also helpful when you must include your sources on your Fact Sheet.)
- After completing your research, make a rough copy of your Fact Sheet. Try to find a design that is easy to read and attractive. Consider how you would like to organize your information. You might organize your facts according to major categories, alphabetically, or numerically in order of size.
- If you have access to a computer and printer, you may want to design your Fact Sheet on it.
- If you design your Fact Sheet by hand, use rulers to draw straight lines on the sheet.
- Use markers or felt-tipped pens for final copies. Correction fluid is useful if you make a mistake.
- You might want to include a drawing of your country's flag, or a map of your country.
- Be sure to include your sources of information at the bottom of your Fact Sheet.

To Be Submitted:

1. Notes
2. Fact Sheet

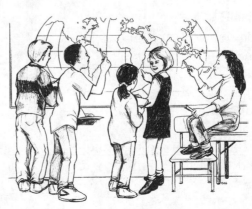

(Data Sheet 18-2)

Name _____

TIPS FOR CREATING A COUNTRY'S FACT PROFILE SHEET

The following categories are often expressed in terms of mathematics. Note that these are just a sample; there are many others.

GENERAL FACTS

Population
Number of States, Provinces
Number of Major Cities and Populations
Largest, Smallest Cities
Percent of People Living in Cities
Percent of People Living in Specific Regions
Number of Major Newspapers
Number of Major Religions:
    Percent of People Belonging to Each
Education:
    Number of Elementary Schools
    Number of Secondary Schools
    Number of Universities
    Number of School-Age Children
    Literacy Rate
Currency (U.S. equivalent)
Size of Armed Forces:
    Army, Navy, Air Force
Number of Languages:
    Percent of People Speaking Each
Government:
    Number of Major Bodies
    Number of Members
Political Parties:
    Percentage of Population Belonging to Each

GEOGRAPHY

Latitude and Longitude
Time Zone
Area
General Elevation (highest mountain)
Longest River
Largest Lake
Percentage of Forested Land
Land Use Facts

CLIMATE

Number of Climate Zones
Average Annual/Monthly Temperature
Average Annual/Monthly Precipitation
Average Annual Snowfall
Average Summer Temperature
Average Winter Temperature
Noteworthy Weather Facts

ECONOMY

Gross National Product
Per Capita Income
Employment Rate
Percentage of White-Collar, Manufacturing, or Service Occupations
Average Length of Work Week
Amount of National Debt (or Surplus)
Imports:
    Total Value and Major Types
Exports:
    Total Value and Major Types
Percentage of Land Used for Farming
Energy:
    Types and Amounts

A LAND OF IMMIGRANTS

The United States is a land of immigrants. Even the ancestors of Native Americans crossed over the land bridge between Asia and Alaska during the Ice Ages. Unfortunately, although all of our ancestors have emigrated to America, newcomers have not always been welcomed by the general population. This is especially true today when many Americans feel that the number of immigrants permitted into the country should be reduced.

GOAL: Working in groups of 2 to 3, students will research immigration, identifying those decades in which the most immigrants came to the U.S. They will also note from which countries the most immigrants came. Groups will then design graphs to illustrate their data. *Suggested time*—3 to 4 class periods.

MATH SKILLS TO HIGHLIGHT:

1. Researching mathematical data
2. Organizing data
3. Using percents
4. Designing graphs to illustrate data

SPECIAL MATERIALS/EQUIPMENT: Reference books on immigration; poster paper; felt-tipped pens; markers; rulers. *Optional*—Computers and printers.

DEVELOPMENT: This project is ideal for incorporating technology into your math curriculum. Many computer programs will enable students to create graphs. This project also offers an excellent opportunity for collaboration with your students' social studies teacher, who may assume responsibility for research and discussion, while you handle the analysis of information and graphing.

- Start the project by explaining to students that they will work in groups of 2 or 3. They will research the history of immigration to the U.S., identifying the years in which immigration was the greatest, and noting from which countries the immigrants came.

- Discuss the concept of the "Melting Pot," and that the U.S. is a land of immigrants.

- Explain that a great controversy rages over immigration today. Many Americans feel that immigration should be reduced. These people believe that immigrants take jobs from Americans and put a strain on social services. Although many facts about immigration are in dispute, that doesn't ease the arguments.

- Hand out copies of Student Guide 19–1, and review it with your students. Especially emphasize the following:

  —Groups will need to do several graphs for this project. Some will focus on the number of people who came to this country during specific time periods, while others will show the countries from which most immigrants came.

  —Suggest that students design graphs according to decades. Trying to do each year individually will make the graphs too tedious.

- Distribute copies of Data Sheet 19–2, "Researching Immigration." This sheet will help students with their research, analysis, and design of graphs.

- To facilitate research, schedule a period for your class in the library. Ask the librarian in advance to reserve books that contain information on immigration.

- If you have access to computers, encourage students to enter their data on spreadsheets and from there create graphs to illustrate their information. Students may also create their graphs using poster paper and markers.

WRAP-UP: Display the graphs of your students.

EXTENSION: Encourage students to examine the issue of immigration today. Suggest that they investigate the number of legal versus illegal aliens in our country. What are the numbers? What are the implications, problems, and concerns? Discuss their findings with the class.

Name _____   Project Due Date _____

A LAND OF IMMIGRANTS

Situation/Problem:

Working with a partner(s), you are to research the history of immigration to the United States. You are to find the decades in which immigration was the greatest, and also identify from which countries the most immigrants came. You are then to create graphs to illustrate your findings.

Possible Strategies:

1. Divide the task of research with your partner(s). For example, one of you might investigate the years 1789–1899, and the other might research the years 1900 to the present.

2. Discuss which graphs will best present the information you find. It is likely that you will need to create several graphs.

Special Considerations:

- Take accurate notes and maintain a list of your sources. This is important if you need to go back and check information.

- Don't try to record immigration for every year since Colonial Days. Rather, focus on decades from 1789 (the year of the first meeting of the U.S. Congress) to the present.

- Use Data Sheet 19–2 to help you with your research, organize your information, and select your graphs.

- If you have access to computers, use them to create spreadsheets and generate graphs.

- If you use markers and pens for creating your graphs, use pencils and rulers to make light lines on your paper so that your graphs and letters will be straight. Use colors that stand out and highlight your information. Be sure to label your information.

To Be Submitted:

Your graphs

© 1996 by The Center for Applied Research in Education

Name _____

RESEARCHING IMMIGRATION

To help you with your research about immigration, use the following guidelines. Use separate sheets of paper for your notes.

1. Find the total amount of immigration for each decade. Start with 1789–1799, then do 1800–1809, 1810–1819, 1820–1829, etc., to the present.

2. List the seven countries from which the greatest numbers of immigrants came. Remember that people have come from all around the world to start new lives in the United States. Compare the numbers of immigrants from these countries with the overall number of immigrants. Express these numbers as percents.

3. After gathering your data, determine how you will illustrate your information with graphs. Here are some suggestions:

   —Bar graphs are useful for comparing years or decades.

   —Line graphs are a good choice to show how immigration increased or decreased over a specific period.

   —Circle graphs (pie graphs) are useful for showing percentages of immigrants and the countries from which they came.

   —Pictographs use symbols to represent data, and offer a good visual perspective for comparison. Values are approximations.

   Note: Make sure the information on your graphs is accurate and clear.

THE GAMES PEOPLE PLAY

Mathematics has always been relevant to people everywhere for work and play. Too often students think of mathematics in association with work. They seldom pause to consider how math is found in virtually every game we play, from the most basic application—keeping score—to strategies based on mathematical probabilities—for example, in games such as chess, poker, and dice. Math is a vital element of games that have originated around the world. In this project students will learn about games that involve math and that have originated in various countries or regions. This activity could be an excellent addition to a multicultural event in your school, or may simply be an enjoyable activity of its own.

GOAL: Working as partners or groups of 3, students will select a game that originated in a country other than the U.S., research its development, and write a short historical report about it. They will then teach and play the game with at least two other students. *Suggested time*—2 to 3 class periods.

MATH SKILLS TO HIGHLIGHT:

Math skills will vary according to the game, strategies, and scoring

SPECIAL MATERIALS/EQUIPMENT: Since students will either obtain or make the games on their own, materials will vary and should be supplied by students.

DEVELOPMENT: Ask students what they do for recreation. Some students probably watch TV, play or watch sports, play video games or board games, solve puzzles, go to the movies, dance, participate in crafts or art, or simply "hang out." Emphasize that there are plenty of recreational activities from which to choose. Prior to the advance of technology, however, there were far fewer choices. In the past, people often turned to board and card games to relax and pass time. Games were played almost everywhere, and the most popular were carried across borders and spread around the world.

- Begin by explaining that for this project, students—working with a partners—will select a game that originated in another country. They will obtain either the game, or make a sample copy of it, research its history, then share their findings with the class. They will also have the opportunity to teach and play the game with other students.

- Distribute copies of Student Guide 20–1, and go over it carefully with your students. In particular, review the checklist that is provided. Emphasize that students should not go out and buy an expensive version of the game they select. (If it is inexpensive, however, they may wish to purchase it. Some games, for example, need nothing more than a deck of cards.) If the game is expensive, or if they cannot find a version of it, they should make their own, using poster paper, cardboard, and markers.

- Hand out copies of Data Sheet 20–2, "Games From Around the World," which provides a list of possible games students might select. Note that this is only a partial list; encourage students to look for other games in the library.

- Discourage students from choosing games that require physical activity. These will be difficult to manage in the classroom.

- Once students have decided on a game, they should research its history. Many games were invented because of unusual circumstances. Solitaire, for instance, was created by a Frenchman in the eighteenth century, who had been imprisoned and sentenced to solitary confinement. Apparently he had plenty of time in which to think of things to do. (Today, there are several versions of solitaire, some of which have different names.)

- Caution students that various sources may report different rules or a different history for the same game. For some games, it might be hard to pinpoint a single country of origin. Instruct students to pick one version of the game, and record their source.

- Upon completion of their research, students are to write a brief historical background of their game, and provide a sample of the game for the class. Students will explain the history of their game, its rules, and play a sample round with other students. Set aside a period to play "games."

- *A note on evaluation:* Rather than collecting all the games, you might instead circulate around the classroom as students are playing the games. If you need to grade the games, doing it now eliminates the need for collecting them and handing them back out. (This is certainly a consideration for games that have a number of small pieces.)

WRAP-UP: Students play their games in class.

EXTENSION: Students may wish to pursue other contributions to mathematics from other countries, such as origami, tangrams, or tessellations.

Name _____   Project Due Date _____

THE GAMES PEOPLE PLAY

Situation/Problem:

You and a partner(s) are to select a game that involves math and which originated in another country. You are to write a historical background of the game, obtain or make the game board or other materials, and teach others how to play.

Possible Strategies:

1. Select a game you have played and which you know originated in another country.
2. Choose a country or a region of the world in which you are interested, and research a game that originated there.
3. Choose a game from Data Sheet 20–2.

Special Considerations:

- Look at Data Sheet 20–2 and carefully go over the list of possible games. Choosing one with which you are familiar will make your research easier.

- Choose board games, card games, or pen-and-pencil games. Avoid games that require physical action.

- Set aside library time to research the game you selected.

- Be aware that many games have several variations. Choose one.

- During your research, you may find that the country of origin for your game is in dispute. Try to find at least two sources that agree and use the information they provide. If all of your sources provide different information, choose one. Be sure to record the source.

- As you research, look for the following information:

  —History of your game

  —Object of the game

  —Number of players

  —Types of playing pieces

  —Rules

  —How math is involved in your game

  —Any special evidence of the culture from which the game evolved

© 1996 by The Center for Applied Research in Education

- After you have finished your research, write a short historical report about your game.

- Obtain or make a sample of your game. If you make it, create a board (if necessary), playing pieces, spinners, dice, etc. Include the object of the game and a copy of written rules.

- To avoid losing pieces, store game pieces in a shoe box or similar container.

- Become the expert on your game. With your partner, explain it to some of your classmates and show them how to play.

To Be Submitted:

Historical report

Name _____

GAMES FROM AROUND THE WORLD

Following are some popular games and the country or region of their origin.

Achi—Ghana

Alquerque—Arabia

Checkers—Europe

Derrah—Nigeria

Dominoes—Egypt

Draughts—France

Dreidels—Germany (although the game has been a part of Jewish culture)

Goose Game—France

Hala-tafl (Fox Game)—Scandinavia

Konane—Hawaii

Ko-no—China and Korea

Lu-lu—Polynesia

Magic Squares—China, Egypt, India, Western Europe

Mu-Torere—New Zealand

Nim—China

Nine Men's Morris (also known as Mill, Morelles, and Muhle)—Europe

Ninuki-Renju—Japan

Nyout—Korea

Paiute Walnut Shell Game—Paiute Indians (Nevada)

Parcheesi—India

Patolli—Aztecs (Mexico)

Pipopipette (also known as Boxes)—France

Pong Hau K'i—China

Safragat—Sudan

Seega—Egypt

Senet—Egypt

Sey—West Africa

Shut the Box—France

Sir Tommy—England

Snakes and Ladders—India

Solitaire (the board game)—France

Tac Tix—Denmark

Tapatan—Philippines

Tawlie—Iraq

Totolospi—Hopi Indians (Southwestern U.S.)

Wari—West Africa

Who Crosses the River First?—China

Yote—West Africa

BACK TO THE PAST

Mathematics has been a part of virtually every civilization throughout history. From the most primitive times when people tallied numbers by making slashes on cave walls, to the vast empires of the ancient Romans and Chinese, and now to our modern world linked by computers, people have needed numbers for counting and calculating. While the need for math hasn't changed, its methods certainly have. People have always adapted mathematics to fit their needs.

GOAL: Working in groups of 3 or 4, students will select a country or region and research how mathematics was used in the past. They will present their information to the class via oral reports. *Suggested time*—2 to 3 class periods over two weeks.

MATH SKILLS TO HIGHLIGHT:

1. Researching mathematical data
2. Organizing data from a mathematical perspective
3. Communicating ideas about math

SPECIAL MATERIALS/EQUIPMENT: History and other reference books; 3 × 5 note cards for notes.

DEVELOPMENT: Consider working with your students' social studies or history teacher for this project. While you may permit students to research countries or regions anywhere in the world, most students will find it more relevant to research places they have studied in their social studies or history classes.

*   Begin this project by explaining that students will work in groups of 3 to 4. They are to select a country or region, and research its use of mathematics in the past. They may choose to research a specific period, for example, the Middle Ages, or they may decide to trace the use of math from ancient times to the present.

- Hand out copies of Student Guide 21–1, and review it with your students.
- Distribute copies of Data Sheet, 21–2, "An Outline to Organization." Go over it with your students. Especially point out the areas on which they might concentrate their research, but note that these are merely suggestions. Groups may find many other ways math was used in the places they are researching. This data sheet also offers a plan to organize the information they find.
- Emphasize the importance of dividing the task of research for this project. Some topics may require quite a bit of research. If group members consult different research sources, they will be able to collect information more efficiently than if they consult the same sources.
- To help students with their research, reserve a period in the library. Confer with the librarian in advance, and ask him or her to set aside books that will help students with their research efforts. Encourage students to conduct research on their own time.
- Remind students that their research should focus on how mathematics was used in the past.
- Remind students to take accurate notes and record their sources.
- After students have completed their research, provide some class time for the groups to organize their information. Recommend that they use note cards to write down notes they will use in their presentation.
- For the oral presentations, we suggest you limit each group to about 3 minutes.

WRAP-UP: Students conduct oral presentations.

EXTENSION: Students may write a report on their topic, and compile the works in a math history anthology. Some students may wish to make a table of contents and index. This would be a great exercise in organization and cross referencing.

Name _____   Project Due Date _____

BACK TO THE PAST

Situation/Problem:

Your group is to select a country or region of the world, and research how mathematics was used there in the past. You may pick a specific time period, or you may investigate the use of math from ancient times to the present. After you have finished your research, you will present your findings orally to the class.

Possible Strategies:

1. Brainstorm with your group to determine which country or region you'd like to research. Selecting one that you have already studied (or are studying) in social studies or history class will make your research easier, because you will be somewhat familiar with your topic.

2. After deciding on a country or region, select a time period. Again, it might be best to choose one you are studying or have studied.

3. Divide the task of research. Some countries may require more research than others. By having each member of your group consult different reference books, your group will be more likely to uncover information.

Special Considerations:

- Focus your research efforts on the use of mathematics in the time period you have chosen.
- Accurately record your sources.
- After you have completed your research, work together to organize your information. See Data Sheet 21–2 for some suggestions.
- Select a spokesperson or persons to present your oral report. Use note cards to write down notes.
- Rehearse your presentation so that you may share your findings clearly and smoothly.

To Be Submitted:

1. Notes for your presentation
2. A list of sources of your information

(Data Sheet 21–2)

Name _____

AN OUTLINE TO ORGANIZATION

The development of mathematics has progressed through the centuries. In researching the use of math in a specific country or region in the past, consider investigating the following topics:

Math in Trade and Commerce

Math and Farming

Math and Money

Math in Education

Math in Science

Math in Weights and Measures

Math and the Number System

Math in Time

Math and Calendars

Math in Exploration

Math and Inventions

Math in Architecture

Math in Recreation and Sports

Math—Computation Machines or Tools

Math in Art

Math in Music

While there are many ways to organize reports, two of the most effective are the *chronological pattern* and the *logical pattern*.

Chronological Pattern: In this form for organization, ideas are arranged in the order in which they occurred. What happens first appears first in the report; what happens second appears second, and so on. This organizational method works best when ideas follow in sequence.

Logical Pattern: In this form, ideas are grouped according to a plan. For example, related ideas may be grouped together. Ideas may be arranged from least important to most important, or most important to least important.

Section 3

•••

MATH AND LANGUAGE

project 22

BECOMING THE EXPERTS

Few students appreciate the role and responsibilities of their teachers, yet many would welcome the opportunity to teach their classmates. This project offers them the chance by allowing students to assume the role of the teacher and teach a math lesson to the class. Placed in this role, students are required to develop, organize, and articulate their thoughts on a topic in math, thus becoming experts on it.

GOAL: Students will work in groups of 4 or 5 and present a math lesson to the class. *Suggested time*—3 to 4 class periods.

MATH SKILLS TO HIGHLIGHT:

Using math as a means to communicate ideas. Specific math skills will vary, depending upon the topic and content of the lesson individual groups select.

SPECIAL MATERIALS/EQUIPMENT: Students should provide a list of materials and equipment they will need a few days prior to teaching their lesson. Typical materials might include an overhead projector, manipulatives, calculators, protractors, etc.

DEVELOPMENT: Before introducing this project to your students, decide if you want them to focus on particular topics or subjects. For example, if your current unit of study is geometry, you might provide a list of topics or let students develop their own topics but only in geometry. Of course, you can leave the scope of this project open, and permit students to select a subject or topic they wish.

- Begin this project by explaining to your students that they will become experts and teach the class a math lesson. Tell them which topics they may cover, or if they have the freedom to select a topic of their choice.
- Emphasize the importance of researching, developing, organizing, and planning their topic.

- Distribute copies of Student Guide 22–1 and review it with your students. Suggest that they divide tasks equally among group members.

- While you should provide a class period for students to work in groups and prepare their lessons, encourage students to meet and work outside of class if necessary. Depending upon the lessons your groups present, it's likely that you'll need at least two class periods for the groups to teach their lessons.

- Hand out copies of Data Sheet 22–2, "A Student Sample Lesson Plan Guide," and discuss it with your students. Explain that this is a guide, similar to ones that teachers use to develop and present lessons. Following it will help students to develop an effective lesson. We recommend that groups try to limit their lessons to about 10 minutes.

- Hand out copies of Worksheet 22–3, "A Sample Lesson Plan," and suggest that students use it in the planning of their lesson. Review the worksheets before students present their lessons to the class. Offer suggestions for improvement, but allow students to make the final decisions for their plans.

- Make sure you obtain the materials students will need to present their lessons. Securing materials in advance reduces the chances for oversights.

- Encourage students to practice their lesson ahead of time.

- Schedule the lessons and assign each group a date to present their lesson.

WRAP-UP: Students present their lessons to the class.

EXTENSION: Invite students to present their lessons to students in other classes.

Name _____   Project Due Date _____

BECOMING THE EXPERTS

Situation/Problem:

Your group will plan and teach a math lesson to your class.

Possible Strategies:

1. Brainstorm with your group to decide upon a lesson you would like to teach.
2. Divide tasks among group members to make the project easier to manage.

Special Considerations:

- Because there are various tasks to researching and developing a lesson, divide them. For example, individual group members may be designated to handle some of the following:

  —Research

  —Making visual aids (models, charts, posters, transparencies, graphs, etc.)

  —Writing the plan

  —Obtaining and using computers and software if they are necessary to your lesson

  —Teaching the actual lesson

  —Preparing activities for students (sample problems, worksheets, quizzes, etc.)

- Review Data Sheet 22–2 and use it to develop your material.

- Fill out Worksheet 22–3, which will help you to produce a good lesson. Submit the worksheet to your teacher for approval.

- Select who will present the lesson to the class. You may decide on one group member, or have two, three, or everyone take a part.

- Practice and coordinate the presentation of your lesson. Make certain you have any special materials or equipment you need ahead of time.

- When presenting the lesson, speak clearly and be willing to answer questions.

- If you distribute any handouts to students, make sure they understand what they are for and what they are to do with them. Any directions should be clear.

To Be Submitted:

A copy of your group's lesson plan

(Data Sheet 22-2)

Name _____

A STUDENT SAMPLE LESSON PLAN GUIDE

There are many kinds of lesson plan formats that teachers may use. Following is a common one you can use in the planning of your math lesson.

Objective: What do you want the students to know after you've taught the lesson? What should they be able to do?

Method: How are you going to teach the lesson? Some suggestions include:

- Pose a problem.
- Demonstrate, using a model.
- Show examples on the board.
- Illustrate the concept on a poster.
- Make a table, chart, or graph.
- Draw a transparency and use the overhead projector.
- Use calculators or computers.
- Provide practice problems.

Procedure: What are you going to do first? Second? Third?

Materials: What do you need to assemble or prepare in advance? What supplies will you need?

Evaluation: How will you know if you accomplished what you set out to do? In other words, how can you show that students learned what you taught?

(Worksheet 22–3)

Name _____   Lesson Plan Due Date _____

A SAMPLE LESSON PLAN

Topic: _____

Objective:

Method:

Procedure:

Materials:

Evaluation:

GREAT DEBATES

A debate in math class? Yes, absolutely. While debates are usually associated with English classes because they promote skills in the use of language, they offer a unique and enormously beneficial activity for math students. To prepare for a debate, students must research their topics, clarify their thinking, and formulate arguments. They must understand topics thoroughly and be in command of their facts. Such things fit in perfectly with a mathematician's skills. Moreover, because there is an element of competition in debates, they appeal to students, most of whom find debates enjoyable.

GOAL: Working in groups of 4 to 5, students will prepare and engage in debates about issues, problems, and topics in math. *Suggested time—4* to 5 class periods spread over two to three weeks.

MATH SKILLS TO HIGHLIGHT:

Skills will vary according to the material of each debate. Accuracy of facts and arguments should be emphasized.

SPECIAL MATERIALS/EQUIPMENT: Reference books on a variety of issues and topics in math; two long rectangular tables students may use during the actual debates.

DEVELOPMENT: There are many formats for debates, ranging between the formal and informal. For this project, we suggest you use an informal format (see Data Sheet 23–2), which will be easier to manage.

- Begin this project by explaining to your students that they will take part in debates on problems or issues in math.

- There are many possible topics for math debates. Here are some:

  —Should calculators be used in the primary grades?

  —Are standardized test scores a good indication of student achievement?

—Should students help their teachers decide what to study in math?

—Should homework be counted in the evaluation of students?

—Should all students have the opportunity to take "honors" or "accelerated" math courses?

—Is learning mathematics necessary to all students?

—Should the history of mathematics be studied in the typical math class?

—Is it necessary to learn fractions any more?

—Should parents help their kids with math homework?

- If you wish, you may generate debate topics with your class. Conduct a brainstorming session, and ask students to suggest topics. As they do, write them either on the board or an overhead projector. Don't take the time to expand or focus them now; simply generate as many possible topics as you can. Afterward, go back and eliminate those that won't lend themselves to a debate, and focus those that will.

- While you can have all groups debate the same topic, it's usually better to give each set of debate teams their own topics. This allows more issues to be addressed and adds variety to the arguments. If a group feels strongly about a topic, let it debate the topic. Few things add more to a debate than passion.

- When you organize your students into teams, be sure to mix abilities. (If your school has a debate team and some members of the class are members, divide them among your groups. Allowing seasoned debaters to be on the same team will stack the odds.) If a team has one fewer member than its opponent, a member of that team may speak twice during the debate.

- Hand out copies of Student Guide 23–1. Review it with your students and emphasize the suggestions for conducting effective debates.

- If you decide to use the suggested debate format, distribute copies of Data Sheet 23–2, "An Informal Debate Structure." While there are many debate formats, this one works well with most classes. You may adapt it to your particular class. Note that the times provided are flexible and may be changed to fit your needs.

- If possible, reserve library time in advance and take your class there for research. Depending on the topics, you'll probably need at least one period for this. Recommend that students also conduct research on their own.

- After students have completed their research, give them a class period to work in their teams and organize their material. Remind them to refer to their Student Guides. Be sure students understand the debate format and their roles.

- Long tables provide an excellent atmosphere for a debate. If you can't obtain tables, have students push their desks together at the front of the room.

- You should serve as the moderator and timekeeper. It is probable that you'll have to remind some students of the debate process.

- Although scoring is an important part of formal debates, we recommend avoiding scoring. Many students will feel undo pressure if their arguments are being evaluated. Concentrate the activity on the debate of topics related to math.

- Requiring students to hand in their notes and sources is a good way to monitor that each group member contributed to the project.

WRAP-UP: Stage the debates. Depending on how long the debates are, this may take two or three class periods. You may schedule the debates over time so that they don't disrupt your normal schedule.

EXTENSION: Videotape the debates and make the tape available to others. Students will enjoy watching themselves in the debate process.

Name _____   Project Due Date _____

GREAT DEBATES

Situation/Problem:

Your group will participate in a debate about a problem or issue in math.

Possible Strategies:

1. Once you receive your topic and position, analyze it carefully so that group members understand it.
2. Divide the tasks of research equally among group members.
3. Formulate ideas and arguments to support your position.

Special Considerations:

- Be accurate in your note-taking. Focus your research on evidence that will support your position. Such evidence often comes from:

    —Authorities and experts

    —Studies

    —Government or business statistics or research

    —Documented facts

    —Personal experience

- Record all your sources in case you need to recheck some information. Be sure your facts are accurate.

- As you research and find support for your position, be alert to facts that may support your opposing team's position. Noting them will help you to respond to their arguments.

- After gathering your information, analyze it and identify the strongest points that support your position. Build your arguments around these points.

- Decide which members of your group will present which points. Your first speaker, who will present your opening statement, should be one of your team's better speakers.

- Be familiar with the debate format you will follow. Each member should know when and on what he or she will speak. (If you are not sure of the debate format, check with your teacher.) In case a team member is absent on the day of the debate, have another member be ready to take his or her place.

- Before the debate, practice your presentation. Other members of the team should feel free to offer advice. Remember, though, comments should be positive and helpful.

- During the debate, take notes of your opponent's arguments and facts. Be ready to rebut (or argue against) them as the debate continues.

- When debating, speak clearly, and use facts. Support your statements with evidence. Keep aware of the time, and don't get sidetracked on minor issues.

- In preparing to rebut your opponent's arguments, look for mistakes in facts, opinions not based on evidence, weakness in examples, or weakness in logic.

To Be Submitted:

Copies of your notes and sources

Name _____

AN INFORMAL DEBATE STRUCTURE

A debate involves taking sides on an issue, and then presenting your arguments for or against that issue. A statement of that issue is called a *Proposition*.

The people who support the proposition are called the *Affirmative Team*. They agree with the statement. Those who disagree with it are called the *Negative Team*.

While formal debates follow a strict format, informal debates have various structures. Following is an example of a format for an informal debate. Each statement is usually given by a different team member.

Opening Statement by Affirmative Team—3 minutes.
Opening Statement by Negative Team—3 minutes.

(3 minutes allotted for teams to prepare rebuttals.)

Rebuttal by Affirmative Team—2 minutes.
Rebuttal by Negative Team—2 minutes.

Second Affirmative Statement—3 minutes.
Second Negative Statement—3 minutes.

(3 minutes allotted for teams to prepare rebuttals and closing statements.)

Rebuttal and Closing by Affirmative Team—2 minutes.
Rebuttal and Closing by Negative Team—2 minutes.

Note: An *opening statement* introduces a team's position and offers important evidence.

A *rebuttal* is a team's response to its opponent's arguments.

A *second statement* is a team's chance to expand upon their ideas and evidence.

project 24

THE MATHEMATICS PUBLISHING COMPANY

Creating, designing, and publishing a mathematics magazine can be an excellent project for a math class. Class magazines provide students with an opportunity to work together on various topics in math in ways that move beyond the typical classroom setting, especially in the integration of mathematics and writing. Although producing a math magazine may sound like a lot of work, it's not so much as you may think and the rewards are significant. High quality magazines can be produced using word processors, personal computers, and photocopiers.

GOAL: Working in groups of 4 to 6, students will create and produce a mathematics magazine. *Suggested time*—4 to 5 class periods, although this will vary based on the length of your magazine. Work time on the magazine may be divided over several partial class periods.

MATH SKILLS TO HIGHLIGHT:

Using writing as a method to communicate ideas about math

SPECIAL MATERIALS/EQUIPMENT: Black pens; correction fluid; white tape; scissors; lettering stencils; transfer letters; graph paper; clip art; glue; paste; rulers; computers; printers; word processors; and photocopier.

DEVELOPMENT: This is a fine interdisciplinary project, and you may wish to work with your students' English teacher. He or she can help students with the actual writing of the magazine, while you handle the math and production. If this is your first experience in doing a class magazine, we suggest you limit its size. Four pages (two sides back to back) will be long enough for several articles and short enough to manage easily.

- Before beginning the actual project, establish guidelines regarding the content of the magazine. You might make such decisions yourself, or discuss them with your students. All of the material should have a math slant. You might choose to do a general magazine, or concentrate on a particular topic such as geometry, fractions, or integers.

- Start the project by explaining to your students what they will be doing. If you have copies of magazines that other classes produced, distribute them so that students can see what a math magazine can be. It's likely that many of your current students have never been involved in the production of a class magazine. If you wish, you might brainstorm possible names for the magazine.

- Distribute copies of Student Guide 24–1 and discuss it with your class, highlighting what you feel are its most important points.

- Assigning different responsibilities to the groups divides the work and makes it easier for you to coordinate and oversee students' efforts. Group 1, for example, might focus on writing articles; Group 2 might be responsible for news items; while Group 3 is to handle design, layout, and artwork. Group 4 may be responsible for puzzles and Group 5 might create tricky math problems. Consider arranging the groups according to student interests. Artsy types will probably prefer to work on design and illustrations, while those who like to write will most likely want to handle the articles. To ensure that groups work efficiently, assign a group leader for each group. It is the leader's responsibility to keep the group on task.

* To support your students in their writing, hand out copies of Data Sheet 24–2, "Possible Ideas for a Math Magazine," which offers suggestions for possible articles. Emphasize that these are just some ideas, and that students might come up with many more.

- You may wish to distribute and discuss copies of "The Writing Process" in Part I's Chapter 2. The information on the handout may be helpful to students as they develop, research, and write their material.

- If you have access to personal computers, word processors, or typewriters, encourage your students to enter articles on them. If students don't have access to such equipment, you might seek parent volunteers to enter and print out the material.

- Artwork and graphics may be added to your magazine either through computer software, clip art, or line drawings. Hand-drawn illustrations should be kept simple and dark for photocopying. Complex drawings with heavy shading don't reproduce well on copiers. Avoid having students draw on a finished page. Instead, illustrations should be drawn on a separate page, cut out, and pasted or taped to a finished page. This reduces the chances of ruining the page during illustrating. Headlines and titles can be easily created using graph paper and stencils or transfer letters. (The art teacher can be a good source of materials and advice.)

- With many activities going on simultaneously, it will be necessary to set deadlines to ensure that work gets done on time. Set reasonable deadlines for having articles completed, and stick to them.

- When all the work is finished, have students proofread the material once more to catch any final errors or oversights. The magazine can then be photocopied. Photocopying on both sides of a page not only results in a more attractive magazine but saves paper as well.

WRAP-UP: Publish enough magazines so that each student gets a copy, and there are enough left over for distribution to other classes, administrators, and display in the school library.

EXTENSION: Make this project an ongoing one. Produce additional magazines throughout the year. If you have several math classes, you might have each class produce a magazine at a different time. Consider having students submit material to a schoolwide math magazine.

Name _____   Project Due Date _____

THE MATHEMATICS PUBLISHING COMPANY

Situation/Problem:

Your class will be divided into groups, and together you will create and produce a mathematics magazine. The groups will be responsible for the entire production of the magazine. Upon completion, copies of the magazine will be printed and distributed.

Possible Strategies:

1. Break your group's tasks into small parts, and divide the parts among group members.
2. Communication is important between groups to avoid duplication of effort. Groups should keep each other informed of their progress.

Special Considerations:

- Generate ideas for articles by brainstorming with your group.
- Some topics may require research. Any research should be thorough.
- You will need to establish deadlines for material to be completed. Managing time is important.
- Try to finish articles well in advance of deadlines. This will give you time for editing and revision. Expect things to go wrong.
- Use computers, word processors, and typewriters to print your material. Desktop publishing software can produce outstanding magazines.
- If your magazine will include artwork, you'll need to decide on what types. Possibilities include computer art, clip art, or line illustrations drawn by students.
- If you are writing math problems, puzzles, or games, be sure to include an answer key.
- Design your magazine. Create a "dummy" layout where you place copies of the articles on a white background sheet that serves as the magazine page. Arrange articles and artwork attractively. Use white tape or paste to attach pieces. (*Note:* Many software programs can do this for you.)
- Before printing, the magazine should be proofread a final time. Special care should be given to any math problems that appear in the magazine. Accuracy is important.

To Be Submitted:

Your group's contribution to the magazine in its final form

© 1996 by The Center for Applied Research in Education

Name _____

POSSIBLE IDEAS FOR A MATHEMATICS MAGAZINE

The following are just some suggestions for articles that might appear in a mathematics magazine.

General articles about math

Historical pieces

Biographical sketches of famous mathematicians

Women in mathematics

Information about math contests

Updates about the school math team

Pieces about student math projects

Self-help articles

Features about class mathematicians

Math shortcuts

Articles on measurement

Articles on estimating

Articles about money

Articles on math and science

Short articles about the math club

Games

Puzzles

"Math Problem of the Month"

Tricky math problems

Articles on careers

Reviews of math software

Guides for purchasing home computers

Math trivia

Math cartoons

Examples of possible titles:

Informational article—"Math in Our Lives"

Self-help feature—"How to Study for Math Tests"

Biographical sketch—"Karl Friedrich Gauss: The Boy Genius"

Article about money—"Budget Tips for Teens"

GREAT MATHEMATICIANS—A PLAY

During their study of math, many students only receive a glimpse of the great mathematicians and their accomplishments. Names and achievements may be mentioned, but few students have the opportunity to learn much about the men and women who have advanced the frontiers of math. The following project is designed to introduce students to some of these men and women, and encourage them to learn about their lives as well as their contributions to math.

GOAL: Groups of 3 to 5 students will select a mathematician, research his or her life, then write a play that highlights a great achievement of this person. If you wish, students may perform the play for the class. *Suggested time*—4 to 5 class periods; perhaps a bit longer depending upon the length of student plays.

MATH SKILLS TO HIGHLIGHT:

Writing as a means to express ideas about math. Specific math skills will vary, depending upon the mathematician and accomplishments. (Students should understand the mathematical concepts inherent in their subject's accomplishments.)

SPECIAL MATERIALS/EQUIPMENT: Reference books on mathematicians; props that students may create or obtain to support the performance of their play. *Optional*—Word processors or computers and printers on which to write the plays.

DEVELOPMENT: You might wish to collaborate with your students' English teacher for this project. Before introducing the project to your students, consider how extensive you want it to become. For example, you may limit the plays to a few minutes each, or permit students as much time as they wish. Students can become quite involved with this type of project, and you'll likely find that some of the plays will be interesting, entertaining, and informative.

- Start the project by organizing the groups and explaining what the project will entail. Set a deadline for the plays to be completed.

- Distribute copies of Student Guide 25–1 and discuss it with your students.

- Distribute copies of Data Sheet 25–2, "A Play Structure," and review it with your students. This sheet offers information on the elements of plays.

- To make sure students understand a common play format, hand out copies of Data Sheet 25–3, "A Sample Play." (Although this is not the form professional playwrights use, it is used in many reading texts and students are likely to be at least somewhat familiar with it.) Emphasize that this is only a part of a play, a sample. Plays are usually divided into acts and scenes; however, your students may wish to write only one act—a major part of a play—and a few scenes. Make certain that students understand SETTING refers to where the play takes place, and AT RISE describes the action as the curtain goes up.

- Hand out copies of Data Sheet 25–4, "Some Famous Mathematicians." Mention that these are just some of the world's great mathematicians. Also point out that the list contains ethnic origins and major areas of expertise. (Another source on famous mathematicians is our book *The Math Teacher's Book of Lists*, Prentice Hall, 1995. See List 261, "Famous Mathematicians through History.")

- Spend at least one class period at the library to get your students started on their research. Encourage them to conduct additional research on their own.

- Note that encyclopedias may offer general information about mathematicians, but biographies and special references will provide better material.

- Encourage students to be creative. They may use humor if they wish, but any depiction of mathematics should be accurate.

- Provide class time for students to meet in their groups and organize their material.

- Insist that students use sound writing skills when writing their plays. Recommend that each group designate a proofreader to go over the final work.

- We require students to hand in their notes and sources at the end of the project. If this is one of your requirements, be sure to tell them exactly what you expect. Suggest that they write these requirements on their copies of the Student Guide.

- Suggest that students create or obtain simple props to support their play.

- When students perform their plays, permit them to use their scripts. Requiring students to memorize their lines may be burdensome to some, causing undue frustration and anxiety.

WRAP-UP: Have each group perform the play it wrote for the class.

EXTENSION: Videotape the performances. Lend the tape to staff members or students who may wish to share it with their friends or families.

Name _____   Project Due Date _____

GREAT MATHEMATICIANS—A PLAY

Situation/Problem:

Working with your group, you are to select a famous mathematician, research his or her life and work, then write a play that highlights one of his or her achievements in mathematics. When you are done writing your play, you may perform it for your class.

Possible Strategies:

1. Brainstorm with your group which mathematician you'd like to study and write about. Think about accomplishments that would lend themselves to a play performance.
2. Divide the tasks of researching, writing, and editing among group members so that the project runs smoothly.

Special Considerations:

- Be organized during your research. Keep accurate notes and record all your sources carefully. Always write full bibliographical information on your notes. This makes it easier to find that source again if you need to recheck some fact. You can find bibliographical formats in you English textbook, a grammar reference book, or a writer's handbook.

- Research your mathematician thoroughly. Consider the following suggestions for zeroing in on important facts:

   —When did he or she live? What was the world like then?

   —How hard did the person work? Did he or she make a discovery by accident?

   —Was the person recognized during his or her lifetime?

   —Why were his or her discoveries important? What significance, if any, do they have today?

   —Did anyone expand upon the contributions of your mathematician?

- Discuss the best way to highlight your mathematician's achievements.

- Set general deadlines for group members to complete specific tasks.

- Use good form in writing your play. Consult Data Sheets 25–2 and 25–3.

- If possible, write your play on a computer or word processor. Not only will this make revisions easier, but you will also have a printed script to read.

- Create or obtain simple props for your play.

- Assign parts for your play. If necessary, recruit additional students from class.

- Rehearse your play so that you may present it smoothly.

To Be Submitted:

1. A final version of your play
2. Research notes
3. Bibliography

Name _____

A PLAY STRUCTURE

A play is a story that is performed on a stage. Although the stories may vary, all follow a similar structure. Plays may contain several acts and scenes.

OPENING

In the opening of a play, the major characters are usually introduced, a problem is revealed (or at least hinted at), and background information is offered.

PLAN

Solving the problem becomes the lead character(s)' goal. They create a plan to solve the problem.

OBSTACLES

As the characters try to solve the problem, they run into obstacles that cause the problem to grow. Conflict arises.

COMPLICATIONS

The problem worsens and the characters try new plans.

CLIMAX

The characters either solve the problem, or fail to solve it.

RESOLUTION

By solving the problem, the characters have achieved their goal. If they fail to solve the problem, they realize that reaching their goal is not possible.

Name _____

A SAMPLE PLAY

"Pi or Pie?"

CHARACTERS: Sara, 17 years old
                Akeem, 16 years old
                Tom, 15 years old
                Jessie, 16 years old

ACT I
Scene 1

SETTING: After school in a high school library. Bookshelves line the wall. Several long tables are arranged throughout the room. The place is empty because it is late.

AT RISE: Sara, Akeem, Tom, and Jessie are sitting at a table, looking at several opened math books. The students look somewhat frustrated.

TOM (*closing a book*): I give up. We'll never find an idea for a math project we can all agree on.

SARA (*frowning*): You give up too easily.

TOM: Too easily! We've been looking for fifteen minutes.

AKEEM (*grinning*): She's right. Give it at least twenty.

JESSIE: Be serious, guys. (*She looks at a page and suddenly brightens.*) How about pi?

AKEEM: Yeah. Pizza. I'm starved. Let's go.

JESSIE: No. Pi. (*She spells it.*) P . . . i . . . . What if we research its importance?

Name _____

SOME FAMOUS MATHEMATICIANS

The following list contains some of the great mathematicians through history. It offers dates, ethnic origins, and major fields of study. You may select one of these mathematicians for your project, or you may select another.

Abel, Niels (1802–1829); Norwegian; Algebra.

Ahmes (about 1650 B.C.); Egyptian; Geometry.

Aiken, Howard (1900–1973); American; Computers.

Al–Khowârizmî, Muhammed (about 780–850); Arabian; Algebra.

Archimedes (287–212 B.C.); Greek; Algebra, Calculus, Pi.

Aristotle (384–322 B.C.); Greek; Logic, Geometry.

Celsius, Anders (1701–1744); Swedish; Measurement.

Copernicus, Nicolaus (1473–1543); Polish, Trigonometry.

Cray, Seymour (1925–   ); American; Computers.

Descartes, René (1596–1650); French; Coordinates.

Dodgson, Charles L. (Lewis Carroll, 1832–1898); English; Logic.

Einstein, Albert (1879–1955); German; Geometry, Infinity.

Escher, Maurits Cornelis (1898–1971); Dutch; Geometry.

Euclid (about 365–300 B.C.); Greek; Geometry.

Fahrenheit, Gabriel (1686–1736); German; Measurement.

Fermat, Pierre de (1601–1665); French; Number Theory.

Gauss, Carl Friedrich (1777–1855); German; Geometry, Number Theory.

Germain, Sophie (1776–1831); French; Symmetry.

Hypatia (370–415); Greek; Conic Sections.

Kovalevsky, Sonya (1850–1891); Russian; Number Theory.

Leibniz, Gottfried (1646–1716); German; Logic, Calculus.

Murasaki, Lady (about 978–1031); Japanese; Combinations.

Napier, John (1550–1617); Scottish; Computers, Decimals.

Newton, Sir Isaac (1642–1727); English; Algebra, Calculus.

Noether, Emmy (1882–1935); German; Algebra.

Oresme, Nicole (1323–1382); French; Functions.

Pascal, Blaise (1623–1662); French; Algebra, Computers.

Ptolemy, Claudius (about 85–168); Greek; Trigonometry.

Pythagoras (about 585–507 B.C.); Greek; Geometry.

Romanujan, Srinivasa (1887–1920); Hindu; Algebra.

Venn, John (1834–1923); English; Sets.

Vinci, Leonardo da (1452–1519); Italian; Geometry.

Von Neumann, John (1903–1957); Hungarian; Computers.

FICTIONAL NUMBERS—WRITING A STORY

Students have been writing stories in their English classes since the time they could hold a pencil. But how many of your students have ever had the chance to write a story in math? This project offers them the opportunity, along with allowing their creativity to fire up.

GOAL: Each student will write a story in which mathematics plays a major role. *Suggested time*—2 class periods.

MATH SKILL TO HIGHLIGHT:

Writing as a means to express ideas about math.

SPECIAL MATERIALS/EQUIPMENT: A few dictionaries and thesauruses. *Optional*—Word processors; computers; and printers.

DEVELOPMENT: Begin this project by explaining to your students that they are to write a story in which math has a central role. We recommend that you permit students to write any type of story they wish—romance, science fiction, fantasy, mystery, historical, or comedy. While you should give students the freedom to be creative, you should also consider some boundaries. For example, you may prefer that they do not write stories of gory horror, graphic sex (just think about some of the shows kids watch on TV these days), or that have foul language. Here are some other suggestions.

- Two class periods should be enough for this project. A Monday and Thursday or Tuesday and Friday will give students a chance to work on their stories at home as well as in school.
- Emphasize that mathematics in some way should be an important part of the stories.
- If you have some students who are reluctant writers, consider allowing them to work with a partner and be co-authors. This will reduce anxiety.

- Hand out copies of Student Guide 26–1 and review it with your students. In particular, emphasize the elements of a story's plot, as noted on the Guide. Although some of your students are probably familiar with a basic plot structure from their English classes, others will need to be reminded. Understanding the components of a plot will help students in creating their stories. Also, be sure to mention the sample story ideas. They can give students a boost in starting.

- Distribute copies of Data Sheet 26–2, "A Revision Checklist for Stories." Discuss it with your students, pointing out that the sheet provides valuable suggestions for revising stories.

- Encourage students to use sound writing skills; they should edit and revise their work. You may wish to hand out copies of "The Writing Process" in Part I's Chapter 2.

- Encourage students to use word processors and computers in the writing of their stories. This will make the work of revision easier.

WRAP-UP: Display the finished stories on a bulletin board. You might also set aside some time for class readings in which students swap and read each other's stories.

EXTENSIONS: Compile stories in a class anthology. Brainstorm a title with your students, photocopy and bind the stories, and distribute them around the school. If you find a story that is suitable for reading to younger children, arrange an opportunity for the author to visit students in that class and read his or her story to them.

Name _____   Project Due Date _____

FICTIONAL NUMBERS—WRITING A STORY

Situation/Problem:

You are to write a story in which mathematics has a major part in the plot.

Possible Strategies:

1. List as many potential ideas for stories as you can.
2. Select the story idea you like best and expand it, adding characters, action, and details.

Special Considerations:

- When creating your story, keep in mind these important parts of a plot:

  —A lead character(s) has a problem that he or she must solve.

  —Conflict, in the form of hostility, anger, or resentment, is associated with the problem. In trying to solve the problem, the character may come into conflict with other characters, nature, or himself or herself.

—The lead character makes plans to solve the problem, but each plan fails and the problem grows worse. These setbacks are called complications.

—The lead character keeps running into complications and the problem keeps getting worse until the story reaches a climax.

—At this point the character either solves the problem and triumphs, or he or she fails to solve it.

—Most stories have either a happy or sad ending, depending on whether the character has solved the problem. Some stories conclude with unresolved endings in which the character neither succeeds nor fails.

- Remember to make math a major part of the story. Be creative. Here are some examples of story ideas:

  —Inspector Integer solves his biggest case in which a computer genius electronically empties people's bank accounts.

  —A future team of space explorers is mapping the distance to a nearby star where alien life is thought to exist. Their goal—first contact.

  —Your lead character needs to come up with cash, quick. The story shows why and how.

  —A thief in the school breaks into lockers. Your character discovers a pattern to the thefts. The thief chooses lockers according to a special sequence of numbers.

  —Your character, who is a numbers whiz, thinks that winning the math contest will be easy. But solving the puzzle for the grand prize proves to be harder than she thinks.

- Use dialogue and action in your story.

- Describe scenes with vivid details.

- If possible, write your story on a word processor or computer; this will make revision easier.

- Edit and revise your story so that your finished copy is an example of your best writing.

To Be Submitted:

A copy of your finished story

Name _____

A REVISION CHECKLIST FOR STORIES

The following list can be helpful when you are revising your story. Apply these questions to your writing.

1. Does my story make sense? Is it realistic and believable?

2. Do my characters act like real people? Do they speak like real people? Do they dress like individuals, according to their natures? Have I described them so that my readers can picture them clearly?

3. Do my characters behave according to their natures? Are their actions logical?

4. Does my story have a problem that the characters must solve? Is the problem big enough to hold the interest of readers?

5. Does my story have conflict?

6. Have I described my scenes with color, sounds, and other details? Do my scenes paint pictures in the minds of my readers?

7. Does every scene in my story build to the climax? Is my climax exciting?

8. Have I used periods, commas, and other punctuation marks correctly? Have I used quotation marks to show dialogue?

9. Have I used correct spelling? Have I used words in their proper contexts?

10. Am I satisfied that this story is the best I can make it?

A MATHEMATICAL AUTOBIOGRAPHY

Our lives are interwoven with numbers. We use numbers to mark significant events (birthdays, for example), as a means of identification (Social Security numbers), and as a way of ranking and comparison (most students prefer a test average of 98 in math over an average of 68). Numbers help us to track the condition of the economy, and tally the score in sports. They even tell us our height, weight, and waist size. Most students accept numbers as a part of life without realizing their true significance. This project may help them to understand just how much they rely on numbers.

GOAL: Working individually, students will write a mathematical autobiography. *Suggested time*—2 class periods.

MATH SKILL TO HIGHLIGHT:

Writing as a means by which to examine and express ideas about math.

SPECIAL MATERIALS/EQUIPMENT: A few dictionaries and thesauruses. *Optional*—Word processors; computers; and printers.

DEVELOPMENT: Begin this project by explaining that an autobiography is an account written by an individual about his or her life. Most students should be familiar with examples of autobiographies, and you might ask them to volunteer titles of some they have read. An autobiography might run several hundred pages and cover everything from a person's birth to old age, or it may be only a few paragraphs or pages focusing on an important aspect of the author's life. In that case, it is usually referred to as an autobiographical sketch. For this project, most students will be writing sketches.

- Hand out copies of Student Guide 27–1 and review it with your students. Answer any questions they may have. It's important to reduce any anxiety they may feel about writing.

- Instruct students to concentrate on the ways numbers play a part in their lives. If a student has experienced a major event in which numbers were important, he or she may wish to focus the writing on that topic. (Most students will find it easier to write about a specific topic or event rather than writing generally about numbers.) For example, one boy wrote about his best Little League baseball season. He managed the highest batting average in the league, led the league in home runs, and had the most wins and strikeouts as a pitcher. He noted that it was the only season he played that well, and he will always remember "the numbers." Another good example is a piece about a health/exercise program in which a student may keep track of workout time, repetition of specific exercises, nutrition, and the caloric content of foods. All involve numbers.

- Distribute copies of Data Sheet 27–2, "Organizing Your Autobiography." While there are many ways students may organize their material, the plan suggested on this sheet is simple and should make the task of writing easier.

- Consider giving students a chance at the beginning of the project to discuss the project with a partner or small group. This will help generate ideas for writing.

- Allow enough time for generating ideas, organizing the material, writing, and revising. For most students two class periods should be enough. If you decide to set aside two periods, we recommend that you reserve a Monday and Thursday or Tuesday and Friday. Spacing the days will give students time to work on the project at home.

- Encourage students to use sound writing skills; they should edit and revise their drafts to polish their work. You may wish to hand out copies of "The Writing Process" in Part I's Chapter 2.

- Encourage students to use word processors or computers for writing. These will make the task of writing and revision easier.

WRAP-UP: Display the finished autobiographies in the room or on a hallway bulletin board.

EXTENSIONS: Compile the autobiographies in a class book. Photocopy them and make them available to others. Display the collection of autobiographies in the school library.

Name _____   Project Due Date _____

A MATHEMATICAL AUTOBIOGRAPHY

Situation/Problem:

You are to write a mathematical autobiography, a personal account of the importance of numbers in your life.

Possible Strategies:

1. List various ways numbers affect your life. Take a sheet of paper and write every way numbers are important to you. Don't worry about expanding any of the ideas now—just write as many as you can.
2. Identify the most important ways numbers are important to you. Rank them in importance from most significant to least.
3. Select the most important way numbers affect your life. Expand your ideas on this topic, and use them as the focus of your writing.

Special Considerations:

*   In listing the ways numbers are important to you, think about:

Special dates	Exercise
Sports	Nutrition
Grades	Recreation
Money	Vacations
Height, weight	Goals, ambitions

Note: These are only some categories you may consider. There are likely to be many more ways numbers are important to you.

*   Organize your information logically, then use good writing skills to express your ideas.
*   If possible, use word processors or computers for your writing.
*   Be sure to revise your writing before submitting a final copy.

To Be Submitted:

A final copy of your mathematical autobiography

(Data Sheet 27–2)

Name _____

Who? What? Where? When? Why?

ORGANIZING YOUR AUTOBIOGRAPHY

Most nonfiction writing follows a three-part plan: opening, body, and conclusion. Using this plan will help you to organize the information you have gathered for your mathematical autobiography.

- Your *opening* should:

  —Capture the interest of the reader by introducing your subject. Try using an interesting or surprising statistic, state a problem in which numbers played a role, offer a joke or anecdote, or exaggerate a common situation in which numbers are important.

  —Lead smoothly into the body of your autobiography.

- Your *body* should:

  —Relate ways that numbers are important to you. Use the five W's to include details about events:

    What happened?

    Who was involved?

    When did the event happen?

    Where did it happen?

    Why did it happen?

  —Add a "How." How do numbers fit in with what you are writing about?

- Your *conclusion* should:

  —Contain a final idea for the reader to consider.

  —Briefly tie together the ideas of the piece.

IT'S PUZZLING

Puzzles can make any kind of learning fun. Most students enjoy solving math puzzles, particularly those created by their peers. Puzzles may serve as an introduction to new material, provide practice in reinforcing skills, and review concepts previously introduced. With a little guidance, students can design math puzzles of their own to share with their friends. They may even wish to publish their puzzles in math magazines, or place them in their portfolios.

GOAL: Students will work individually or in pairs to create math puzzles to share with the class. *Suggested time*—2 class periods.

MATH SKILLS TO HIGHLIGHT:

Specific skills will vary according to the types and contents of puzzles. Care should be taken to ensure that puzzles and their answer keys are accurate.

SPECIAL MATERIALS/EQUIPMENT: Graph paper; rulers; correction fluid; nonreproducible blue pencils (the color of which will not appear on photocopied pages); black felt-tipped pens. *Optional*—Computers and printers that may be used in the design of puzzles.

DEVELOPMENT: When you introduce this project, many students may be at a loss as to how to create a math puzzle. A few days before actually starting the project, you might mention that the class will create mathematical puzzles, and suggest that students consult math puzzle books or their texts for ideas. Your school or local library will likely have many sources in the recreational math section. If you have examples of math puzzles created by students from other classes, or examples from books, make them available. Data Sheet 28–2 provides some examples, but there are many more. Also, prior to beginning the project, decide if you want students to concentrate on a particular unit of study or topic, or if they will be permitted to create puzzles on any topic they wish.

- Start this project by explaining what students will do. Tell them that puzzles should be designed with a particular purpose or objective. Puzzles may be used to introduce new material, review previously learned skills, or practice computation. Some ideas for the content of puzzles include:

  —Learning definitions or properties

  —Identifying figures

  —Learning relationships between definitions and numbers

  —Practicing computation or using calculators

  —Solving proportions

  —Applying order of operation rules

  —Using percents

  —Finding perimeter, area, and/or volume

  —Solving equations

- Distribute copies of Student Guide 28–1, and review it with your students. Note that graph paper can be used to draw boxes for puzzles.

- Inform students if you want them to concentrate on specific topics.

- Distribute copies of Data Sheet 28–2, "Puzzles, Puzzles, Puzzles," which contains examples of puzzles students might do. Go over the sheet with your students, but emphasize that these are only some of the many types of puzzles they may create.

- Mention that students can add twists to common puzzles. A good example is a simple crossnumber puzzle. Although the puzzle may focus on the basic operations of addition, subtraction, multiplication, and division, a new wrinkle to it would be to have the puzzle solvers use calculators and work against a time limit. Another idea would be for students to compete against each other, with a champion being determined by the best time. Such a puzzle would be fun, exciting, and give students practice in working with calculators.

- If you have access to computers, students may be able to design their puzzles on them. Various types of software may be utilized for drawing and writing. Many word processing programs come with easy-to-manage clip art, while art programs come with drawing capabilities. Most include geometric figures that can be easily manipulated on the screen. (Before permitting students to utilize computers for the creation of puzzles, you should demonstrate how the programs work. This will reduce confusion with using the equipment.)

- Suggest that students create a "rough" or "dummy" version of their puzzles before attempting to complete them.

- Emphasize that all math must be accurate, and that each puzzle should have an answer key.

WRAP-UP: Make copies of the puzzles and allow students to work on them. This may be done as a class activity upon completion of the project.

EXTENSION: Compile copies of the puzzles in a class book. Make the puzzle book available to other students and classes.

Name _____   Project Due Date _____

IT'S PUZZLING

Situation/Problem:

You will create a math puzzle that other members of your class will try to solve.

Possible Strategies:

1. Obtain examples of math puzzles in magazines and textbooks. Study them carefully to see how they are created.

2. Determine your purpose or objective, and decide which type of puzzle you want to do.

Special Considerations:

- Gather the math facts you will use. Be sure all your information is accurate.
- Create a "dummy" version of your puzzle. Carefully sketch out on graph paper or a blank sheet how your puzzle will be set up.
- If you are using a blank sheet, use rulers to divide distances equally.
- If you need to draw boxes or spaces, use a fine-tipped black felt pen. This will reproduce well.
- Use a light blue pencil to make marks that you don't want to be reproduced on a copier. This is useful for answer keys.
- Mistakes can be "whited-out" using correction fluid.
- Consider creating your puzzle on a computer. Word finds, word scrambles, and tricky questions may easily be done on computers. Some software enables you to draw and arrange geometric shapes.
- Double-check your work by exchanging your puzzle with a friend. He (or she) checks yours while you check his (or hers).

To Be Submitted:

1. A final copy of your puzzle
2. An answer key

(Data Sheet 28-2)

Name _____

PUZZLES, PUZZLES, PUZZLES

Math puzzles come in countless forms. Here are just a few examples.

- **Word Finds:** Pick mathematical terms, and arrange the words horizontally, vertically, backwards, forwards, and diagonally.

Find all the math terms.

```
E  R  A  U  Q  S
A  V  R  B  C  U
E  A  E  C  F  M
D  O  R  N  E  X
```

Solution

```
(E  R  A  U  Q  S)
A  V  R  B  C  U
E  A  E  C  F  M
D  O  R  N  E  X
```

- **Magic Squares:** In these squares, the sum of the numbers in each column, row, and diagonal of the square are equal.

Find the missing numbers.

9	2	
4		8
5	10	

Solution

9	2	⑦
4	⑥	8
5	10	③

- **Crossnumber Puzzles:** These puzzles are similar to crossword puzzles, except that digits are used.

DOWN

1. The area of a square whose side is 5
2. 9^2
3. The volume of a cube whose side is 3.

ACROSS

1. The perimeter of a square whose side is 7
3. $3 \times 6 + 3$

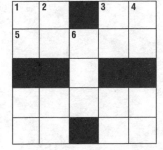

Solution

```
²2  ²8      ³2  ⁴1
⁵5   1  ⁶   7
```

(Data Sheet 28–2 continued)

- **A Maze of Basic Facts and Computation**: Solving problems helps you to find your way through the maze.

Use the solutions to the problems to guide you through the maze.

$5^2 - 1$

$2 \times 5 + 2^3$

$-7 + 7$

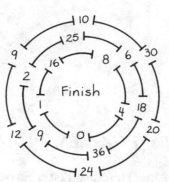

Solution

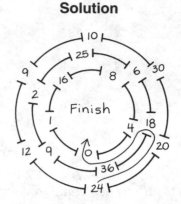

- **Mathograms**: These are puzzles in which letters are substituted for the digits of numbers. The object is to find the digit represented by the letter.

Find what digit each letter represents.

TWO	
+ TWO	
FOUR	

Solution

```
   928
 + 928
 1856
```

T = 9
W = 2
O = 8
F = 1
U = 5
R = 6

- **Word Scrambles**: The letters of math words are mixed-up.

Unscramble each word to spell a math term.

enev

remip

Solution

even

prime

- **Rebuses**: A math term is written with words, numbers, and illustrations. The goal is to figure out what it is.

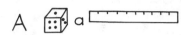 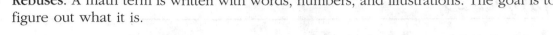

Solution

A diameter equals
two radii

- **Secret Messages**: Answers to a list of math problems provide a secret message. Possible answers (in numbers) are paired with letters of the alphabet. By finding the correct mathematical answer, the correct letter is discovered. Once all the answers are solved correctly, the message is revealed.

Solve each problem. Match the answer with the letter of the alphabet to reveal a secret message.

C $(6 + 3) \times 2 =$ _____
P $(3 \times 5) - 1 =$ _____
A $4 \times 3 =$ _____ $\times 4$
E $200\% =$ _____

I $4^2 =$ _____
L $8 \div 1/4 =$ _____
R $3.4 + 4.6 =$ _____
S $5 1/4 - 1/4 =$ _____
Y $3^3 =$ _____

__ __ __ __ __ __ __   __ __ __   __ __ __ __   __ __   __ __.
18 16 8 18 32 2 5   3 8 2   2 3 5 27   3 5   14 16

Solution

$(6 + 3) \times 2 = 18$
$(3 \times 5) - 1 = 14$
$4 \times 3 = 3 \times 4$
$200\% = 2$

$4^2 = 16$
$8 \div 1/4 = 32$
$3.4 + 4.6 = 8$
$5 1/4 - 1/4 = 5$
$3^3 = 27$

Circles are easy as pi.

LENDING A MATH HAND

Students teaching students is a great learning activity with many benefits. This is certainly true when older students teach younger ones. Before they can present material to younger students, however, older students need to master their topics and articulate them in a manner that younger students will understand. Older students gain satisfaction (and often a boost in self-confidence) from helping younger children, while the younger ones learn math from a novel approach. Younger students are often more receptive to instruction from older students. Although there are many details to manage with this project, the overall benefits are well worth the effort required.

GOAL: Working in groups of 3 to 4, students will select a topic in math appropriate for younger students. They will write about it, creating a booklet that explains both concepts and applications, then present their booklet to the younger students. *Suggested time*—2 to 3 class periods; additional time will be necessary to present the booklets to the students in other classes.

MATH SKILLS TO HIGHLIGHT:

Writing as a method of expressing ideas about math. Specific skills will vary, depending on the topic.

SPECIAL MATERIALS/EQUIPMENT: Black pens for line illustrations, examples, or practice worksheets; scissors and glue for cutting and pasting; clip art; and staplers and staples for binding. *Optional*—Computers, printers, and word processors on which students may write their booklets.

DEVELOPMENT: Before beginning this project, speak with teachers of students in lower grades in your district, and ask if they would like to have groups of your math students write and present booklets (focused on specific topics) to their classes. We suggest you consider students in grades 1 through 6, for these are often the most receptive to visitors from other classes. Find out what types of material their teachers might want your students to cover. If possible, get a list of potential topics from each teacher. In the typical sixth grade, for example, basic operations are covered, along with fractions, decimals, and percents. Once other teachers have agreed to have your students visit, set up tentative time frames. In planning visitations, be sure to obtain any necessary permission from building principals, supervisors, or other administrators.

- Introduce this project by explaining to your students that you have arranged the opportunity for groups to create math booklets that describe concepts and applications. They will write the booklets for students in lower grades (mention the grades). Once the booklets are finished, they will be photocopied and stapled. Your groups will then visit the classes they've written their booklets for, and present the booklets to the younger students.

- If you have several grades and topics, you might permit your groups to choose which one they'd like to do. If you have several teachers who have volunteered their classes, try to have a group write a booklet for each one. (If people volunteer and are left out, they may not volunteer next time.)

- To give your students an idea of what material for younger students is like, obtain some sample texts or workbooks from teachers of younger students and share them with your class.

- Distribute copies of Student Guide 29–1 and review it with your students. Encourage students to refer to their guides as necessary throughout the project.

- Hand out copies of Data Sheet 29–2, "Creating a Math Booklet," and go over it with your students. Note that they are to choose a specific topic and write about it, including concepts and applications. They may include practice sheets and examples. Point out that two sheets of paper will provide a booklet with eight pages (which includes the front and back covers). That should be enough for most groups.

- If students have access to computers or word processors, suggest they use this equipment for writing. Not only will revisions be easier, but many word processing programs also come with features that can help in the design of booklets. Some even include clip art.

- Review the rough drafts of the booklets and offer suggestions for improvement before the final copies are completed.

- Have enough copies of the booklets photocopied so that everyone in the classes that are to be visited will receive his or her own copy.

- Encourage your groups to rehearse their presentation. The actual presentation may be little more than talking about the math topic, handing out the booklets and going through them, or may be an actual lesson that uses the booklet as a type of text. The final decision here should be based upon the needs and abilities of the class your group is visiting, as well as the ability of your students, your schedule, and time constraints.

- Check your schedule and make travel plans well in advance. If your students will need to travel to an elementary school across town, arrange for buses, costs, chaperones (if necessary), and permission slips with plenty of lead time.

- Check back with the teachers whose classes you will be visiting and confirm meeting times and topics.

- If possible, arrange for your groups to visit the same school (for different classes) on the same day. Having them make their presentations at about the same time is a plus. This reduces the logistics concerns. You can get one group started in one classroom, then head to the next.

WRAP-UP: Students present their math booklets to other classes.

EXTENSION: Set up a tutoring program in which your students can help younger students with their math on a regular basis.

(Student Guide 29-1)

Name _____   Project Due Date _____

LENDING A MATH HAND

Situation/Problem:

Your group will select a math topic that is applicable to younger students. You will write a booklet that explains the topic, then you will present copies of your booklet to the students in their classroom.

Possible Strategies:

1. Review with your group possible math topics you want to develop in a booklet.
2. Divide the tasks of the project to make the work easier to manage.

Special Considerations:

- Select material that is appropriate for the age group you will be working with.
- Think about dividing tasks according to research, writing, layout, illustrations, and any practice worksheets that will be needed.
- Make sure you write clearly and explain your topic fully. Use language that your audience will understand. (*Hint:* Check some books at the library that are written for the grade level of your audience. This will give you an idea of the vocabulary you should use. Material for second graders, for instance, is very different from material for sixth graders.)

- Consider teaching a math concept in story form. Young children often learn easily through stories.

- Keep any illustrations and practice sheets simple. Use black pens to make distinct lines. If possible, use clip art to highlight your work. Avoid complex drawings, shading, or colors because these won't reproduce well on copiers.

- If available, use computers or word processors to write your material. Because a booklet is set up differently from a page on a computer screen, you will either have to arrange your writing in columns (some word processing programs can do this for you), or write only on half of the screen. After printing your material, cut out the writing and paste it on the pages of your booklet.

- Refer to Data Sheet 29–2 for suggestions on how to produce your booklet.

- Practice how you will present your booklet to younger students. There are many possibilities. One group member may be selected as the lead presenter, while other members may act as assistants. If you divide the class, each group member may work with a group of younger students.

- When you travel to other classes, be sure you have all of your materials.

- When you present your booklets to other students, always be polite, considerate, and patient.

To Be Submitted:

A final copy of your booklet

Name _____

CREATING A MATH BOOKLET

There are several ways to create a math booklet that highlights math skills for younger students. Here's one:

- Select a topic that is appropriate for the age and curriculum of the students who make up your target audience.
- Focus your topic. It's impractical to want to teach fifth graders fractions; that topic is far too broad. Try something more focused like simplifying fractions or multiplying mixed numbers.
- Include concepts as well as steps to do the math in your booklet.
- Write steps to performing mathematical procedures in order.
- Provide examples for the steps.
- An easy way to make a booklet is to take two sheets of blank paper, then:
  —Put them together, one on top of the other. Turn the pages lengthwise, so that the longer sides are across the top and bottom. Now fold them down the center, bringing the left side over the right.
  —Staple the outside of the fold (a staple on the top, the bottom, and in the middle).
  —To help design the contents of your booklet, make a "dummy" layout. Think of this as practice. Experiment with where you might put writing, illustrations, and sample problems. You might need to try several possible layouts before you find the design you like the best. Make sure to number the pages correctly.
  —If you want a longer booklet, simply add more sheets of paper.
- Leave ample space on each page. A page that is too crowded will not be attractive or easy to read.
- Add illustrations or clip art to your booklet.
- Design an attractive cover.
- Include practice worksheets or sample problems in your booklet.
- Proofread your work carefully, and make sure all the math examples are accurate.
- After your booklet is in its finished form, but before you have stapled it, have the separate pages photocopied. Remember to photocopy the pages of your booklet on the front and back. You'll then need to staple the pages to produce the actual booklets. Be sure to make enough copies so that you, the teachers, and each person of your audience may have one.

SHARING THE MATH WORD

Having an article published can be a most satisfying experience for a student (or even an adult). Although math students, and their teachers, generally don't think much about publishing articles, there are many magazines and newsletters that are open to student writing on numerous topics, including math. That's the focus of this project—encouraging students to write articles about mathematics with the aim of publication.

GOAL: Working individually (although you might allow students to work in pairs as co-authors), students will write articles on topics in math and submit them for publication. *Suggested time*—1 class period to get the project started. Students will then work at their own pace doing most of the work on articles at home.

MATH SKILLS TO HIGHLIGHT:

Writing as a means by which to express ideas about math. Specific skills will vary, depending upon the topic of the article.

SPECIAL MATERIALS/EQUIPMENT: Computers and printers; word processors; photocopiers; regular business envelopes for letters; 9 × 12-inch mailing envelopes for student manuscripts; postage stamps.

DEVELOPMENT: Since a major part of this project is writing, you may wish to work with your students' English teacher. He or she can handle the actual writing while you focus your efforts on the mathematics. Due to the strong competition for getting an article published, you might want to make this an optional project only for students who indicate a desire to write and submit their work.

Many magazines and newsletters regularly publish the writing of students. Start looking for potential markets right in your school. If your school board or PTA publishes a magazine or newsletter for parents or the community, see if the editors are interested in your students submitting math articles. Perhaps they would be willing to run a regular column.

Local newspapers or magazines are also potential markets. Contact the editors either through a letter or a phone call, and ask if they are interested in having your students submit material.

For lists of other potential markets, consult the *Market Guide for Young Writers* by Kathy Henderson (published by Writer's Digest Books, 1507 Dana Avenue, Cincinnati, OH 45207). This reference contains over 150 markets for student writers. Older students who are serious about writing should be referred to *Writer's Market*. Also published by Writer's Digest Books, this source offers a listing of several thousand potential markets for writing. Your local library may have copies, or you may contact the publisher.

- Begin this project by telling your students that there are many markets for articles written by students. Although writing for publication is usually associated with English classes, the markets are as open to well-written math articles as they are to articles written on other subjects.

- Note that submitting writing to magazines and newsletters is an excellent way to share ideas.

- Distribute copies of Student Guide 30–1 and review it with your students. Emphasize the importance of closely following the suggestions for submission.

- Recommend that students obtain sample copies of magazines to which they are interested in submitting articles, and also write to editors for guidelines for submissions. Many magazines will send guidelines informing authors of the types of articles they need.

- Distribute copies of Data Sheet 30–2, "A Sample Query Letter." Explain that a query is a letter an author sends to an editor of a magazine, in which the author describes his or her idea for an article. In the letter the author asks the editor if she or he would be interested in receiving a copy of the article. Queries save time and effort. If the author doesn't receive any positive responses to a query letter, it saves her or him the effort of writing an article for which there is little interest.

- Discuss the query letter in detail. Explain that queries are written as business letters. Note the headings, greeting, and closing. Next point out that query letters have distinct parts. Most begin with a statement of a problem or a direct question to the editor. In the sample, the statement is in the first paragraph. Some details are then offered (paragraph two). After the details, the author asks the editor if she or he would be interested in the article, and usually offers some detail about how the article would be structured (paragraph three). Finally, the author offers his or her qualifications— why the author is suited to write this article.

- Suggest that students use computers or word processors for writing. Such tools make writing and revision easier. Also, most editors frown on handwritten material.

- To help students generate ideas for articles, you might let them work in small groups for part of the period.

- If you assign this project to all of your students and wish to collect articles at a specific time so that you may review them, set a deadline.

WRAP-UP: Students submit their articles to magazines and newsletters.

EXTENSION.   Encourage students to write additional articles and submit them for publication. Make writing articles an ongoing activity in your class.

(Student Guide 30-1)

Name _____   Project Due Date _____

SHARING THE MATH WORD

Situation/Problem:

You are to write an article on a topic in math and submit it to a magazine for publication.

Possible Strategies:

1. Obtain copies of several magazines or newsletters that publish the material of students. Review the articles they publish, noting the types, lengths, styles, and tones.
2. Write to magazines you are thinking about sending an article to, and ask the editor if he or she can forward guidelines. Some magazines will even send free sample copies if you request them.
3. Generate a list of potential topics, and narrow it down to a topic you'd like to write about. (Articles that are sent to magazines are called *manuscripts.*)

Special Considerations:

- Try to select a topic that is fresh; in other words, it hasn't been done before. You might write about an old topic in a new way.

© 1996 by The Center for Applied Research in Education

- Query magazines to see if they would be interested in your article idea. See Data Sheet 30–2 for an example of a query letter.

- Always follow the magazine's guidelines. If they want articles of 800 words, avoid sending them an article of 1,200 words.

- When submitting a manuscript to a magazine, always include a SASE (self-addressed, stamped envelope). If they reject your manuscript, many magazines won't return your article without a SASE.

- Be sure the copy of your article that you send is clear (no smudges) and has clean lettering. Always keep a copy for yourself.

- Your article should be typed or printed on 8 $\frac{1}{2}$ × 11-inch white bond paper. Avoid erasable paper which smears easily. Margins should be at least one inch on all sides. Your name and address go at the top left corner of the title page; the word count, rounded to the nearest hundred, goes at the top right. The title, with your name beneath it, should be centered and started about one-third down the page. Starting with page two, your last name and a key word from the title should be placed at the top left. This is called the pageheading. It makes it easier for busy editors to find pages of your manuscript should they become separated. Number your pages at either the bottom center or top right. Use paper clips to keep your manuscript together; never use staples.

- When you mail your manuscript, include a brief cover letter in which you introduce yourself.

- Remember that the competition is very stiff. Submit only your best work. If you receive a rejection, meaning your work is returned to you because the magazine can't use it, don't give up. All writers suffer rejection. Keep trying.

To Be Submitted:

A finished copy of your article

Name _____

A SAMPLE QUERY LETTER

Author's Name
Address
City, State ZIP Code
Date

Editor's Name
Name of Magazine
Address
City, State ZIP Code

Dear (Editor's Name):

Studying for math tests is a problem for many math students. Most just don't know how to study.

At Tom Paine High School, students have organized a math study club. The purpose of the club is to help students learn how to study for math tests and quizzes by introducing students to various study strategies. The club boasts a great success rate. All members have seen their grades improve, and almost half have seen their grades rise 15% or more. The club has recently begun to help interested groups organize study clubs for other subjects.

Would (Name of Magazine) be interested in an article describing how the Math Study Club at Tom Paine High School helps students improve their math grades? I would include interviews with club members to highlight the writing.

I feel I am very qualified to write this article. I am one of the founders of the club and serve as its current president.

Thank you for your time.

Sincerely,

Author's Name

KEEPING A MATH JOURNAL

A math journal contains written accounts of a student's ideas, questions, failures, successes, and musings regarding mathematics. It becomes a record of a student's experiences and progress. Journals are generally written in the first person and may explore a variety of topics and issues: summaries of important concepts, frustrations, solutions to particular problems, or simply the student's impressions, opinions, or observations about math. Sometimes journal entries may be rather general; sometimes they may be personal. Always they present the student with the opportunity to explore his or her understanding of math.

Since journals can provide a written record of a student's growth in learning math, entries are often an excellent addition to a math portfolio. A math journal provides you with a means of getting to know your students in a unique way.

GOAL: Each student will maintain a math journal for a marking period, semester, or school year. *Suggested time*—a partial class period to introduce the project and get students started.

MATH SKILLS TO HIGHLIGHT:

Writing as a means by which to express ideas about math. Specific math skills are dependent upon the unit of study.

SPECIAL MATERIALS/EQUIPMENT: A spiral notebook, or composition book, for each student to use as a journal.

DEVELOPMENT: Before you begin this project you must consider and decide on some guidelines for journals. How often should entries be made? How often will you look at the journals? Will students be encouraged to share entries with others? If students are maintaining portfolios, will they be encouraged to select journal entries for inclusion with their portfolios? Will there be any limits to the types of entries?

We recommend that you review student journals periodically. This gives you the opportunity to respond to students and make sure they are writing in their journals regularly. You may collect journals every few weeks, or get in the habit of reading a few from each class two or three times per week. This kind of schedule makes your workload more manageable.

We don't recommend grading or correcting the writing in journals. Grading will cause students to write what they think you want to see, rather than take risks with their ideas and write about concepts or ideas they are not sure of. You should respond to the writing of your students by offering suggestions, constructive comments, questions, and encouragement. It's not unusual for students to write back to you in their journals, and you and they may even correspond through journals.

- Begin this project by explaining the purpose of a math journal. Distribute copies of Student Guide 31–1, and review it with your students.

- Discuss how often students should make entries. While some students will write in their journals regularly without your prompting, others will need guidelines. A minimum of three times a week is a reasonable goal.

- Tell students how often you will collect journals.

- Mention that while you won't be grading journals, you will offer comments. Encourage students to respond to your comments. Tell them that while you will respect their ideas and privacy, you must report anything you read that you feel endangers the student or someone else.

- Emphasize that a math journal is a place to write about reflections and insights regarding math.

- Since many students may be unfamiliar with the types of entries that may be included in a journal, copy and hand out copies of Data Sheet 31–2, "Possible Entries for Math Journals." Note that these are just a few examples of topics students might consider writing about.

WRAP-UP: Review journals periodically and respond to the writing of your students.

EXTENSIONS: Suggest that students select some of their best entries, polish and publish them in a math or class magazine or school newspaper, or include them in a math portfolio.

(Student Guide 31-1)

Name _____   Project Due Date _____

KEEPING A MATH JOURNAL

Situation/Problem:

You will maintain a math journal. Your journal will be a place for you to write about topics and issues in math.

Possible Strategy:

1. Respond to daily math assignments, classwork, and projects in your journal.

2. Select topics of interest in math that you would like to write about. Write about things that are important to you, about the solutions of specific problems, questions you may have, summaries of concepts, insights, reflections, or your opinions about issues in math.

Special Considerations:

- Use a standard spiral notebook or composition book for your journal. Be sure your name and class are on the cover. If you run out of pages, continue your journal in a similar book. Number your journals.

- Use your math journal only for math entries. Don't use it for other subjects.

- Bring your journal to class each day. Feel free to write in it at home as well as in school.

- Strive to write in your journal at least three times each week. Of course, you may write in it every day.

- Date your entries.

- Remember that your teacher will periodically read your journals, and offer suggestions and comments.

- Take some of what you feel are your best entries, and share them with others.

- Review your journal from time to time and reflect on your growth in mathematics.

To Be Submitted:

The math journal

Name _____

POSSIBLE ENTRIES FOR MATH JOURNALS

The following are some examples of topics you might wish to consider writing about in your math journal. There are countless others, limited only by your imagination and interest in math.

- Describe steps to solving a specific problem.
- Write about a concept or idea you find puzzling or fascinating. Explain why it interests you.
- Select a concept and explain it.
- Describe a situation in which you use math in your life.
- Write about your greatest triumph in math.
- Describe how you used a computer to help you solve a math problem.
- Explain what makes a particular problem especially frustrating.
- Write on what you don't like about a topic in math.
- Explain situations when calculators are useful.
- Write about why estimation is an essential skill.
- Write about your feelings regarding a problem, situation, topic, or issue in math.
- Write about how you felt in math today.
- Write about shortcuts to solutions.
- Write about what you understand now that you had trouble with before.

project 32

MATH PORTFOLIOS

A math portfolio is a collection of various types of a student's work gathered over a period of time. It may be compared to an artist's portfolio that contains samples of the work an artist does, but in this case the portfolio holds examples of math work. A student's portfolio may include items such as assignments, quizzes, tests, reports, writing samples, projects, and/or project summaries. A good portfolio becomes a repository of a student's work, revealing not only the student's overall progress in math but also his or her attitudes toward mathematics. It can provide a far broader scope of a student's achievement than just tests and quizzes. Regular review of a portfolio can be helpful for students, teachers, parents, and administrators.

There are two types of portfolios: a work portfolio and an assessment portfolio. While some teachers require students to maintain only a general work portfolio, most require students to periodically select what they feel are their best papers from their work portfolios and compile an assessment portfolio for evaluation. Specific criteria are used in evaluation. (See "Portfolio Assessment Criteria" at the end of these notes.) Whether you decide to have students maintain one or two portfolios, you undoubtedly will find that portfolios are an important tool in a math curriculum.

GOAL: Each student will maintain a math work portfolio and an assessment portfolio for a specific length of time, perhaps a marking period, semester, or the whole year. *Suggested time*—a partial class period to introduce the project and get students started.

MATH SKILLS TO HIGHLIGHT:

Evidence of specific math skills will vary according to the unit of study. Portfolio items should reflect examples of a variety of problem-solving strategies that show evidence of student progress, growth, and reasoning abilities.

SPECIAL MATERIALS/EQUIPMENT: Two heavy envelopes or folders for each student (one will serve as a work portfolio and the other as an assessment portfolio); milk crate or box for each class to store the portfolios; felt-tip pen to write students' names on portfolios.

DEVELOPMENT: Decide whether you will require students to maintain only a work portfolio, or a work portfolio and an assessment portfolio. We suggest both. Since not all of the items that go into a work portfolio will be examples of a student's best efforts, an assessment portfolio offers students a chance to select examples of their work that show their greatest progress and learning. You must also decide what type of work students will file in their portfolios, and how long they will maintain their portfolios.

- Start this project by explaining the purpose of a portfolio to your students. You may find that some of your students were never required to maintain one and will be uncertain of what they are to do.

- Distribute copies of Student Guide 32–1, and review it with your students. Especially note the types of material that may be placed in a portfolio.

- Hand out copies of Data Sheet 32–2, "Portfolio Assessment Criteria." Explain that the abilities and skills noted on the sheet are the criteria you will concentrate on when you review the portfolios of your students. (Some teachers prefer to focus their assessment efforts on two or three specific criteria. They feel this helps them to remain more objective.) Of course, you may include additional criteria based upon your program and needs.

- Distribute large envelopes or folders to serve as the actual portfolios. Have students clearly print their names on their portfolios with a felt-tip pen. If possible, provide a milk crate or box in the classroom to store the portfolios. Keep the portfolios in alphabetical order, and instruct students to file their own work. This relieves you of the burden of filing. (If you can't store portfolios in the classroom or another central location, you may permit students to maintain them at home.)

- Emphasize that any work put into the portfolio should be dated and placed in sequential order according to the date.

- At the end of the specific time frame—a unit or marking period, for example—have students review their work, and select items to place in an assessment portfolio. You may provide guidelines as to the number of items to include. You may also require that specific assignments be included so there is some consistency among the portfolios.

WRAP-UP: Review portfolios with individual students and discuss their growth in math. Use the assessment of portfolios as a means to focus on future achievement. *A note regarding grading:* Since most items that go into a portfolio are already graded, it is not usually advisable to place a grade on the portfolio. A portfolio's greatest value lies in its identifying student growth and mastery of mathematical concepts and skills. Moreover, when students know that a portfolio will be graded, many won't always choose work that shows growth or reveals original thinking, but instead will select samples they feel are most likely to result in the best grade.)

EXTENSIONS: If you had students maintain portfolios for only a unit or marking period, consider extending the time frame. Share portfolios with parents and administrators.

Name _____   Project Due Date _____

MATH PORTFOLIOS

Situation/Problem:

You will create a math assessment portfolio. Your portfolio will show your progress in math through various samples of your work.

Possible Strategy:

Select examples of your work in math to be stored in your portfolio.

Special Considerations:

- While you may select work for your portfolio, check with your teacher to find out if he or she requires that some specific examples of your work be included. Some of the work you may wish to put in your portfolio follows:

  —solutions to open-ended questions

  —a report

  —a math project

  —a summary of your contribution to a math project

  —an article you've written about a topic in math

  —homework

  —tests

  —quizzes

  —work that was done in another class but that relates to math

  —a math problem you've written

  —an explanation of a math concept

  —an entry from your math journal (if you are keeping a journal)

  —comments from teachers

  —any work required by your teacher

- Be sure to place all required math work in your portfolio.

- Make sure your name is on your work, and date all assignments.

- File all assignments in chronological order.

- Clip or staple multi-page assignments together so that individual sheets do not become separated or lost.

- Include a Table of Contents, which lists the items in your portfolio.

- Include a Letter of Introduction to the reader of your portfolio. Your "reader" may be your teacher, your parent, or an administrator. Your Letter of Introduction should contain the following:

   —an explanation of what you chose to put in your portfolio, and why you chose these items

   —a description of the major concept(s) your portfolio illustrates

   —how this portfolio shows your progress

   —what work you liked best and why

To Be Submitted:

A portfolio, including a table of contents and letter of introduction

(Data Sheet 32–2)

Name _____

PORTFOLIO ASSESSMENT CRITERIA

The following criteria can show your overall growth in learning math.

- Understanding specific problems in math
- Understanding specific concepts
- Evidence of effective mathematical reasoning
- The ability to choose effective problem-solving strategies
- The ability to gather, analyze, and organize data in the solving of problems
- The ability to interpret results and draw conclusions
- The ability to support conclusions
- The use of appropriate math vocabulary, notation, and labels in written work
- The construction, manipulation, and understanding of models
- The use of technology
- Accuracy
- Evidence of self-assessment of work
- Evidence of critical thinking
- Enthusiasm in the learning of mathematics
- Understanding and appreciation for the wide scope of mathematics in our world

Section 4
···
MATH AND ART
AND MUSIC

MAKING A MATH POSTER

Math posters can make a classroom more attractive and interesting. This is especially true when students design and make posters that focus on a math idea, concept, formula, or term.

GOAL: Working individually or in pairs, students will create a math poster for the classroom or school. The subject matter is up to them. *Suggested time*—1 to 2 class periods.

MATH SKILLS TO HIGHLIGHT:

1. Representing mathematics in the format of a poster
2. Using math as a means to communicate ideas

SPECIAL MATERIALS/EQUIPMENT: Poster paper; rulers; colored pencils; markers. Sample posters, old magazines, catalogs, and clip-art books can be good sources of illustrations for posters. *Optional*—T-squares; drafting materials.

DEVELOPMENT: Show students a variety of posters; math posters would be most useful although any posters will be helpful. Explain that the purpose of a poster is to share an idea. Effective posters are visually "catchy." They gain attention by attracting the reader's eye with vivid colors, interesting photos or pictures, or compelling headlines. If you are showing examples of posters, ask students to point out what they find most interesting about each poster. Ask what they feel the poster is trying to convey.

- Begin the project by telling students that they will work alone or with a partner to create a math poster.
- Distribute copies of Student Guide 33–1, and review it with your students; especially note the possible topics for posters. Ask students to suggest more possible topics, and list them on the board or on an overhead projector. This will help students to get started.

- Hand out copies of Data Sheet 33–2, "Pointers About Posters." Review the material with your students, and discuss the various suggestions for creating effective posters. Emphasize that their posters should contain as many of the components of effective posters as possible.

- Discuss the importance of neatness and clarity. A poster's message might be negated if the poster is sloppy. Conversely, the message of a neat poster might be lost if it is bundled with too much information.

- Encourage students to design their posters in a way that best shares their ideas about math.

WRAP-UP: Display the finished posters in your classroom. If there is not enough space, perhaps a hallway or section of the library might be used.

EXTENSION: You may want to have a school or class vote on the best poster. Award math prizes for the first-, second-, and third-place winners.

Name _____   Project Due Date _____

MAKING A MATH POSTER

Problem/Situation:

You are to design a math poster to be displayed in your math class or elsewhere in your school.

Possible Strategies:

1. Study examples of posters. Determine what you feel makes some posters more effective than others.
2. Review Data Sheet 33–2 and compare what you feel makes an effective poster to the information on the Sheet.
3. Browse through your math text to find an idea, concept, formula, or term that you can convey in a poster.

Special Considerations:

- Be sure the topic you select is not too broad or complex to be communicated in a poster.
- If your topic at first seems too broad, try narrowing it down. Perhaps you can pick a part of it to illustrate.

- Following are some samples of possible topics for posters. There are many more:

    —Properties in Math

    —Exponents

    —Simplifying Fractions

    —Decimals

    —Percents

    —Scientific Notation

    —Rounding

    —Area Formulas

    —Circumference

    —Perimeter

    —Types of Triangles

    —Types of Polygons

    —Types of Quadrilaterals

    —Parts of Circles

    —Types of Lines

    —Math and Your Future

    —The Importance of Math

- Be sure to review Data Sheet 33–2. It will help you to create an effective poster.

- Try to make your poster unified and balanced.

- Try to create a clever illustration. Good sources of illustrations include magazines, catalogs, and clip-art books. Some computer programs offer many examples of clip art you might use. Of course, you may draw your own illustrations.

- Be neat. Make sure your illustrations, graphics, and lettering are precise and arranged attractively. Lines should be straight.

- If you have drafting tools, you may wish to use them.

- If you enjoy calligraphy, you may wish to use this type of lettering to highlight your poster.

To Be Submitted:

Your poster

Name _____

POINTERS ABOUT POSTERS

We see posters everywhere—from a store window advertising an upcoming local event to movie posters announcing the next great flick. A poster is usually larger than a standard sheet of writing paper, and usually—but not always—includes a picture or graphic design with the text. The elements of effective posters are listed below. You should try to incorporate them in your poster.

1. *Selling Point.* The purpose of any poster is to announce something or sell something.
   - The message may be direct and include words such as "buy," "ask," or "attend."
   - The message may simply announce or communicate an important idea.

2. *Benefits.* The poster tells readers what they have to gain by following the poster's advice or suggestions, or at least offers important information.

3. *Gaining Attention.* Every poster attempts to gain and hold attention. They may do this in several ways:
   - The poster may employ bold headlines, or amusing or eye-catching pictures.
   - Posters may use dramatic situations, slogans, a play on words, rhymes, popular sayings, or may appeal to the conscience of people.
   - The element of surprise helps to gain and keep attention. This may include unexpected, bizarre, or exaggerated illustrations, or pictures taken from unusual perspectives or dramatic angles, such as tilting the picture on its edge.

4. *Simplicity.* The best posters are simple and easy to read. Too many colors, pictures, or fancy lettering will detract from the poster's message.

5. *Unity.* Everything in a poster should work toward its purpose.
   - Main ideas may be highlighted by using devices such as arrows, dots, or pointing fingers.
   - One or several elements in the layout may touch or overlay others.
   - The poster may be surrounded with a border.
   - The background may be painted, or the poster may be on colored paper.

6. *Balance.* No part of a poster should overpower another. Balance can appear in two ways: Formal Balance and Informal Balance.
   - Formal Balance—a line of symmetry divides the poster where one half balances the other.
   - Informal Balance—the various elements of the poster, such as size, color, and shape, are in harmony and give an impression of being in balance.

7. *Workmanship.* This is the overall quality of the poster, including lettering, coloring, pictures, and message. Quality workmanship results in outstanding posters.

CREATING A LOGO

A logo is a visual representation that establishes an identity. Since effective cooperative learning depends upon a feeling of interconnectedness, this project can be an excellent team-building activity.

GOAL: Working in groups of 3 to 5, students will think about their group and design a logo that best portrays or describes them. Students will show their logo to the class, and explain why they chose their design. *Suggested time*—2 to 3 class periods.

MATH SKILLS TO HIGHLIGHT:

1. Making and testing conjectures
2. Communicating math strengths and goals
3. Synthesizing information related to math

SPECIAL MATERIALS/EQUIPMENT: Colored pencils; markers; compasses; rulers; stencils; 8-$1/_2$ × 11-inch white paper; sample logos. *Optional*—Computers and printers.

DEVELOPMENT: Since students will create logos that will represent their group, this project works best after students have worked together previously as a group. Students will be better able to identify their individual and collective strengths and weaknesses. Prior to starting this project, cut out logos from advertisements and product packages and bring them to class.

- Introduce this project by explaining to your students that they will work in groups and create a logo for their group.
- Discuss logos as visual representations of organizations, companies, or products. Logos convey a message and remind people of the group or product they represent. Show students examples of logos, and ask them if they can identify the logos. In many cases, they will be able to. This demonstrates the power of logos.

- Hand out copies of Student Guide 34–1, and review it with your students.
- Distribute copies of Data Sheet 34–2, "Creating an Effective Logo," and discuss the information on the sheet. Emphasize that students should refer to this sheet when creating their logos.
- Provide students with the time necessary to discuss the characteristics of their group, which they may incorporate in their logo. Stress that each student should contribute to the discussion. Consider requiring each student to contribute his or her own design. The group then selects the best design, or they may wish to combine the best features of two or more designs. Whichever way they pick their logo, students should have reasons for their choice.
- If you have access to computers, suggest that students design their logos on them. Many art and drawing programs have the capability to produce outstanding logos.
- If you do not have access to computers, the logos may be drawn and illustrated by hand. Encourage students to color their logos.
- Remind students that they should choose a spokesperson to explain the selection of their logo to the class.

WRAP-UP: Each group introduces its logo and explains its design. You may wish to display the logos in the classroom or elsewhere in your school.

EXTENSION: Use a silk-screening technique to print each group's logo on T-shirts. Your school's art teacher may be willing to help you with this.

Name _____   Project Due Date _____

CREATING A LOGO

Situation/Problem:

You and your team are to design a logo to represent your group. This logo will be drawn on 8-1/2 × 11-inch paper and will project an image of "your group." After finishing your logo, you will show it to the class and explain why you chose its design.

Possible Strategies:

1. Look at various logos. Discuss what makes some more effective than others.
2. Brainstorm with your group to determine your unique characteristics, both as individuals and as a group.
3. Review Data Sheet 34–2 to learn about the elements of effective logos.
4. Individually create rough sketches of what each of you thinks your group logo should be like. Discuss the logos and pick the best one, or combine features of different ones.

Special Considerations:

- As you study various logos, try to decide what message is communicated, what you like about it, what makes it memorable, and what you don't like about it.

© 1996 by The Center for Applied Research in Education

- To find the characteristics of your group, ask yourself questions like the following:

  —What are our strengths?

  —What are our goals?

  —How do we differ from other groups?

  —How do we differ from each other?

  —What do we wish to share or communicate through our logo?

- Give your group a name.

- Design a logo that best describes your group. Sketch several possible logos. Compare them and select the best one.

- When creating your logo, pay attention to design, especially the spacing between letters and/or pictures. Your logo should be visually appealing.

- Write your reasons why you selected the logo you did. Select a spokesperson who will later share your reasons with the class.

- If you have access to computers, you may wish to design your logo on them. Many art and drawing programs have the capability to create logos.

- You may draw your logo on white paper. Be neat with your artwork and lettering.

To Be Submitted:

Your logo

Name _____

© 1996 by The Center for Applied Research in Education

CREATING AN EFFECTIVE LOGO

A logo is a visual representation that conveys a meaning. It may be a picture, a name, or a picture and a name. You probably would recognize many, including the NBC Peacock, MTV graphic, the Hallmark Crown, and the Golden Arches of McDonald's. Big companies pay thousands of dollars to consultants to design logos that will provide positive, memorable impressions. Following is some information that will help you design your own logo.

AN EFFECTIVE LOGO MUST:

1. Make a good first impression.
2. Describe who you are, and also your ideas and attitudes.
3. Possess something unique or interesting to help you stand out from the crowd. Your logo should be your mark of distinction.

TO DESIGN AN EFFECTIVE LOGO:

1. Think of a symbol that uniquely depicts you. This symbol may be an illustration, name, or a combination of both.
2. Carefully consider the lettering you will use. For example:

    —Italics (slanted) denotes action or speed. It projects a modern or progressive image.

    —Capital letters suggest formality, steadiness.

    —Lower-case letters suggest an informal manner or casual image.

    —Outlined letters also project an informal image.

    —Thin letters denote professionalism.

    —Thick or bold letters project strength or dependability.

    —Script denotes gentleness or caring.

3. Keep your logo clear and simple. Avoid cluttering it with unnecessary letters or art. Eliminate any unnecessary details.
4. Strive for balance in your spacing of letters, pictures, and designs.
5. Be neat in drawing and sketching. Use a ruler or compass, if needed. Draw letters carefully.

project 35

I WANNA BE LIKE ESCHER

Maurits Cornelis Escher (1898–1972) was a Dutch graphic artist. Although he began to study architecture, he soon abandoned it for graphics. Until 1937 he drew and sketched mostly landscapes, but then concentrated on constructing images that exist only on paper or in abstract theory.

While his graphics may be grouped according to several different themes, the division of the plane is the focus of this project. A tiling design which covers a plane with no gaps or overlaps is called a *tessellation*. A *pure tessellation* is a design in which only one figure is used. A *regular tessellation* uses only one regular polygon to tile the plane. A *semiregular tessellation* is a design that covers the plane using two or more regular polygons. Escher created over 150 different tessellations in his drawings, yet he had no formal math training.

GOAL: Working individually, students will make a drawing similar to those Escher used to tile a plane. *Suggested time*—3 to 4 class periods.

MATH SKILLS TO HIGHLIGHT:

1. Defining and discussing tiling the plane, tessellations, including pure tessellations, regular tessellations, and semiregular tessellations

2. Reviewing the names of polygons, including triangle, quadrilateral, rectangle, square, parallelogram, rhombus, and regular polygon

3. Using the protractor to measure angles, or using the formula $[180(n-2)]/n$ to find the measure of each interior angle of a regular polygon (n stands for the number of sides)

4. Discussing transformations, including slides, reflections, slide reflections, and rotations

SPECIAL MATERIALS/EQUIPMENT: Books containing Escher's graphics; protractors; scissors; envelopes to store patterns; rulers; transparent tape. *Optional*—Colored pencils or crayons.

DEVELOPMENT: Show students examples of Escher's graphics in books about Escher. An excellent source is *Fantasy and Symmetry: The Periodic Drawings of M. C. Escher* by

Caroline H. MacGillavry, Harry N. Abrams, Inc., 1976. Another is *M. C. Escher: His Life and Complete Graphic Work* by F.H. Bool, et al., edited by J. L. Locher, Harry N. Abrams, Inc., 1982. Many other sources are probably in your local library.

- Begin the project by discussing pure, regular, and semiregular tessellations, and the differences among them.

- Distribute copies of Student Guide 35–1 and review it with your students. Note that the guide provides step-by-step instructions for students.

- Hand out copies of Data Sheet 35–2, "Polygon Patterns." Ask students to cut out the large regular triangle, square, and other regular polygons. Distribute an envelope to each student, and instruct students to keep all of their pieces in it to prevent the pieces from becoming lost. The small squares and triangles (the ones that have a one-centimeter side) will only be used in the extension for this project. Do not cut them out yet.

- You may permit students to work in small groups to determine which regular polygons will make a regular tessellation. Remind students that only one shape may be used per design. Polygons may not overlap and no spaces should be left between the tiles. Students should discover that only the regular triangle, square, and regular hexagon tile.

- Explore why some figures tile. The key here is the measurement of the angles. You may ask students to measure the angles of the regular polygons, or you may use the formula [180 (n – 2)]/n to determine the measure of an interior angle of a regular polygon. Students should discover that in order for a figure to tile, the sum of the angles around any point is 360 degrees. As an option students may generalize that any triangle and quadrilateral will tile. They may require slides, reflections, slide reflections, and/or rotations.

- Distribute copies of Data Sheet 35–3, "Steps to Making an Escher-like Drawing." These steps are illustrated with examples for clarity. Be sure your students understand the steps.

- Hand out copies of Worksheet 35–4, "Isometric Dot Paper." Students are to cover the worksheet by sliding, reflecting, sliding and reflecting, and/or rotating the shape. By adding details and color, the drawings should resemble some of Escher's works.

WRAP-UP: Students should share their drawings with other members of the class. You may wish to display drawings in a central location.

EXTENSION: By using the smaller regular triangles, squares, and other regular polygons, students can create semiregular tessellations through manipulating the patterns. Combinations may include:

octagon and square

hexagon, square, and triangle

hexagon and triangle

square and triangle

Students may also wish to make an Escher-like drawing, consisting of two figures.

Name _____   Project Due Date _____

I WANNA BE LIKE ESCHER

Situation/Problem:

Maurits Cornelis Escher (1898–1972) was a graphic artist. One of his most famous themes was tiling the plane. A tiling design that covers the plane with no gaps or overlaps is called a tessellation. Escher created over 150 different tessellations in his drawings. His designs are truly fascinating. Can you be like Escher and create a tessellation of your own? When your drawing is complete, share it with your class.

Possible Strategies:

1. Study examples of Escher's graphics on tiling.
2. Determine which polygons will make a regular tessellation. List them.
3. Design a shape of your own by using a polygon that will tessellate.

Special Considerations:

- From Data Sheet 35–2 choose a polygon that will form a regular tessellation. You may select a triangle, square, or hexagon.
- Refer to Data Sheet 35–3 for instructions on how to make an Escher-like drawing. Follow the suggestions carefully.
- Use Worksheet 35–4 for your drawing. Be creative.
- You may color your design.

To Be Submitted:

Your worksheet

(Data Sheet 35-2)

Name _____

POLYGON PATTERNS

Regular Triangles

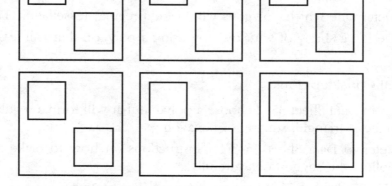

Squares

Regular Pentagons

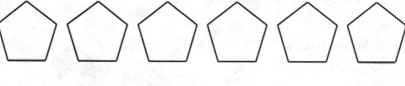

Regular Hexagons

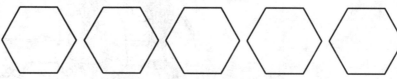

Regular Octagons

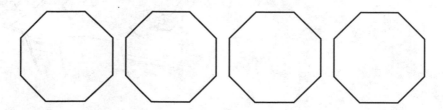

Name _____

© 1996 by The Center for Applied Research in Education

STEPS TO MAKING AN ESCHER-LIKE DRAWING

1. Start with a shape that will tessellate. (A hexagon is used in the example.)

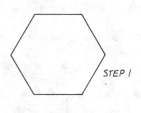

2. Cut a portion of the figure on one side, slide it to the opposite side, and tape it. (In the example, this was done 3 times.)

3. What does the shape resemble? (In this case, the shape resembles a snowflake.)

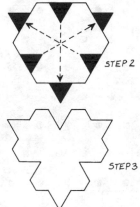

4. Cover the paper by sliding, reflecting, sliding and reflecting, and/or rotating the shape.

5. Add details.

ISOMETRIC DOT PAPER

project 36

THE PLUS AND MINUS COMIC STRIP

Comic strips are regular features in most newspapers. Combining unique characters, witty dialogue, and good art, popular comic strips attract a strong following and transcend generations of readers. This project gives your students a chance to create comic strips with a focus on math.

GOAL: Students will work in pairs or groups of 3 to make a math comic strip. *Suggested time—*2 to 3 class periods.

MATH SKILLS TO HIGHLIGHT:

1. An awareness of spatial relationships
2. Other skills will vary, depending on the storyline students select for their comic strip

SPECIAL MATERIALS/EQUIPMENT: White drawing paper; black pens; rulers. *Optional—*Computers and printers.

DEVELOPMENT: Consider collaborating with your students' art teacher for this project. He or she might permit them to work on their comic strips in art class. If you arrange such collaboration, you should handle the introduction to the project and help students focus their storyline on mathematics, while the art teacher manages the actual creation of the comic strips.

Before beginning the project, collect several examples of comics from newspapers and magazines. Since some math texts intersperse comics and cartoons throughout their chapters, go through your text and list pages on which cartoons or comics are located. Providing students with examples of comics that have a mathematics slant will help them generate ideas for their own comic strips.

- Start this project by explaining that students are to work in pairs or small groups and create a comic strip focusing on some aspect or idea in mathematics. Encourage students to invent their own characters; however, if they wish, they may use the characters Plus and Minus in their comic strips.

- If you have examples of comic strips, distribute them. Point out how comic strips usually focus on an idea, developed in a narrative, which usually ends with a punchline. Also note the artwork. Cartoonists must remain aware of spatial relationships as they work. Because the action must fit within a box, the artwork must be carefully designed. Too much detail crowds the box; too little may not be visually appealing or may not express the cartoonist's ideas.

- Hand out copies of Student Guide 36–1, and review it with your students. Especially note the Special Considerations, which help students to generate ideas for their comic strips. Emphasize that the comic strips must have a math angle or punchline.

- Recommend that students keep their comic strips to four frames or less. More than that will require a rather complex narrative and artwork.

- Some students may complain that they can't draw well. Tell them that you don't expect them to be professional artists. Their ideas are more important.

- Distribute copies of Data Sheet 36–2, "Comic Tips." Discuss the information with your students, which offers background on some of the techniques cartoonists use.

- If you have access to computers and art and drawing software, encourage students to create their comic strips on them.

WRAP-UP: Display the comic strips in class, or make copies and bind them in a class comic book. Hand out copies of the book to students, and be sure to display some in your school's media center.

EXTENSION: Some students may wish to explore creating flip books. Your library probably has several sources. Here's a good one: *Making "Movies" Without a Camera* by Lafe Locke (Cincinnati, OH: Betterway Books, 1992). Another good source is *Copier Creations* by Paul Fleischman (New York: HarperCollins, 1993).

Name _____   Project Due Date _____

THE PLUS AND MINUS COMIC STRIP

Situation/Problem:

You and your partner(s) are to create a comic strip that focuses on math, or uses a math idea or concept in some way. You may use Plus and Minus as your main characters, or you may create your own.

Possible Strategies:

1. Study various comic strips. Identify their features, and analyze how they are done.
2. Consider inventing your own characters. Brainstorm possible characters for your comic strip.

Special Considerations:

- Identify an idea in math that can be used in a comic strip.
  - —Think about your characters, what they are like, and how they relate to math. What situations could you create that show them using or discussing math?
  - —Brainstorm for ideas. Jot down ideas, possible topics, phrases, words. Doodle to generate ideas. Use your imagination. Let your thoughts roam. Think of associations. Look for a play on words or funny circumstances. Try to make connections.
  - —Look through your math text for ideas.

- Once you have an idea, sketch it out on paper. Try keeping your comic strip to four frames or less. Be aware of spatial relationships. Since you are limited by the size of each frame, you must design your art carefully. Try to keep things in proportion. Remember, you'll need room for the narrative and dialogue.

- Refer to Data Sheet 36–2 for suggestions for creating a comic strip.

- You may need to try several sketches before you are pleased with your comic strip.

- When drawing your comic strip, use rulers to make straight lines, and be neat with your artwork. Dialogue should be written clearly.

- If you have access to a computer, and your computer has art and drawing software, you may wish to create your comic strip there.

To Be Submitted:

Your comic strip

Name _____

COMIC TIPS

From *Peanuts* to *Dick Tracy*, *The Wizard of Id* to *Blondie*, comics vary. Yet, all have common elements. The most important include:

1. A narrative related by a series of pictures. Called frames or panels, the narrative is usually humorous, but may be serious.
2. Continuing character(s). The characters are unique and have their own personalities. They may be human, animal, or even aliens.
3. Dialogue within the pictures, usually in the form of "speech balloons," from the characters' mouths.
4. Captions that tell the story. This is called the narrative.
5. Background art that enhances the scene, but does not overshadow the characters.
6. A punchline. The punchline may be a joke, an amusing situation, an insight or observation, or a play on words.

CREATING A COMIC STRIP

1. You'll need a cast—people, animals, or other characters.
2. You'll need dialogue in the form of speech balloons. You may use captions to describe the action. (Some comics don't have dialogue or captions. These rely on the art to deliver the punchline.)
3. Your comic strip will need a setting, a specific place the story occurs.
4. You'll need a narrative that shows action in proper sequence.
5. You'll need a punchline that is developed out of the narrative.
6. You'll need to be selective in deciding what to put in and what to leave out of your comic strip. Remember, you have a limited amount of space.

project 37

NUMBERS AND SONGS

A novel and enjoyable way for students to highlight math concepts or facts is to write a song about them. Even if they don't have any particular musical talent, most students will plunge into this project with great enthusiasm.

GOAL: Working in groups of 2 to 4, students will compose songs that express an idea in mathematics. Upon completion of the project, students will be encouraged to perform or record their song for the class. *Suggested time*—2 to 3 class periods.

MATH SKILLS TO HIGHLIGHT:

Skills will vary depending on student songs

SPECIAL MATERIALS/EQUIPMENT: Rhyming dictionaries; for students who have a musical background, you may wish to provide examples of songs and music sheets.

DEVELOPMENT: Consider working with your students' music teacher for this project. While you work with students on the math for this project, he or she can help them write songs.

- Begin this project by explaining to your students that they will work in groups to write a song that identifies a math concept or fact. If you have students who study music or play musical instruments, try to organize groups so that each group has at least one of these students. Students who have a musical background can assume roles of leadership in this project.

- Distribute copies of Student Guide 37–1, and review it with your students. Encourage them to select the type of music they like, and write their song in that style. Writing a song will be easier if they choose a type of music with which they are familiar.

- Hand out copies of Data Sheet 37–2, "Tips for Writing a Song," and discuss the information with the class. Note that students who don't have a musical background might simply compose a song using a beat, much like a rap song.

- Discuss that most songs use lyrics that rhyme. If you have access to rhyming dictionaries, encourage students to use them. If these dictionaries are not available, encourage students to generate their own lists of rhyming words. Using the board or an overhead projector, ask students to help you create examples of rhyming words, such as the ones below:

  —run, fun, sun, son, done, none, ton . . .

  —high, sigh, cry, tie, pie, lie, try, multiply . . .

  —dad, pad, tad, bad, add, sad, fad . . .

  —hide, cried, tried, divide, wide, sighed . . .

  The lists can go on and on. Do a few examples and your students will understand what to do.

- For students who have a musical background, and who want to set their lyrics to musical notes, hand out copies of Worksheet 37–3, "Music Sheet." Suggest that if they play musical instruments, they might use their instruments to match the notes to their lyrics. Note, however, that only students who have the interest and musical ability will be able to manage this.

- If groups have a member who plays a musical instrument, encourage the group to include the use of the instrument with its song.

- If some groups have no members who play an instrument, assure them that using only lyrics in their songs is fine.

- If your students have access to a computer and software that allows songwriting, encourage them to use it. It is truly astonishing what students can do using such equipment. (Your students' music teacher may have this type of equipment.)

- Suggest that students videotape or tape-record their songs. Perhaps they can do this in the music room or at home.

WRAP-UP: Encourage students to perform their songs for the class. *A note here:* If a group is reluctant to perform, accept a tape or video, or even just a written copy of its song.

EXTENSION: Videotape your students performing their songs in a "Festival of Math Music."

Name _____   Project Due Date _____

NUMBERS AND SONGS

Situation/Problem:

You and your group are to compose and perform a song that highlights a concept or fact in mathematics.

Possible Strategies:

1. Discuss favorite types of music with the members of your group. Select one that most group members enjoy. It will be easier to write a song in a familiar style of music.
2. Brainstorm math concepts or ideas. Have a recorder write down the group's ideas. Use your math text to generate ideas.

Special Considerations:

- Choose a math concept or fact that can be expressed in a song.
- Refer to Data Sheet 37–2 for suggestions on songwriting.
- Remember that your song doesn't have to be long; but it should contain an idea about math.
- Use a rhyming dictionary to help you write lyrics that rhyme, or generate your own list of rhyming words.
- If possible, write musical notes as well as lyrics for your song. This will be easier if a group member has had training in music or plays an instrument.
- You may find it easier to write your lyrics according to a specific beat. Each syllable of a word in the lyrics would equal one beat. You may wish to try various beats.
- If a member or members of your group play a musical instrument, try using the instrument with your song.
- If you have access to a computer and software that supports songwriting, try using it to compose your song.
- If necessary, meet outside of class to rehearse the singing of your song.
- Tape-record or videotape your song.
- Consider performing your song "live" for the class.

To Be Submitted:

A copy of your song

(Data Sheet 37-2)

Name _____

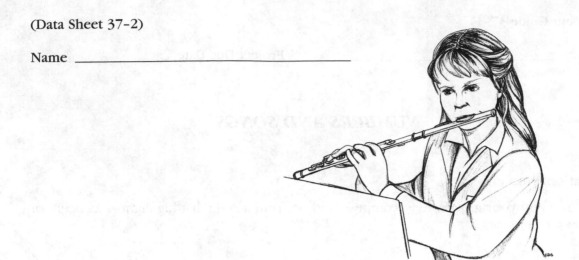

TIPS FOR WRITING A SONG

Songs are a form of communication in which a songwriter expresses his or her ideas about a particular topic. Here are some suggestions for writing a song.

- The words of songs are called *lyrics*. A lyric is similar to a poem, but the words of a lyric are set to music.
  - —Lyrics usually include rhyme. This helps make the song pleasing to the ear of the listener.
  - —A rhyming dictionary can be helpful in writing lyrics.
- Many popular songs contain *verses* and a *chorus*. The chorus is the part of the song that is repeated.
- *Rhythm* is the pattern of musical notes in a song.
- The *beat* is the underlying pulse in a piece of music. It may be fast or slow. The speed is called the *tempo*.

To write a song, try the following:

1. Find a topic or idea. It should be one that listeners can easily understand.
2. Compose lyrics that express your idea. (Although many professional songwriters compose the music first, for beginners it's usually easier to write lyrics, then explore rhythm and beat.)
3. Set your lyrics to a beat. The beat in a song is unchanging. Often, the lyrics of a song will fit a particular beat. Experiment with several possibilities. A four-beat count is one of the easiest to work with.
4. If you have an understanding of musical notes, write the notes that go with the lyrics.
5. Create a videotape or tape recording of the performance of your song.

Name _____

MUSIC SHEET

Write the lyrics and music for your song below.

Song Title: _____

project 38

THE MATH IN MUSIC

When most people think of music, they think of things like a favorite song, a rhythm, or the feelings a memorable melody evokes. Few think of mathematics, even though math is an integral part of music. This project gives students the opportunity to learn just how music is based on numbers.

GOAL: Working individually, students will research the ways mathematics is fundamental to music. They will then write an essay based upon their research. *Suggested time—* 1 to 2 class periods, with additional research time outside of class.

MATH SKILLS TO HIGHLIGHT:

1. Researching information about mathematics
2. Using writing to express ideas about math

SPECIAL MATERIALS/EQUIPMENT: Reference books that contain information about music and math. *Optional*—Word processors; computers; printers.

DEVELOPMENT: This project will require some real "digging" for facts, and you may wish to assign it as a challenge.

- Start this project by explaining to your students that music is based on mathematics. An *interval*, for example, is the space between two notes. An *octave* is the space of eight notes or tones of a major or minor scale. The sound of two notes an octave apart is explained as the *frequency* of the higher note being twice that of the lower note. *Rhythm* is founded on the lengths of notes and the interrelationship between them. *Beats* are a metrical structure that provide the pulse of a piece of music. Some common beats in popular music are meters in 4/4, 2/4, 3/4, and 6/8 time.
- Distribute copies of Student Guide 38–1, and review it with your students.

- Prior to beginning the project, consult your school librarian about this topic and ask her or him to set aside reference books for your students. Schedule at least one period in the school library to help students get started with their research. Suggest that, if necessary, students continue their research on their own time.

- Since students will likely require time outside of class to complete this project, set a deadline. A week to ten days should be enough time.

- Distribute copies of Data Sheet 38–2, "Tips for Essay Writing," and review the suggestions with your class.

- Encourage students to use word processors or computers to write and print their essays.

WRAP-UP: Display the essays of your students.

EXTENSION: Produce a book containing the essays of your students. You may title it *Math in Music: A Collection of Student Essays.*

Name _____   Project Due Date _____

THE MATH IN MUSIC

Situation/Problem:

You are to research the role mathematics plays in music. You are then to write an essay based on the information you found.

Possible Strategies:

1. Review some general reference books about music and look for topics and key words that relate to math.
2. Access electronic databases (such as computerized card catalogs), focusing your search on words that relate to math and music.

Special Considerations:

- Some key words you might wish to concentrate your research on include: octave, meter, beat, interval, and rhythm.
- Take accurate notes.
- Be sure to record your sources.
- Refer to Data Sheet 38–2 for suggestions on organizing and writing your essay.
- If possible, use word processors or computers and printers to write your essay. Include your sources.

To Be Submitted:

Your finished essay

Name _____

© 1996 by The Center for Applied Research in Education

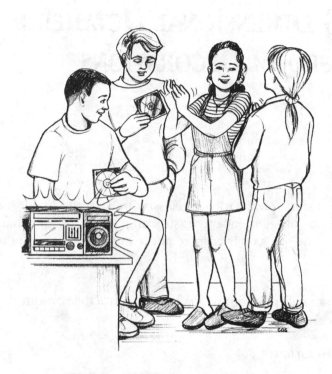

TIPS FOR ESSAY WRITING

An essay is usually a short piece of writing in which the author focuses his or her efforts on a specific topic. Following are some guidelines for writing an effective essay.

- The typical essay uses a simple format:

  —An *introduction* in which the main point of the essay is stated.

  —A *body* that explains the main ideas. Depending on the length of the essay, the body might be a few paragraphs or several pages long.

  —A *conclusion* that summarizes the main points of the essay.

- An essay should be written in a clear, concise style.

- In organizing your essay, identify the main ideas you found in your research. List them on a piece of paper. These main ideas will probably make up the body of your essay.

  —Organize your main ideas in order, from most important to least important. This will be the basic outline of your essay.

  —Support your main ideas with details and examples.

MAKING 3-DIMENSIONAL OCTAHEDRA AND CLASSROOM DECORATIONS

This project can add some pizazz to your classroom, as well as your teaching. Students will likely enjoy the hands-on element of constructing 3-D octahedra that may serve as classroom decorations. The project is also a good introduction to solid geometry and the Platonic Solids.

GOAL: Students will work individually to construct classroom decorations. *Suggested time*—2 class periods.

MATH SKILLS TO HIGHLIGHT:

1. Inscribing an equilateral triangle in a circle
2. Using a compass
3. Identifying the parts of a circle
4. Identifying regular octahedra and their faces, edges, and vertices
5. Evaluating Euler's Formula

SPECIAL MATERIALS/EQUIPMENT: At least 8 pictures per decoration; which relates to a theme; compasses; straight edges; scissors; glue; spring clothespins; a hole puncher; cord for hanging the decorations. Old magazines; catalogs; brochures; newspapers; and even greeting cards and wrapping paper are good sources for pictures.

DEVELOPMENT: Prior to starting this project, we suggest that you make a sample decoration. Seeing an example of what they are to do will make it easier for your students to complete this project. A few days before the project, tell your students that they will make decorations for the classroom, and show the one you've created. You might select a theme in advance—Christmas, Math in Architecture, or Pictures of Geometric Shapes are some examples—or you may leave the theme open to your students. Instruct them to start collecting pictures, 3 × 3-inch in size, on their topic. You may have students bring to class materials from which they may choose pictures, or have them find pictures at home. In either case you should have extra sources of pictures on hand. Remind students the day before the project to bring their materials or pictures to class.

- Begin the project by explaining to your students that they will make decorations for the classroom. Mention that the decorations will be 3-dimensional octahedra. Once again, show them your example.

- Distribute copies of Student Guide 39–1, and review it with your students.

- Hand out copies of Data Sheet 39–2, "Constructing a 3-Dimensional Octahedron," and discuss the information. Note that the Data Sheet provides instructions for making the decorations. Consider having students practice following the directions on plain pieces of paper before they try to make their decorations. This will help them to avoid ruining pictures.

- You may wish to introduce the concept of an equilateral triangle and segment of a circle, as well as review the meaning of diameter of a circle and arcs.

- If the construction is too difficult for your class, you may adapt the steps by making several circles whose diameter is 3 inches. Students may then use these as a pattern. You may also cut out and distribute an equilateral triangle you've inscribed to serve as a pattern. In this case, make your patterns out of light cardboard or oaktag, and ask students to trace the circle, place the triangle on it, and trace the triangle.

- Emphasize that students should have eight inscribed triangles, each inscribed in a circle. They will then cut out each circle and fold the segments toward them so that the triangle is flat.

- Point out that upon completion of their decoration, the resulting figure will have eight faces, each of which is an equilateral triangle. It is one of the Platonic Solids called a regular octahedron. You may also wish to discuss Euler's Formula: $V - E + F = 2$, where V stands for the number of vertices (in this case 6), E stands for the number of edges (12), and F stands for the number of faces (8).

WRAP-UP: Display the decorations by hanging them in your classroom. (Because a large number of decorations will be cumbersome to carry, we suggest you evaluate them as students complete and submit them to you.)

EXTENSION: Discuss the other Platonic Solids. Students may use the same procedure to construct a regular tetrahedron by using four faces.

Name _____   Project Due Date _____

MAKING 3-DIMENSIONAL OCTAHEDRA
AND CLASSROOM DECORATIONS

Situation/Problem:

You will make a decoration for your classroom by selecting pictures, drawing circles, and inscribing equilateral triangles in them. Your finished decoration will be a 3-dimensional octahedron.

Possible Strategies:

1. Choose a theme or idea that interests you, and select appropriate pictures.

2. Although you will be working individually, you might work cooperatively with other students in searching for pictures. For example, you may wish to share old magazines. Tell your friends what type of pictures you are looking for and they may find some; likewise, if you find pictures your friends might be able to use, show them.

Special Considerations:

- You will need eight pictures for your decoration. Finding more than eight will give you a choice of several. Good sources for pictures include old magazines, catalogs, brochures, greeting cards, wrapping paper, and newspapers.

- Make sure your pictures are at least 3 × 3 inches.

- Note that the main part of your pictures will be the center of the circles. (If your teacher shows you a model, study it carefully.)

- Review Data Sheet 39–2 carefully. It provides instructions on how to inscribe an equilateral triangle in a circle and construct your 3-dimensional octahedron.

- Before trying to make your decoration, try making a rough copy, using plain pieces of paper. This will give you valuable practice.

To Be Submitted:

Your decoration

Name _____

© 1996 by The Center for Applied Research in Education

CONSTRUCTING A 3-DIMENSIONAL OCTAHEDRON

To create your decoration, follow the steps below.

- Inscribe an equilateral triangle in your circle by doing the following:
    - —Set your compass to make a circle with a 3-inch diameter, and don't change the setting as you draw the circle around your pictures.
    - —The main part of your picture should be at the center of your circle.
    - —Lightly draw the diameter and label the endpoints A and B.
    - —Place the compass point on A and construct an arc, labeling the endpoints C and D.
    - —Place the compass point on B and construct an arc, labeling the endpoints E and F.
    - —Use a straight edge to connect points A, E, and F, or you may connect B, C, and D, depending upon the placement of your picture.
    - —Make all lines lightly so that they won't interfere with the picture.
- Repeat this process for each of the eight pictures you've selected.
- Cut out the circles.
- Use the sides of the triangles as lines for folding, and make all folds on the triangle toward you. The folds will result in making flaps, which you will use for gluing.
- Take four of the circles and place glue on two flaps of each circle. (One flap of each circle will not be glued yet.)
- Place the glued flaps together in pairs so that all four circles are connected, using clothespins to hold the circles in place until the glue dries. You should now have a 3-dimensional object with a circle as the base.
- Follow the same procedure with the remaining four circles. You should now have two parts of your decoration.
- Glue the two parts together to complete the decoration. Use clothespins to hold the parts in place until the glue dries.
- Using a hole puncher, make a small hole in your decoration and attach a thin cord so that your decoration can be hung up.

CREATING A GREETING CARD FOR MATH EDUCATION MONTH

The National Council of Teachers of Mathematics traditionally designates April as Math Education Month. A unique way to support math education is for your students to create greeting cards that wish others a Happy Math Education Month.

GOAL: Students will work individually to create a greeting card that expresses a thought about mathematics in the context of Math Education Month. Upon completion of their greeting cards, students will give (or mail) their cards to friends. *Suggested time*—1 to 2 class periods.

MATH SKILL TO HIGHLIGHT:

Communicating ideas about mathematics

SPECIAL MATERIALS/EQUIPMENT: Assorted colors of construction paper; white drawing paper; rulers; compasses; scissors; stencils; felt-tipped pens; markers; colored pencils. (If you intend to have students mail their cards, we suggest you use 5 × 8-inch envelopes.) *Optional*—Computers and printers.

DEVELOPMENT: Consider working with your students' art teacher, who may be willing to help create the greeting cards. Before you begin the project, decide if you want students to merely exchange cards with a friend, or mail them to a friend. While having students exchange their cards with a friend in class makes the overall management of the project easier, students enjoy mailing their cards to friends. If the cards are mailed, students may send them to friends in other towns. Mailing will require envelopes and postage.

- Start the project by explaining to your students that they will create a greeting card about math, and give (or send) their card to a friend.
- Discuss Math Education Month with your students. Note that its purpose is to promote mathematics in schools and communities. By participating in this project, your students will be promoting math by wishing their friends a Happy Math Education Month.

- Distribute copies of Student Guide 40–1, and review it with your students.
- Distribute copies of Data Sheet 40–2, "Tips for Creating Math Greeting Cards," and discuss the information on the sheet with your students. Emphasize that the Data Sheet provides suggestions for making greeting cards.
- If you have access to computers and software that have the capabilities to create greeting cards, encourage your students to use the equipment.
- If students are to mail their cards, we suggest you obtain 5 × 8-inch envelopes. (If your school doesn't have them, you can obtain them at most office supply stores for a nominal fee.) These should be sufficient for mailing. Using bigger envelopes will increase postage costs. Of course you can use smaller envelopes, but these will limit the size of the students' cards. Remind students to create cards of a size that will fit inside their envelopes.

WRAP-UP: Students exchange or address and mail their cards.

EXTENSION: Suggest that students write letters about math topics and send them to friends regularly. They might establish pen-pals with whom they correspond about math.

Name _____   Project Due Date _____

CREATING A GREETING CARD FOR MATH EDUCATION MONTH

Situation/Problem:

Working individually, you will create a greeting card containing a thought about math, and exchange or send it to a friend, wishing him or her a Happy Math Education Month.

Possible Strategies:

1. Decide to whom you will send your greeting card. Try to include a thought or idea about math that is "just right" for this person.
2. Think about how you might express an idea about math for Math Education Month.
3. Write as many possible ideas as you can. Later, go over them and select the best one.

Special Considerations:

- Select an idea that can be expressed on a greeting card.
- Refer to Data Sheet 40–2 for suggestions on how to generate ideas and create a greeting card.
- Consider the design of your card. A simple card may lie flat, or you may design one that folds in half.
- Consider the size of your card. If you intend to mail it to a friend, plan on fitting it inside an envelope. To fit your card inside an envelope, make your card $1/4$ inch less than the envelope's length and width. If you create a card that is to be folded over, its folded dimensions should be $1/4$ inch less than your envelope's dimensions.
- Sketch your card on scrap paper first. Consider various designs.
- When you start your actual card, draw your letters and illustrations lightly with pencil. You can go over the lines later with pens or markers.
- If you have access to computers and software that support the creation of greeting cards, try designing your card on this equipment.

To Be Submitted:

Your finished greeting card

Name _____

TIPS FOR CREATING MATH GREETING CARDS

There are various ways to create a greeting card, depending on your ideas, interests, and skills. While the following suggestions will help you to make a math greeting card, they cover only the basics. Use your imagination and experiences to create a truly unique card, designed especially for your friend.

FIND AN IDEA

- Think about topics in math you are studying.
- Think about associated ideas or topics.
- Consider your feelings about math.
- Write any ideas you may have, then pick the one you like best.

DECIDE ON YOUR DESIGN

- What color paper will you use?
- Will you express your idea as a short poem? Will you simply write your thought in clear prose?
- Will you use stencils for lettering? Do you know calligraphy? Will you print the words on your greeting card? Will you use script? What color(s)?
- Will you use a computer to design your card?
- Will you draw an illustration? Use computer graphics? Will you use clip art?

THE IMPORTANCE OF UNITY

Your letters, illustrations, and overall design should reflect your message. Outstanding greeting cards are those cards whose parts complement each other.

THE GEOMETRY AND ART OF ARCHITECTURE

All too often, students study the concepts of geometry in class but don't connect them to the real world. In this project, students have the opportunity to relate their study of geometry to architecture around the world.

GOAL: Working with a partner or in groups of 3, students will relate their study of geometry to architecture. They will select a building or structure, and identify its geometric shapes and properties. Each group will then make a poster of the building or structure it chose, and label the examples of geometry it found. The group will also write a brief description of the structure. *Suggested class time*—2 periods, although students might need to spend some time outside of class to complete the project.

MATH SKILLS TO HIGHLIGHT:

1. Identifying types of angles
2. Recognizing two- and three-dimensional geometric shapes
3. Recognizing parallel and perpendicular lines
4. Identifying types of symmetry

SPECIAL MATERIALS/EQUIPMENT: Reference books on buildings and architecture; poster paper; rulers; felt-tipped pens; markers; colored pencils; stapler and staples.

DEVELOPMENT: Discuss examples of geometry found throughout your school and classroom. Point out some examples—circular clocks, square tiles, rectangular door frames, corners that are right angles, floor and ceiling that are parallel planes, and rectangular walls that form line segments where they meet.

- Begin the project by explaining that students will work with a partner or in a small group and study the architecture of a building or structure such as the Empire State Building, pyramids, or London Bridge. They will identify as many examples of geometry as they can, create a poster of their building or structure, and write a brief description.

- Consider the level of your class. For students who don't have a strong background in geometry, you may suggest that they look for basic shapes—circles, rectangles, squares, triangles, etc. For advanced students, suggest they identify the basics as well as arcs, the Golden Rectangle, and specific types of triangles.

- Hand out copies of Student Guide 41–1, and review it with your students. Note that the Guide contains a list of examples of geometry students should look for. You may wish to add more to it.

- Distribute copies of Data Sheet 41–2, "Famous Architecture Around the World." Encourage students to select a building or structure that interests them. This list is certainly not exclusive, and you may wish to open up the project and allow students to select other buildings or structures.

- Provide at least one class period in the library for students to conduct research. Prior to starting this project, consult with your school's librarian and ask her or him to reserve books on buildings and architecture for your class. Additional sources where students may find pictures of the buildings they wish to research include encyclopedias, atlases, travel brochures, and magazines (especially *National Geographic* and travel magazines). If possible, have these additional sources available for your students to use.

- When students do their posters, remind them to draw their building or structure as accurately as possible. They should label as many examples of geometry or geometric principles as they can.

- The reports students write should be brief, highlight the geometry represented in their building or structure, and also provide some background information. The reports should be attached to the bottoms of the posters.

WRAP-UP: Display the posters. You might have each group briefly discuss the geometry shown on its poster.

EXTENSION: Have students select a building in town—it may be their own home or even the school—and identify the geometry the building displays.

Name _____   Project Due Date _____

THE GEOMETRY AND ART OF ARCHITECTURE

Situation/Problem:

You and your partner(s) will make a poster of a building or other structure, and identify various geometric shapes and properties. You will also write a brief description of your building or structure.

Possible Strategies:

1. List any famous buildings or structures that you and your partner(s) know. Decide if you would like to explore any of these for examples of geometry.

2. Consider choosing a building or structure that is a part of a topic that interests you. For example, if you like medieval history, you might select a castle to study. If you like ancient history, the pyramids may interest you.

3. Review Data Sheet 41–2, and select one of the buildings or structures that is listed.

4. Once you've chosen a building or structure, think about dividing tasks. While you and your partner(s) may work together to identify examples of geometry, you may draw the poster and your partner(s) may write the description. Both of you may color and label the poster.

Special Considerations:

- You'll need to conduct research to find a picture or photograph of the building or structure you've chosen. Check books on buildings and architecture, encyclopedias, atlases, history books, geography books, magazines, and similar sources. Magazines such as *National Geographic* often contain photos of buildings and structures around the world.

- In examining your building or structure, try to find as many examples of geometry as possible. Look for the following:

  —Types of angles: acute, obtuse, and right

  —Regular polygons such as equilateral triangles and squares

  —Other polygons such as right triangles, rectangles, and diamonds

  —Circles and semicircles

  —3-dimensional shapes such as prisms, pyramids, cones, domes, and spheres

  —Parallel and perpendicular lines

  —Symmetry including reflections, rotations, translations, and combinations

- Draw your building or structure on your poster paper as accurately as you can. Title your drawing, and neatly label the examples of geometry on the poster.

- When you write your description, be sure to include the history or background of your building or structure, as well as a summary of the geometry it represents. Write your description on only one side of the paper (use additional sheets if necessary), and staple it to the bottom of your poster. Be sure to answer the following questions in your description:

  —Who designed the building or structure?

  —What are its dimensions?

  —Where is it located?

  —When was it constructed?

  —Why was it constructed?

  —Is it used today? If yes, how?

To Be Submitted:

Your finished poster and description

Name _____

FAMOUS ARCHITECTURE AROUND THE WORLD

The following buildings and structures offer excellent examples of geometry.

Alamo (San Antonio)

Arc de Triomphe (Paris)

Blue Mosque (Istanbul, Turkey)

Castle of El Morro (San Juan, Puerto Rico)

Chrysler Building (New York City)

CN Tower (Toronto)

Colosseum (Rome)

Eiffel Tower (Paris)

Empire State Building (New York City)

Flatiron Building (New York City)

Geosphere (Lake Buena Vista, Florida)

Great Wall of China (China)

Hagia Sophia (Istanbul, Turkey)

Hancock Tower (Boston)

Houses of Parliament (London)

Huaca del Sol (Moche, Peru)

Independence Hall (Philadelphia)

Jefferson Memorial (Washington, D.C.)

King Dome (Seattle)

Kyongbok Hall (Seoul, South Korea)

Leaning Tower of Pisa (Pisa, Italy)

Lincoln Memorial (Washington, D.C.)

Parthenon (Athens)

Pei Pyramid at the Louvre (Paris)

Pentagon (Washington, D.C.)

Pont du Gard (Nimes, France)

Pyramid of Cholula (near Puebla, Mexico)

Pyramid of Khufu (near Giza, Egypt)

Pyramid of the Sun (near Mexico City)

Schonbrunn Palace (Vienna)

Sears Tower (Chicago)

Shwe Dagon (Rongoon, Myanmar [formerly Burma])

Space Needle (Seattle)

St. Basil's Cathedral (Moscow)

St. Peter's Square (Vatican City, Rome)

Stonehenge (Salisbury Plain, England)

Sydney Opera House (Sydney, Australia)

Taj Mahal (Agra, India)

Temple of Warriors (Yucatán, Mexico)

Tower Bridge (London)

Transamerica Building (San Francisco)

United Nations Building (New York City)

Washington Monument (Washington, D.C.)

World Trade Center (New York City)

U.S. Capitol Building (Washington, D.C.)

DESIGNING A QUILT PATTERN

People have used quilts for at least a few thousand years. The ancient Russians, Chinese, and Indians of Central America wore quilted clothing for warmth. When the Crusaders returned to Europe, they brought home the idea of quilted fabrics, which they learned from the Saracens who wore quilted shirts. The Europeans soon adapted quilts for undergarments and sleepwear. When the Dutch and English colonists settled the New World, they were kept warm during winter nights by the quilts they laid across their beds. Today, quilt-making is as much art as craft. The elaborate patterns quilts exhibit inspire both admiration and fascination. Although your students won't actually make quilts for this project, they will have the opportunity to design original quilt patterns.

GOAL: Working individually, students will create and color a one-patch quilt design based upon the regular hexagon. A one-patch quilt is made by using only one geometric shape that is repeated throughout the quilt. (The hexagon is a good choice, because it can be "cut" in a variety of ways such as isosceles trapezoids, rhombi, isosceles triangles, equilateral triangles, and kites.) Students will choose a design, draw the pattern on the included worksheet, and color it to highlight a quilt design. *Suggested time*—1 to 2 class periods with some time possibly needed outside of class.

MATH SKILLS TO HIGHLIGHT:

1. Recognizing the properties of regular polygons, particularly the regular hexagon
2. Recognizing the properties of an equilateral triangle
3. Measuring angles
4. Finding the sum of the measures of interior angles of triangles and quadrilaterals
5. Identifying lines and/or points of symmetry
6. Identifying congruent figures

SPECIAL MATERIALS/EQUIPMENT: Rulers; protractors; crayons; felt-tipped pens; colored pencils; markers; pictures of quilts or a real quilt.

DEVELOPMENT: If you have a quilt, bringing it to class to show your students is an excellent way to generate interest in this project. If you can't bring in a quilt, try to obtain books about quilts from your library. These books will have plenty of pictures of quilts that you can share with your students.

- Begin the project by explaining that each student will create a one-patch quilt design, based on a regular hexagon. After completing their designs, students will color them to enhance their quilt patterns.

- When you show pictures of quilts, ask students to identify some of the figures they recognize on your sample quilts, and point out how they are pieced together to achieve an overall effect.

- Distribute copies of Student Guide 42–1. Review it with your students, and emphasize the need for careful measuring and use of congruent figures.

- Hand out Data Sheet 42–2, "Creating a One-Patch Quilt Design," and discuss the suggestions and shapes.

- Remind students that they may use only one shape since they are designing a one-patch quilt.

- Hand out at least two copies of Worksheet 42–3, "Quilt Design," to each student. Have extra copies ready for students who wish to try various patterns or who make mistakes with their designs. Mention that the worksheet has a border, which is not part of the design, and suggest that students use the dots for guidelines. The designs will stretch beyond the border, but students should continue to draw as much as they can in order to fill the worksheet.

- Explain that the use of color can enhance their designs. Note that the selection of colors may enhance or detract from their designs. Particular colors can make some shapes stand out while others may make some shapes difficult to see.

- Once the designs are finished, ask students to measure the angles and test a conjecture about the sum of the measures of the interior angles of a polygon. You may wish to introduce the formula $(n - 2)180$ where n stands for the number of sides.

- Depending on the abilities of your class, you may wish to discuss the properties of regular polygons and discuss congruent figures. Another aspect of this project is the important role of symmetry. Symmetry with respect to a point or a line may also be introduced or reinforced.

WRAP-UP: Display the quilt designs on the bulletin board.

EXTENSION: Invite a quilter to the class with examples of her (or his) work. Have her (or him) explain quilting to your students.

Name _____   Project Due Date _____

DESIGNING A QUILT PATTERN

Situation/Problem:

You will create a design for a one-patch quilt based on a regular hexagon. A one-patch quilt is made by using only one geometric shape that is repeated throughout the quilt. You will not have to select fabrics or sew—you only have to make the design on the worksheet. You should color your design to highlight its pattern.

Possible Strategies:

1. View examples of quilts and study their patterns.
2. Review Data Sheet 42–2 to help you create a possible design.
3. Use Worksheet 42–3 to draw a rough sketch of your design and add color. This will help you to better visualize what the finished design will be like. Revise your initial design as necessary.

Special Considerations:

- Draw in pencil. Use a straight edge.
- You are making a one-patch quilt so you may use only one shape. Be sure to consult Data Sheet 42–2 for details.
- Use Worksheet 42–3 to help you make your design.

  —The border around the page will not be part of your design.

  —Use the dots on the worksheet to help you draw your design.

  —Start near the middle of the grid, and draw your design, repeating until the grid is nearly filled. Your design will stretch to the border.

- Once your design is finished, color it. Keep in mind the following suggestions:

  —Choose colors you like.

  —Decide what you wish to be highlighted on your design. Choose colors that will help this part of your design to stand out.

  —Select colors that are pleasing to the eye and that complement each other. For example, purple and a close shade of blue may run together and weaken any contrast. Green and yellow, on the other hand, will provide a contrast.

  —Color the border.

To Be Submitted:

Your quilt design

(Data Sheet 42–2)

Name _____

CREATING A ONE-PATCH QUILT DESIGN

To create a quilt design based on a regular hexagon, you may use one of the following patterns or create one of your own. Remember, once you select a shape, it is the only one you can use in your design.

A regular hexagon ⬡ can be divided to form:

1. Two isosceles trapezoids

      Each isosceles trapezoid ⬯ may be repeated

      and arranged as

2. Three 60°–120°–60°–120° rhombi

      Each rhombus ▱ may be repeated and

      arranged as

3. Six isosceles triangles

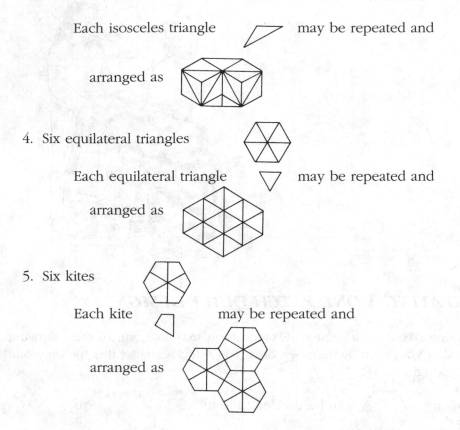

Each isosceles triangle   may be repeated and

arranged as

4. Six equilateral triangles

Each equilateral triangle   may be repeated and

arranged as

5. Six kites

Each kite   may be repeated and

arranged as

Can you find other ways to divide a regular hexagon? If so, you may use this shape to design your quilt.

There are several other possible quilt arrangements for each shape pictured above.

Name _____

QUILT DESIGN

Section 5

•••

MATH AND SPORTS AND RECREATION

CHOOSING A MEMBERSHIP PLAN AT A HEALTH CLUB

Students and adults are constantly forced to make choices based on a variety of factors. This project, which requires students to evaluate the membership plans of a health club, provides a glimpse of one of those real-life choices.

GOAL: Working individually, students will pretend they are about to join a health club. They are to analyze various membership plans and select the one that is "right" for them. Upon selection of their plan, students will write an explanation, detailing their reasons for choosing the plan they did. *Suggested time*—1 to 2 class periods.

MATH SKILLS TO HIGHLIGHT:

1. Using estimates to solve problems
2. Determining the best options
3. Comparing and contrasting different membership plans

SPECIAL MATERIALS/EQUIPMENT: Calculators for comparing costs.

DEVELOPMENT: Discuss problem-solving as a basis for making intelligent decisions. This is particularly true in many common activities such as choosing a car, buying admission plans to amusement parks, and vacation planning. While cost is usually a factor, it is not the only factor. What seems to be a good deal (in terms of price) may not, in fact, be very good if you are paying for a lot of "extras" you don't need. Conversely, a basic plan, while not offering any extras, may present the best value out of several plans because it contains the things people need the most.

- Begin this project by asking students if any of them belong to a health club. If you teach high school, particularly the upper grades, it's likely that some of your students will. You might also ask how many of their parents belong to health clubs. Briefly discuss what a health club is—it's a place that offers activities for keeping fit. Such activities might include weight-training and exercise equipment, aerobics classes, tennis, racquetball, volleyball, basketball, and even swimming.

- Distribute copies of Student Guide 43–1, and review it with your students. Emphasize that students are to select a membership plan that satisfies their needs at the lowest cost.
- Note that in comparing plans students may have to estimate the number of times they will be able to use the club.
- Hand out copies of Data Sheet 43–2, "Power Health Club—Membership Plans." Review the Sheet with your students. Be sure to point out the different plans, and note that each has different features. They should be especially careful not to buy a membership that contains a lot of options they won't need. This simply increases the cost with very little benefit.
- Remind students that they are to write an explanation of why they chose the plan they did.

WRAP-UP: Ask volunteers to explain what plan they chose. Collect the written explanations and display them.

EXTENSION: Ask students to speculate on why the various membership plans are set up the way they are. Why might a health club offer yearly commitments or "pay as you go"? Why might they offer several different plans? What advantages might a health club gain by offering various plans to people? What are the advantages, if any, to the potential members?

Name _____   Project Due Date _____

CHOOSING A MEMBERSHIP PLAN AT A HEALTH CLUB

Situation/Problem:

Imagine that you have decided to join a health club. You visit the club and ask for information about its membership plans. When you review the information, you find that there are several plans from which you may choose. You want to choose the plan that best suits your needs, but at the most reasonable cost. After making your selection (from Data Sheet 43–2), you are to write an explanation, offering your reasons for choosing the plan you did.

Possible Strategies:

1. Think about your needs. What types of activities would you like to do at a health club? Weight-training, exercising on different kinds of equipment, aerobics, basketball, tennis, racquetball, volleyball, etc.?
2. Examine the various plans to see which ones offer what you want most.
3. Consider the times you could go to work out. Are all of the activities you want to participate in available when you can go?
4. Compare the plans and evaluate the costs of each.

Special Considerations:

- Review Data Sheet 43–2, which contains several membership plans from which you can choose.
- Carefully consider whether you would be satisfied participating in only your favorite activities. Or do you want the privilege of taking part in everything the club offers?
- Check the "off-hour" rates. If the activities you are most interested in are offered then, you may be able to save on costs.
- To compare the costs per visit of different yearly plans, estimate the number of times per month you expect to work out and multiply by 12. This will give you the total number of visits for the year. Now divide the cost of the plan by the number of visits. Your answer will be the cost per visit. Compare that with the cost of "pay as you go."
- Some activities require partners (tennis and racquetball), and others require teams (volleyball and basketball). Does the club offer leagues, which will provide you with partners or teams? Or will you have to join with friends? If you were to join with friends, would they be able to work out when you could?
- After selecting your membership plan, write an explanation detailing your reasons for choosing this plan over the others. Be prepared to orally explain your reasons.

To Be Submitted:

Your explanation

Name _____

POWER HEALTH CLUB—MEMBERSHIP PLANS

The Gold Membership: One-year membership, $499. Unlimited use of facilities during times the club is open. Activities include weights, exercise equipment, aerobics classes, tennis, racquetball, basketball, and volleyball.

The Two-for-One Gold: Join with a friend. One year membership for two, $899. Includes same privileges as the Gold Membership.

The Silver Membership: One year membership, $399. Unlimited use of weights, exercise equipment, and aerobics classes during times the club is open.

The Pay-As-You-Go Membership: $10 per visit for use of the weights, exercise equipment, and/or participation in aerobics classes during times the club is open. $15 per visit for tennis, racquetball, basketball, or volleyball during nonprime time. (Prime time is between 7 P.M. and 9 P.M., Mon.–Fri.) $20 during prime time. *Note:* Leagues are available for tennis, racquetball, basketball, and volleyball. A one-time registration fee of $10 is required for joining each league.

The Aerobics Membership: One-year membership, $249. Includes unlimited participation in aerobics classes.

The Off-Hours Membership Plan: One-year membership, $229. Unlimited use of facilities between 2 P.M. and 6 P.M., every day. (Activities are the same as the Gold Membership.)

EQUIPMENT FOR THE SCHOOL'S WORKOUT ROOM

Ask students what their favorite subject in school is and many will answer gym. Of course, most of these students are offering this answer only as a joke, but gym, nevertheless, remains a popular class. In this project, students have the opportunity to imagine they are able to select equipment for a new workout room that has been added to their school gym.

GOAL: Working in groups of 3 or 4, students are to assume they have been asked to help select equipment for a new workout room. They are given a $5,000 budget that they cannot exceed. *Suggested time*—2 to 3 class periods.

MATH SKILLS TO HIGHLIGHT:

1. Using estimation
2. Making choices based on budget constraints
3. Maintaining accurate tallies

SPECIAL MATERIALS/EQUIPMENT: Calculators. *Optional*—Catalogs containing workout equipment.

DEVELOPMENT: To focus this project, think of the workout room containing such equipment as rowing machines, cross-country skiing machines, treadmills, exercise bikes, etc. If you are not familiar with such equipment, consult with your students' physical education teacher. Prior to assigning this project, obtain old catalogs and newspaper advertisements containing workout equipment that students can use to find the machines they might like to buy. Data Sheet 44–2 also contains equipment and prices.

• Begin this project by telling your students to imagine that a workout room has been added to their school's gym; this room may be used during free periods and after school. Groups of students have been given the opportunity to choose equipment for it.

- Distribute copies of Student Guide 44–1, and review it with your students. Note that each group may spend up to $5,000. They should try to buy equipment that will be popular among the greatest number of students.

- Distribute copies of Data Sheet 44–2, "The Cost of Exercising." Review it with your students, and explain that this Sheet concentrates on five major areas of exercise— cycling, weight-training, rowing, walking or running, and cross-country skiing. Students may choose equipment from the Data Sheet.

- If you have obtained catalogs or newspaper advertisements containing workout equipment, allow students to select equipment from these sources as well as the Data Sheet. Students may include machines other than the kinds listed on the Data Sheet, for example, stair climbers and mechanical slides.

- Some students may have workout equipment at home. Encourage them to share their knowledge and experience of these machines with the other members of their group.

- Emphasize that the many types of equipment should be carefully considered. Suggest that students discuss the value of the various products, and choose what they feel will help to create a workout room that most students would like to use.

- Distribute copies of Worksheet 44–3, "Gym Equipment Order Form." Review the Worksheet with your students and explain what the different categories mean. After selecting the equipment it would like to purchase, each group is to fill out the form, being sure to include all the necessary information.

- Remind students to select a spokesperson to share their selections with the class. Each group should be able to justify its choices.

WRAP-UP: A spokesperson for each group presents the members' selections of equipment. Students should also submit their worksheets.

EXTENSION: If students had an additional $2,500 to spend, what else would they purchase? Would they buy more of the equipment they already chose, or would they buy different items?

Name _____   Project Due Date _____

EQUIPMENT FOR THE SCHOOL'S WORKOUT ROOM

Situation/Problem:

Imagine that your group has been asked to select equipment for a new workout room that has been added to your school's gym. This workout room, which will be available to students during free periods and after school, will contain equipment such as rowing machines, cross-country skiing machines, treadmills, and exercise bikes. The school board will provide $5,000 for you to buy the equipment. You can't exceed that amount, and any money you don't spend will be returned to the school board.

Possible Strategies:

1. Brainstorm to list some types of equipment you might consider purchasing. The equipment you consider should appeal to as many students as possible.

2. Divide the tasks for the project. While all group members should be involved with choosing the equipment, one may be responsible for writing the reasons for choosing specific equipment or models over others, another may keep track of estimated costs, a third may be responsible for completing Worksheet 44–3, and the fourth may assume responsibility for presenting the group's selections to the class.

3. As you consider various types of equipment, keep a running estimate of your total costs. If two or three pieces of equipment consume most of your $5,000 allotment, you will not be able to buy much more.

Special Considerations:

- Use Data Sheet 44–2 to review and select equipment.
- If you have catalogs of workout equipment or newspaper advertisements containing such equipment, use them along with the Data Sheet to make your selections.
- Carefully weigh the pros and cons of each piece of equipment you are considering. Choose equipment you believe will benefit the most people.
- After you have decided on which equipment your group would like to purchase, complete Worksheet 44–3. Be sure you total the prices accurately, and include reasons (justification) for selecting the equipment you did.
- Don't calculate sales tax with your order. (If applicable, that will be handled by your school's administration.)
- There is no shipping or handling fee. (Many suppliers will waive shipping and handling for large orders.)
- Appoint a spokesperson to present your selections to the class. Be able to explain why you have made these selections.

To Be Submitted:

Your worksheet

Name _____

THE COST OF EXERCISING

Listed below are several popular types of exercise equipment, their benefits, and prices of specific models.

CYCLING

Equipment—stationary bike

Benefits—excellent aerobic exercise; tones and strengthens legs and circulation

- Model: *Basic Rider.* Standard unit, $295, includes built-in timer, odometer/speedometer.
- Model: *Premium Rider.* $449, includes controls to monitor distance, speed, and resistance.
- Model: *Rider 2000.* Top-of-the-line unit, $1,195. Includes built-in timer, odometer/speedometer; automatically adjusts the resistance on your leg muscles as you cycle.

WEIGHT TRAINING

Equipment—free weights or multi-station weight unit

Benefits—strengthens, tones, and shapes every muscle in the body

- Model: *Barbell Starter Set.* $189. Basic barbell set includes solid steel bar and complete set of weights.
- Model: *Standard Bench Press.* $259. Basic weight-training bench. Includes weights.
- Model: *The Inclined Exerciser.* $569. Features adjustable exercise bench; allows 13 basic exercises. Weights included.
- Model: *Power Weight I.* $1,699. Features six exercise stations for both upper- and lower-body workouts. 170-lb. weight stack.
- Model: *Power Weight II.* $2,879. Features six exercise stations and more than 100 different exercises. Includes 260-lb. weight stack.

ROWING

Equipment—rowing machine

Benefits—strengthens cardiovascular system; tones the overall body

- Model: *Easy Row.* $359. Uses hydraulic pistons to give the feel of rowing; 10 resistance settings.
- Model: *Advanced Row.* $659. Simulates actual rowing, fully electronic; 20 different resistance settings; has pull strap instead of oars.

WALKING AND RUNNING

Equipment—motorized or non-motorized treadmill

Benefits—excellent for strengthening the cardiovascular system; tones entire lower body

- Model: *Walk-well.* $795. Non-motorized, has digital timer and speedometer. Elevation may be adjusted.
- Model: *Powertread.* $2,499. Motorized; computerized control panel shows speed, running time, distance, and pace per mile.

CROSS-COUNTRY SKIING

Equipment—cross-country ski machine

Benefits—strengthens and tones all muscle groups

- Model: *Pro Ski.* $399. Pulley system simulates movement of cross-country skiing. Adjustable tension knob.
- Model: *Pro Ski Plus.* $499. Includes same features as the Pro Ski, plus electronic timer and speedometer.

Name _____

GYM EQUIPMENT ORDER FORM

Item Number	Model Name	Justification for Ordering	Price Each	Total Price

Total = _____

COMPARING SPORTS SUPERSTARS

Most students have favorite sports and are familiar with the stars of that sport. While many athletes are awarded "superstar" status by the media, their actual statistics and value to their teams may not be as good as their reputations. As students compare superstars in their favorite sport for this project, it's likely they will be surprised by what they find.

GOAL: Working in pairs or groups of 3, students will select a sport and at least five athletes generally considered to be superstars in that sport. The students will research the careers of these athletes and compare their statistics, then determine who is the best. They will create graphs, charts, or tables to represent their findings, and orally share their results with the class. *Suggested time*—2 class periods.

MATH SKILLS TO HIGHLIGHT:

1. Researching, analyzing, and comparing statistics
2. Understanding "average," a term often used in sports statistics
3. Making a determination based on statistics
4. Creating graphs, charts, or tables

SPECIAL MATERIALS/EQUIPMENT: Poster paper; rulers; felt-tipped pens; markers; reference books on sports stars and player statistics. *Optional*—Computers and printers for searching electronic reference sources and creating graphs, tables, and charts.

DEVELOPMENT: Prior to beginning this project, ask your school librarian to reserve books on sports (especially those that contain statistics on players). Electronic reference sources for use with computers, such as *Sports Illustrated Multimedia Almanac*, a CD produced by Star Press Multimedia, Inc., as well as on-line databases, may also provide excellent information. Still another source of information is sports cards; baseball, football, basketball, and hockey cards offer plenty of information about players. You might suggest that students who have card collections review them for players and statistics.

- Begin this project by explaining that every sport has its so-called superstars. Many of these athletes enjoy their status because of flamboyant styles, the ability to make great plays under pressure, or simply media hype. Some "superstars," however, don't have great statistics. Other players in their leagues may have better stats, but because they contribute to their teams' success without much fanfare their real value is overlooked.

- Explain that each pair or group of students is to pick a favorite sport, and choose at least five athletes in it who are considered to be superstars. (Obviously this is subjective, but most kids know who the top players in their favorite sports are.) Students are to research the statistics that prove the achievement of these athletes, and decide who is the best.

- Encourage students to choose more than five athletes if they wish. You might also suggest that they compare the statistics of the superstars with the stats of other players.

- Distribute copies of Student Guide 45–1, and review it with your students. Note that they may select any sport for this project, but the more popular ones such as baseball, basketball, football, hockey, tennis, and soccer will be easier to research.

- Schedule a period in the library for students to conduct research, and encourage them to do additional research, if necessary, on their own.

- If you have access to computers, students may use electronic reference sources or on-line references in their search for information. Caution them about charges for on-line time.

- Suggest that students develop criteria by which to compare athletes. Point out that the criteria should be consistent, and that athletes should be compared according to the same categories.

- Distribute at least five copies of Worksheet 45–2, "Sports Superstars," to each group. Recording players' statistics on the Worksheet will make comparison easy.

- Review the word "average" with your students. Many sports statistics are expressed as averages. For example, in basketball, a player's scoring average is the total number of points he scores in a season, divided by the number of games he plays. Averages are an excellent means of comparison. A basketball player who averages 25.4 points per game is a much better scorer than one who averages 8.5. For some sports you might also feel it is necessary to review decimal values with your students, because some averages may be expressed as decimals.

- After students make their determination of which athlete is the best, they should create graphs, tables, or charts to illustrate their findings.

- Remind each group to select a spokesperson to share the members' findings with the class.

WRAP-UP: Student give oral presentations. Display the graphs, charts, and tables.

EXTENSION: Instruct students to compare the salaries of some of the highest-paid players in sports. They should calculate their pay per game or event, and discuss if these athletes are paid fairly, or too much or too little. Set up discussion groups of 6 to 8 students for this.

Name _____   Project Due Date _____

COMPARING SPORTS SUPERSTARS

Situation/Problem:

You and your partner(s) are to select a sport and at least five athletes in that sport who are generally considered to be superstars. You are to research and compare career statistics that show their contributions to their teams. You will then determine if these athletes are truly superstars. After making your determination, you are to create graphs, tables, or charts to support your conclusions. You will also share your conclusions orally with the class.

Possible Strategies:

1. Decide which sport you and your partner(s) would like to research.
2. Discuss what makes a superstar in the sport you've chosen. List specific criteria or examples.
3. List at least 10 athletes who you feel are superstars in this sport. Narrow this list down to 5 to 7.

Special Considerations:

- Research the statistics of the athletes you've selected. Books on specific sports and athletes, references on sports statistics, and almanacs and books of records will likely provide good information. Baseball, football, hockey, and basketball cards are also good sources of facts.

- If you have access to computers, search electronic references such as *Sports Illustrated Multimedia Almanac* (a CD produced by Star Press Multimedia, Inc.). On-line services offer plenty of information about sports, but be cautious of charges for on-line time.

- Be sure to compare the athletes you've selected according to specific criteria. For example, in baseball, you might compare everyday players according to:

  —batting average

  —runs batted in (RBIs)

  —home runs

  —triples

  —doubles

  —total number of hits

  —total number of runs scored

  —fielding percentage

  —games played

  You would need to compare starting pitchers according to different criteria, such as won/lost record, ERA (earned run average), strikeouts, bases on balls, etc.

- Use Worksheet 45–2 to record and help you compare the statistics of players. Try to use one sheet per player; that will make it easier to compare players.

- Consider comparing the superstars to some other players. Are there other players in your sport who are not usually thought of as being superstars, but who have better stats than some superstars?

- Based on your comparison and analysis of statistics, determine which athletes are the true superstars.

- Create graphs, tables, or charts to support and illustrate your conclusions. For example, you might use graphs to compare the stats of the superstars in specific categories. If you have access to computers, create your support materials on them.

- Select a spokesperson to present your conclusions to the class.

To Be Submitted:

Your graphs, charts, or tables

© 1996 by The Center for Applied Research in Education

(Worksheet 45-2)

Name _____

SPORTS SUPERSTARS

Fill in the superstar's name, and label the categories for statistics across the top. *Example:* For a basketball player you might wish to record Games Played, Points Scored, Scoring Average, Rebounds, and Steals. Listing the years along the left will provide you with useful statistics for this player, which you can then compare with others.

Name of Superstar:

Year					

MATH AND THE BIG GAME

Many students are enthusiastic sports fans or at least have a moderate interest in sports. Most are familiar with major sporting events such as the World Series and Super Bowl. This project is for the sports buffs in your class. Students are required to watch a major sporting event and record examples of statistics that are offered throughout the game. Your students will quickly realize that without math the game would lose much of its appeal. Since this project will interest primarily students who enjoy sports, you might wish to make it a voluntary or extra-credit assignment.

GOALS: Working individually, students will watch a major sporting event such as a game of the World Series, the Super Bowl, the NCAA Basketball Finals, or similar contest. They are to record the various statistics offered throughout the game, and note how the use of math helps to enrich understanding of the action. When they are finished, they are to select one or two statistics they felt were most helpful to viewers, and be ready to share their opinions with the rest of the class during a discussion. *Suggested time*—2 partial class periods.

MATH SKILLS TO HIGHLIGHT:

1. Using statistics to understand relationships in sports
2. Gaining an appreciation of the importance of mathematics in sports

SPECIAL MATERIALS/EQUIPMENT: None.

DEVELOPMENT: Because big games will generate the most interest among students, consider assigning this project during the World Series (seventh game, if possible), a major college football bowl game, the Super Bowl, the championship game of the NCAA basketball finals, or another big game. The big games are also the ones in which sportscasters flash countless statistics on the screen for viewers. (After this project is done, your students will probably be surprised at just how many statistics are offered.) Plan on completing the project in two partial periods: a 15- to 20-minute session to introduce it, and another 15- to 20-minute session after the game for the discussion. If you assign the project as an optional activity, you may conduct the discussion with the participants at the back of the room while the rest of the class works on the day's homework.

- Begin this project by telling your students that math has a major role in sports. Aside from the obvious—needing numbers to keep score—games are played on fields and courts of specific dimensions, many rules are based on numbers (for example, baseball's three strikes and you're out), and equipment must conform to precise sizes. Also, players are compared by statistics. The quarterback who completes 60% of his passes is better than the one who completes 45%. It's likely that your students have watched hundreds (maybe even thousands!) of games without thinking about the significance of mathematics.

- Tell students what game you want them to watch. Explain that they are to record examples of statistics displayed on the TV screen, noting their purpose to the action of the game. In other words, they should try to answer the question: Why is each statistic displayed? What does it add to watching the game?

- Distribute copies of Student Guide 46–1, and review it with your students.

- Emphasize that students are to select one or two statistics they found most helpful in adding insight or background to the game. They should be able to discuss their opinions at the conclusion of the project.

- Make several copies of Worksheet 46–2 available to your students. This Worksheet is designed to help them record statistics and note their impressions. Each student should have at least three sheets. If they need more space, instruct them to use the back of the sheets or a separate sheet of paper.

WRAP-UP: Conduct a discussion in which students share their opinions about the statistics used during the big game.

EXTENSION: Expand the discussion to this question: Might the overuse of statistics detract from a game?

Name _____   Project Due Date _____

MATH AND THE BIG GAME

Situation/Problem:

You will watch a major sports event on TV, and record as many examples of the use of statistics as you can. As you record the stats, you will try to identify their purpose and decide whether each stat is effective. After the game you will select one or two stats that you found most helpful to your understanding or appreciation of the game. Upon returning to class, you will share your opinions during a discussion.

Possible Strategies:

1. Watch the game with several copies of Worksheet 46–2 handy. When a statistic appears, write it down. If you wait, you might forget what it was.

2. Include an example of each statistic you record. This will help you to recall them clearly.

Special Considerations:

- Label your statistics according to quarters, innings, or periods. This will make it easier to identify specific stats during the follow-up discussion.

- Try to record as many statistics as you can, but don't worry if you miss a few. Sometimes stats are flashed on the screen fast.

- Try to identify the purpose of each statistic. For example, in football, if one of the teams playing leads the league in defense, what is the significance of that? Obviously, it suggests that this team should be able to hold its opponent to a low score. If the opponent has already scored three touchdowns midway through the first half, the league's leading defense is not playing well. What might that mean for the rest of the game?

- Some statistics are more helpful to understanding a game than others. Try to identify ones that are the most helpful to you. Note them on your worksheet. Be ready to share your opinions and supporting reasons with the class.

- If you run out of worksheets, use the back or a separate sheet of paper.

- If you watch the game with a friend who is also doing this project, be sure that each of you formulates his or her own opinions about the statistics provided during the game.

To Be Submitted:

Your worksheets

© 1996 by The Center for Applied Research in Education

Name _____

TRACKING THE STATS

Use this sheet to record the statistics shown during a major sports event.

Name of event:

Statistic	Purpose and Effectiveness

YOUR UNIQUE EXERCISE PROGRAM

Most adolescents realize the value of exercise. Books and magazine articles that promote fitness, as well as advertisements for exercise equipment, health club memberships, and exercise videos, are common. While many students exercise regularly through sports and dance, many others express an interest in developing a personal exercise program. That's what this project encourages them to do.

GOAL: Students will work in pairs or groups of 3 to design a personal exercise program. They will explain the program they develop to the class, and also write a brief description of it. Upon completion of the project, students will be encouraged to commit themselves to their exercise programs. *Suggested time*—2 to 3 class periods.

MATH SKILLS TO HIGHLIGHT:

1. Using a stopwatch to take a pulse
2. Determining a target heart rate
3. Finding the percent of a number
4. Rounding to the nearest whole number

SPECIAL MATERIALS/EQUIPMENT: Stopwatches; calculators; fitness magazines and books.

DEVELOPMENT: Ask your students what they do for exercise, and their answers may run from participating in sports, dance, and gymnastics to simply working out at home. Ask students why they exercise, and you'll likely receive equally diverse answers—from keeping healthy to staying slim to building muscles.

A cautionary note: Before starting this project, check with your school's nurse and your students' gym teacher regarding any students who, because of medical reasons, are restricted from participating in physical activities. Most students who are restricted in some way will tell you. Occasionally, there's one who won't because he or she wants to participate so badly. Privately remind students who are restricted not to attempt any workouts that violate their doctor's advice.

- Begin this project by explaining that students will work in pairs or groups of 3 to develop a personal exercise program. (In setting up partners or groups, allow friends to work together. Friends often have similar interests for exercising and will more likely "work out" together after they have developed their program.)

- Distribute copies of Student Guide 47–1, and review it with your students. Point out that the Guide contains a list of exercises students may consider in developing their programs. There are many more, of course, and you should encourage students to consult reference books and magazine articles about fitness and exercise.

- Discuss the value of aerobic exercises that cause the heart to beat faster for an extended period (at least 20 minutes). Aerobic exercises strengthen the cardiovascular and circulatory systems and promote general fitness. Jogging, rope-skipping, racquetball, cross-country skiing, swimming, ice skating, basketball, hiking, and vigorous dancing are good examples of aerobic exercises.

- Hand out copies of Data Sheet 47–2, "Finding Your Training Range." Review the information with your students, and discuss the importance of exercising within the target zones as noted on the Sheet. If necessary, review how to find the percent of a number and rounding to the nearest whole number, which students will need to do to determine their own training range.

- Plan to spend a period in the library so that students may conduct research on various exercises. Prior to beginning this project, ask your librarian to reserve books and magazines on fitness and exercise. On-line computer services are also good sources of information.

- Emphasize the importance of developing an exercise program that is reasonable and suited to the person. *Also note this caution:* Students who do not exercise regularly should consult with their doctor before embarking upon any exercise program. During exercise, if students feel they are becoming fatigued, light-headed, or are having trouble catching their breath, they should slow down.

- Encourage students to commit themselves to their exercise routine.

- Note that charting one's progress can be an important part of an exercise program. Although this is not a requirement of the project, encourage your students to keep a record of the progress they make in their exercise program. Recording progress enables students to see how they are improving, and provides continuous motivation. An exercise chart may be little more than a dated log that shows the progress toward goals. Mention that it often takes time to achieve fitness goals, and students should not be discouraged by what may seem to be slow progress in the beginning of an exercise program.

- Remind students to write a description of their exercise plan, and be prepared to share their plan orally with others.

WRAP-UP: Conduct a discussion in which students describe their exercise plans. Also, display their written descriptions.

EXTENSION: About three months after the completion of the project, ask your students to evaluate the exercise plan they developed. Have they met their goals? Have they increased the level of activity? Have they expanded their exercise plan to include other forms of exercise? Have they given up? If yes, why?

Name _____   Project Due Date _____

YOUR UNIQUE EXERCISE PROGRAM

Situation/Problem:

You and your partner(s) will develop a personal exercise program. You will explain your program to the class, and also write a brief description of it. You are encouraged to commit yourself to your program.

Possible Strategies:

1. Choose exercises that you enjoy.
2. In developing your program, include the types of exercises, the number of workouts per week, and the length of time for each workout.

Special Considerations:

- There are many activities you might include in an exercise program. The following is just a partial list. Consult exercise and fitness books for more.

    —Basketball
    —Baseball
    —Softball

—Weightlifting

—Volleyball

—Jogging

—Dancing (especially aerobic dancing)

—Calisthenics (such as sit-ups, push-ups, squats, etc.)

—Exercise videos

—Ice skating

—In-line skating

—Cycling

—Hiking

—Walking (briskly)

—Swimming

—Hockey (field, street, or ice)

—Soccer

—Tennis

—Racquetball

—Cross-country skiing

—Downhill skiing

—Snowboarding

- You may find it necessary to research some of the activities you are considering.

- Most fitness experts suggest a workout plan of at least three sessions a week for at least 20 minutes of steady activity (not including a warm-up and cool-down period). A program of three to four sessions a week of 45–60 minutes per session of steady exercise is considered to be a vigorous program.

- You might develop a program in which you alternate some exercises with the seasons. For example, if you live in a part of the country that receives a lot of snow in the winter, you might substitute cross-country skiing for jogging (which you would do during the late spring, summer, and early fall). Similarly, if you have access to ice in the winter, you might substitute ice skating for in-line skating. If you live near the shore or belong to a community pool, you might swim in the summer.

- As you consider which exercises to include in your program, you should also consider your fitness goals. For example, your fitness goals might include:

—Losing or gaining weight

—Reducing or increasing your measurements

—Improving your energy and stamina

—Reducing stress

—Improving your general health and sense of well-being

- A necessary part of any exercise program is safety. Choose exercises that are suited to you. Avoid selecting exercises that are too difficult or too demanding. Be willing to start at low levels of exertion and build your endurance. For example, if you seldom jog, don't select a three-mile run as the most important part of your exercise program. Start with a quarter-mile slow jog around the high school track and gradually improve your stamina.

- *Note:* If you have not worked out regularly, if you are recovering from an illness, or if you suffer from a serious condition, consult your doctor before beginning any exercise program. In addition, keep the following points in mind:

  —Always warm up before exercising by stretching. Going lightly through the motions you will use while exercising is a good way to warm up.

  —Always cool down after exercise by walking around for a few minutes. This allows your body to ease back to normal. Never just plop down on a chair while your body is still breathing hard.

  —Drink plenty of liquids, preferably water.

  —If you feel you are becoming fatigued, light-headed, or experience pain, stop exercising. These are signs you are pushing your body beyond its safety zone.

- A good guide for safe exercise is to work out within your training range. This range represents a safe zone where your workout is effective but not overly strenuous to your body. By going beyond your training range, you risk hurting yourself. Consult Data Sheet 47–2 to determine and monitor your training range.

- Write a description of your exercise program to share with others, and be prepared to discuss it with the class.

- Plan to work out regularly with your partners. Try to arrange a schedule so that you can work out together. (Working out with friends usually makes it easier to maintain a fitness program.)

To Be Submitted:

The description of your exercise program

Name _____

FINDING YOUR TRAINING RANGE

Your training range (or target heart rate) gives you a safety zone while exercising. It is based on your age and heartbeats per minute. It's called a training range because it enables you to zero in on a level of exercise that's right for you.

FINDING YOUR TRAINING RANGE:

This example assumes the student is 15 years old.

Always start at	220 beats per minute
Subtract your age	-15
	205 beats per minute

Maximum safe heart rate = 205 beats per minute.

For a 15-year-old student, going beyond 205 heart beats per minute can be dangerous. The American College of Sports Medicine recommends that you calculate both 55% and 90% of your maximum safe heart rate to find the low and high end of your training range.

Multiply: $205 \times .55 = 112.75$. Round to 113 beats per minute. This is the low end of the range. Exercising at this rate would result in a light workout. For people who have not exercised regularly during the past few months, exercising near the low end of the range is practical. As their conditioning improves, they can safely increase the level of activity and increase their heart rate.

Multiply: $205 \times .9 = 184.5$. Round to 185 beats per minute. This is the high end of the range. Exercising at this rate would result in a heavy workout.

The training range for this 15-year-old student is between 113 and 185 heartbeats per minute.

TAKING YOUR PULSE:

You can easily keep track of your heart rate if you know how to take your pulse. Here's what to do:

- Use your first two fingers (index and middle; no thumbs).
- Press lightly on your carotid artery, which is located on the right side of your neck, straight down from the corner of your right eye. The artery is just under your chin. Gently put your fingers beneath your chin and feel for the pulse. You may need to move your fingers around a little, but the carotid is simple to find for most people.
- Using a stopwatch or the second hand of a wristwatch, count the number of beats you feel for 10 seconds. This is your 10-second heart rate.
- Since there are 60 seconds in a minute, multiply your 10-second heart rate by 6 to find your heart rate per minute.

Note: Don't take anyone else's pulse or let them take yours.

PUTTING THE NUMBERS TOGETHER:

After finding your training range, take your pulse for 10-second periods several times throughout your workout. Multiply the number of beats times 6 to find your heart rate per minute. It should fall within your training range. If it is near the low end of the zone, and you don't feel tired or out of breath, you can increase the level of your workout. If, however, your heart rate per minute is near the top of your range, you should be careful not to exceed it. Of course, if you are becoming tired or having trouble catching your breath at any point during the workout, slow down.

© 1996 by The Center for Applied Research in Education

THE BIG DANCE

School dances are always popular events. While most students enjoy them, they don't think much about the work that goes into organizing and holding a big dance. They would be surprised at the amount of math (and money) that's involved.

GOALS: Working in groups of 3 or 4, students will plan a big dance for their school. They will consider such factors as entertainment, security, decorations, refreshments, and advertising, as well as raising the money to pay for the dance. They will write a summary of their plan and present their ideas to the class. *Suggested time*—2 class periods.

MATH SKILLS TO HIGHLIGHT:

1. Anticipating and estimating the costs of having a dance
2. Calculating costs
3. Determining the best buy
4. Applying the terms *revenue*, *costs*, and *profit*

SPECIAL MATERIALS/EQUIPMENT: Calculators; 8-1/$_2$ × 11-inch white paper; black felt-tipped pens and markers. *Optional*—Computers and printers; circulars from local grocery stores containing the prices of refreshments.

DEVELOPMENT: Ask students how many of them like to attend dances. Probably most do. Explain that much work goes into organizing a successful dance. Although all the information students will need to complete this project is contained on Data Sheet 48–2, having students obtain prices for refreshments from the circulars of local grocery stores will broaden their choices. If you'd like them to work from circulars, ask students to bring in grocery circulars from home a week or so prior to the project.

- Begin the project by explaining that students will work in groups of 3 or 4 to plan a dance for your school. Their group is responsible for obtaining a disc jockey (DJ) or another form of entertainment, arranging for security, providing refreshments, decorating, and creating advertising. To raise money to pay for the dance, they will need to set the price for tickets.

- Distribute copies of Student Guide 48–1, and review it with your students.

- Explain the term "revenue." Many students may not understand that it is the amount of money that, in this case, is obtained through the sale of tickets and/or refreshments. Also explain that "costs" refer to the money needed to pay for the dance, and "profit" is any money left over after the costs are subtracted from the revenue.

- Depending on your class, you may wish to review rounding and estimating.

- Hand out copies of Data Sheet 48–2, "The Costs of a Big Dance." Review the Sheet with your students. Particularly point out that some assumptions are made on the Sheet. For example, groups are to assume that 300 students will attend the dance if a DJ plays music and provides entertainment, 250 will attend if a DJ simply plays music, and only 150 will attend if the music is supplied by a CD or tape player and managed by student volunteers. The difference in the number of students will affect the revenue. Also note that the PTA will help sponsor the dance by donating $150 towards its cost.

- If necessary, explain the difference between name-brand and store-brand items.

- If you have gathered grocery circulars, make them available to your students. Explain that the circulars give them a wider variety of items they may wish to select for refreshments.

- Explain that most of the revenue to pay for the dance will come from the cost and sale of tickets. To raise additional money, groups may decide to sell refreshments at a price above the cost they were bought. This will result in a profit that can be put toward the overall costs of the dance.

- Emphasize that groups should try to arrange what they think will be the best dance at the most reasonable cost to students.

- Distribute copies of Worksheet 48–3, "The Big Dance—Cost/Revenue Tally Sheet," to the groups. The Worksheet makes it easy to tabulate costs and revenues. Make additional sheets available.

- To publicize their dance, suggest that students design an advertisement. They may use markers, or, if they have access to computers, use computers to create their ads.

- Remind students that each group is to write a summary of its plan for the big dance, including its anticipated costs and revenues. Groups are to designate a spokesperson to share their ideas with the class.

WRAP-UP: Each group shares its plan with the class. You might also display each group's written summary, advertisement, and final Worksheet.

EXTENSION: Create a committee to plan a real dance for your school. Be sure to check with your principal for your school's procedures in organizing a dance. Note that prices, depending on your locality, will vary from those presented in this project.

Name _____   Project Due Date _____

THE BIG DANCE

Situation/Problem:

Your group has been selected to plan a big dance for your school. You will need to provide entertainment, security, refreshments, decorations, and advertising. Your school's PTA will help sponsor the dance through a $150 donation, but you will need to raise the rest of the money to pay for its costs through the sale of tickets and refreshments. Parent volunteers will chaperone the dance, handle the sale of tickets at the door, and sell the refreshments.

Possible Strategies:

1. Discuss what factors make a dance successful. Is a disc jockey (DJ) important? Is it important for a DJ to play a wide variety of music? Is it important for a DJ to take an active role in the night, for example, and teach new dances? How important are refreshments? How important is the cost of tickets? How important are decorations?

2. Consult Data Sheet 48–2 for prices associated with a big dance. Decide on the things you'd like to have at your dance, round off prices, and calculate a "rough" estimate of your total costs. Subtract the $150 that the PTA will donate. This figure will represent how much revenue you will need to pay for your dance. Dividing this number by the total number of students you expect to attend the dance will give you the estimated cost of each ticket.

3. If the cost of your tickets is high, you might want to increase the prices of the refreshments you will sell. This will add to your overall revenue, and help you to lower the prices of your tickets. You might instead decide to find a better price for your refreshments, use less expensive brands, or eliminate some refreshments. This will help you to lower your costs, too.

Special Considerations:

- Decide what type of entertainment you will have. Note the differences in your expected turnout as listed on the Data Sheet. This will affect your ticket prices and revenue.

- Decide which refreshments, if any, you will provide. Estimate how much refreshments you will need. For example, if you decide to buy cans of soda, how many will you need? Also, if you buy cans, you'll need straws. If you decide to buy liter bottles, you'll need cups in which to serve the soda. How many packs of snacks will you need? There are many decisions to make.

- Decide how much security you will need.

- Decide how much you will spend on decorations. You may choose not to decorate to save money.

- Be willing to adjust your original decisions. You may find that costs prohibit you from having all the things you want at your dance. You may need to compromise.

- After you have decided on what you want at your dance, calculate your exact costs. Remember to add the PTA donation to your revenue. Use Worksheet 48–3 to tally your costs and balance them against your projected revenue. *Note:* For some items on the Worksheet, the "Cost Each" won't apply.

- You must be able to pay for the dance entirely. You may not fall short. (To ensure that you have enough revenue to pay for the dance, you should anticipate that a few students you expect to come won't because of last-minute changes in plans. The prices of your tickets and/or refreshments should reflect this.) If you show a profit, any amount up to $150 will be returned to the PTA. Any amount over $150 will go into a general fund and will be used to defray costs for other school events.

- Design an advertisement on 8-1/2 × 11-inch white paper. If you have access to computers, design your advertisement there. Be sure to include all necessary information—day, time, location, price, type of music, and if refreshments are available.

- Write a brief summary of your plan for the dance, and appoint a spokesperson to share your ideas with the class.

To Be Submitted:

1. Summary
2. Advertisement
3. Worksheet

© 1996 by The Center for Applied Research in Education

(Data Sheet 48–2)

Name _____

THE COSTS OF A BIG DANCE

ENTERTAINMENT—DISC JOCKEYS

"Mr. Smooth"—Music from the '80s and '90s. $400 for 3 hours; $75 for 1 hour extra.

"Wild Man"—Your choice of music from the '60s to the '90s. Provides entertainment and teaches new dances. $600 for three hours; $150 for 1 hour extra.

An alternative: Student volunteers play compact discs or tapes for no cost.

Notes on expected attendance: With Mr. Smooth, you can expect 250 students to attend the dance. With Wild Man, you can expect 300. CDs or tapes played by student volunteers will result in 150 students attending the dance.

SECURITY

You will need at least one off-duty police officer for 150 students, and another officer for every 100 additional students after that. *Cost:* $20 per hour for each officer.

REFRESHMENTS

Soda—brand name:	2-liter bottles, $0.99
	12-oz. cans, 6 pack, $2.89
store brand:	2-liter bottles, $0.79
	12-oz. cans, 6 pack, $1.49

Snacks—small, individual packs of potato chips, pretzels, corn chips, and cheese chips; six 1-oz. bags, $2.79.

Additional items—

Straws, 250 for $0.99

Plastic cups, 100, 5-oz., $1.59

Napkins, 120, $1.19

DECORATIONS

A minimal amount of decorations, $25

More elaborate decorations, including assorted streamers, some balloons, and wall displays, $50

Name _____

THE BIG DANCE—COST/REVENUE TALLY SHEET

Costs

Item	Cost Each	Total
	Total Costs	

Revenue

Source	Total
Total Revenue	

Subtract *Total Costs* from *Total Revenue*. The difference should either be zero or show that you have a profit.

Total Revenue – Total Cost = _____

THE NUMBERS GAME

Many students enjoy solving math puzzles and games. In this project, students work with common phrases that are related to numbers. To add excitement to the challenge, you may wish to award prizes to the students who achieve the highest score.

GOAL: ·Working in pairs or groups of 3, students are to find the meaning of each "number" phrase on a list they are given. They will also be encouraged to compile a list of number phrases of their own. *Suggested time*—1 class period; a partial period to introduce the project and a partial period to discuss answers. Much of the work for this project will be done out of class.

MATH SKILL TO HIGHLIGHT:

An awareness of how numbers are a part of our lives in ways other than the obvious tasks of computation and analysis

SPECIAL MATERIALS/EQUIPMENT: None.

DEVELOPMENT: Pose some number phrases such as the "five senses" (hearing, sight, smell, taste, and touch), the "fourth dimension" (time), and "one-way ticket" (a ticket that takes you to one destination only). Discuss what they mean, and explain that number phrases are very common in our language. Ask your students to offer some they know.

- Begin the project by explaining to your students that they will work in pairs or groups of 3. They will be given a list of number phrases and will have to identify the meaning of them.

- Distribute copies of Student Guide 49–1, and review it with your students. Point out the scoring strategy for this project. Groups will earn 2 points for each number phrase they identify correctly, and 3 points for every phrase they can think of that is not on the list.

- If you decide to make this project a competition, point out that the winners will likely be decided by the number of additional phrases they find. Note that any additional phrases must be verified in reference sources. Students should also provide a key for the meanings of their phrases. Consider giving a prize—a homework pass?—to the winners.

- Hand out copies of Worksheet 49–2, "Number Phrases," and review it with your students. The Sheet contains 25 phrases based on numbers. Following is the answer key:

1. *One-liner*—a short joke.
2. *In two shakes of a lamb's tail*—quickly. (Have you ever seen a lamb shake its tail?)
3. *Three-dog night*—a very cold night. (On cold nights in the Arctic, three sled dogs are needed to keep warm when sleeping.)
4. *On all fours*—on hands and knees.
5. *Take five*—to take a break. (A five-minute break.)
6. *Six of one and a half dozen of the other*—equally accepted.
7. *Seven seas*—the seven oceans. (North and South Pacific, North and South Atlantic, Arctic, Antarctic, and Indian. Granted, this stretches modern geography a bit, but that's how the phrase originated.)
8. *Eight-hour day*—the typical workday, 9 A.M. to 5 P.M.
9. *On cloud nine*—very happy. (Originated from the number nine, which was considered to be a perfect number.)
10. *Top 10*—the first ten of a list. (Originally for pop music.)
11. *Eleventh hour*—the latest possible time.
12. *Twelvemonth*—a year.
13. *Catch-22*—a situation for which there is no solution. (Taken from the title of the Joseph Heller novel, *Catch-22*.)
14. *Twenty-three skidoo*—go away. (Refers to 23rd Street in New York City during the 1920s and 1930s. It was from that street that many railroads left the city.)
15. *Twenty-four hour*—a period lasting day and night.
16. *Forty winks*—a short nap. (Thought to be an arbitrary number.)
17. *Fifty-fifty*—equal.
18. *Eighty-eight*—a piano. (A standard piano has 88 keys.)
19. *Ninety-nine times out of a hundred*—often.
20. *Hundred and one*—many.
21. *One hundred percent*—entirely, completely.
22. *Thousand and one*—very many.
23. *Sixty-four-thousand-dollar question*—the most important question. (Based on the 1940s radio quiz show, which featured the $64 question. The $64,000 question is the updated version.)
24. *Feel like a million*—to feel very well.
25. *A million to one*—very low chance for success.

- Discuss where students might find the meanings of the phrases. Some possibilities include dictionaries, writer's stylebooks, and math reference books. Suggest that groups meet in the library during free periods or after school, if necessary. Students might also consider asking their parents or grandparents for help. Older relatives might be familiar with phrases such as "twenty-three skidoo." Getting the family involved with this project can make it an enjoyable activity for everyone.

- Caution teams not to give answers to one another.

WRAP-UP: Provide the answers and ask students to tally their scores.

EXTENSION: Compile the additional phrases that students found into a new list. Make copies of this list and distribute it to students who are interested in continuing the project.

Name _____   Project Due Date _____

THE NUMBERS GAME

Situation/Problem:

You and your partner(s) are to find the meanings of the "number" phrases listed on Worksheet 49–2. Also try to write other number phrases. Each correct answer is worth 2 points, and each additional phrase you add is worth 3 points.

Possible Strategies:

1. Skim the list and write the meanings of any phrases you know.
2. Write any other number phrases (not on the list) that you know. To receive 3 points for each phrase, you must be able to verify it and its meaning through reference sources.

Special Considerations:

- Consult dictionaries, writer's stylebooks, and math reference books for the meanings of number phrases.
- Ask your parents and grandparents if they know the meanings of any of the phrases.
- Correct your answers and compute your score.

To Be Submitted:

Completed worksheet

Name _____

"Cloud 9"

NUMBER PHRASES

Write the meaning of each phrase below. Each correct answer is worth 2 points. On the back of this sheet, write any other number phrases you know. These are worth 3 points each, but you must be able to verify the accuracy of your phrases through reference sources. Write the source after each phrase.

1. One-liner

_____

2. In two shakes of a lamb's tail

_____

3. Three-dog night

_____

4. On all fours

_____

5. Take five

_____

6. Six of one and a half dozen of the other

_____

7. Seven seas

_____

8. Eight-hour day

_____

9. On cloud nine

_____

10. Top 10

_____

11. Eleventh hour

_____

12. Twelvemonth

_____

13. Catch-22

_____

14. Twenty-three skidoo

_____

15. Twenty-four hour

_____

16. Forty winks

_____

17. Fifty-fifty

_____

18. Eighty-eight

_____

19. Ninety-nine times out of a hundred

_____

20. Hundred and one

_____

21. One hundred percent

_____

22. Thousand and one

_____

23. Sixty-four-thousand-dollar question

_____

24. Feel like a million

_____

25. A million to one

_____

PLANNING A SUNDAE PARTY

Students like to have parties. Holiday parties, end-of-the-year parties, good-bye parties, or a party to reward students for their achievements are common in many school systems. The parties are usually planned by teachers and/or parents. In this project, students will plan a sundae party for the class. You may wish to celebrate the completion of this project with a real sundae party, based upon students' suggestions.

GOAL: Students will work in groups of 3 or 4 to plan a sundae party for their class. At the end of the project, a spokesperson for each group will share the plan for the party with the class. *Suggested time*—2 class periods.

MATH SKILLS TO HIGHLIGHT:

1. Using estimates to determine serving size
2. Rounding numbers
3. Estimating the total costs of a sundae party
4. Calculating the total costs

SPECIAL MATERIALS/EQUIPMENT: Calculators. *Optional*—Grocery circulars containing the prices of ice cream and toppings.

DEVELOPMENT: Although Data Sheet 50–2 contains the prices for ice cream, toppings, and other materials needed for a sundae party, you may wish to collect grocery circulars to make the project more realistic for your students. A week or two prior to the project, ask students to bring in circulars from home. *Note:* Before distributing the circulars to your class, check them to make sure they include the prices for ice cream and toppings. Grocery circulars don't always contain these items.

- Begin the project by explaining to your students that they will be working in groups of 3 or 4 to plan a sundae party for the class. They will be required to choose the type and amount of ice cream, any toppings they wish, and any other materials—such as napkins, plastic dishes, and spoons—they will need. Since students will need to pay for the party by contributing an equal sum per student, groups should attempt to keep the costs of the party within reason.

- Hand out copies of Student Guide 50–1, and review it with your students. Emphasize that groups are to plan the best party for the most reasonable cost.

- Distribute copies of Data Sheet 50–2, "Prices for a Sundae Party." Review the prices of the various items with your class. In particular, point out the serving sizes on the bottom of the Sheet. Students will need to know these to estimate how much ice cream and toppings to buy. Also point out the wide variety of toppings, and tell the groups that they don't have to provide all the toppings for the party. They may choose the ones they want. If necessary, explain the difference between name-brand and store-brand items.

- If you are making grocery circulars available, tell students they may use these as well to make their choices. Also, if the circulars contain the prices for fat-free ice cream, ice milk, or sherbet, you may wish to broaden the project and permit groups to choose these items in addition to those on the Data Sheet.

- If necessary, review rounding for estimates.

- Encourage students to estimate the amounts and costs of the items they will need for their party, find out the estimated cost per student, and then work from there to finalize their selections.

- Hand out copies of Worksheet 50–3, "Tallying the Costs of a Sundae Party," for students to use in calculating their costs.

- Remind students that they should appoint a spokesperson to describe their party choices to the class.

WRAP-UP: Students share their sundae party plans with the class.

EXTENSION: Have a real sundae party. You might have students decide on the best plan proposed by the different groups, or simply list the items students want on the board or an overhead projector and together calculate the costs.

If you have the party, here are some tips:

1. Keep things practical.

   —Limit the choices of ice cream. If you provide more than three, some students will have trouble deciding which flavors they want. That slows down the serving process.

   —Avoid ice cream containers that have two or three flavors. It's better to have only one flavor per container. This eliminates the problem of students trying to spoon out only the flavor they want.

   —Use whipped topping that comes in a container and must be spooned out. Avoid the kind you spray. Some students might be tempted to spray it on each other rather than on their ice cream.

2. Collect all the money a few days in advance.

3. Enlist parent volunteers to buy the ice cream and bring it into class at the time for the party. This eliminates the need to store the ice cream at school. If you must buy the ice cream yourself, make sure you have enough freezer space at home and at school to store it.

4. If you have tables, lay plastic tablecloths over them to reduce the mess and cleanup. (Garbage bags are an inexpensive option, especially if the school janitor is willing to give you some.) If you don't have tables, you may simply push desks together and cover them. Better yet, see if you can have the party in the cafeteria.

5. Have ready plenty of napkins, paper towels, a sponge, and small bucket filled with water.

6. Line the classroom wastebasket with a garbage bag. This will prevent the leakage of any melting ice cream.

7. Set the ice cream, toppings, dishes, scoops, spoons, napkins, etc., on your tables and let your students serve themselves, buffet style. Have separate spoons for each container of ice cream and each topping.

8. Enjoy! It'll be a great party.

Name _____   Project Due Date _____

PLANNING A SUNDAE PARTY

Situation/Problem:

Your group will plan a sundae party for your class. Keeping in mind that class members will have to pay for the party, your task is to provide a great party with different flavors of ice cream and a variety of toppings at a reasonable cost. At the end of the project, your group's spokesperson will describe your plan for the party to the class.

Possible Strategies:

1. Discuss the types of ice cream and toppings your group feels would be popular at a sundae party.

2. Decide what you feel is a fair price for individual students to pay for the party.

3. Make a rough estimate of your total costs. See Data Sheet 50–2 for items and prices. Select the items and amounts you'd like for your party, round off the prices, and estimate your costs. Dividing by the number of students who wish to participate in the party will give you an estimate of the cost per student. If the price is higher than what you originally decided was a fair price, you will need to eliminate some items, or discuss raising the price each student must pay. If your estimate is below what you feel is a fair price, you may decide to add some things.

309

Special Considerations:

- Be realistic in your estimates of what students will pay for a sundae party.

- Be willing to compromise over the items you select. To keep the price of the party reasonable, you may need to eliminate some things you'd like.

- Pay close attention to serving sizes when you estimate how much ice cream or toppings to buy. (Unless you use "giant" scoops, two scoops of ice cream would equal about 4 oz., which is the typical serving size.) If you want students to have more than the typical serving size, you will need to buy more ice cream. Also, if students will be serving themselves, they might be "generous" with the amount of ice cream they scoop out. You may want to plan to buy a little extra to make sure you have enough. If you have any ice cream left over, you can always offer seconds.

- You must buy sufficient materials for cleanup.

- As you select the items you want, maintain a running tally of your costs. Use Worksheet 50–3.

- Appoint a spokesperson to share your party plan with the class.

To Be Submitted:

Your worksheet

Name _____

PRICES FOR A SUNDAE PARTY

Following are the costs of various items you'll need for a class sundae party.

ICE CREAM AND SERVING ITEMS

Chocolate, vanilla, strawberry, coffee, cherry vanilla, chocolate chip, etc.:

$1/2$ gal.—Brand name, $4.29; Store brand, $2.29

1 gal.—Brand name, $6.99; Store brand, $4.49

Plastic bowls, 12 oz., 50 for $1.59

Plastic spoons, 24 for $1.99

Napkins, 100 for 1.59

Serving spoons for toppings, 2 for $1.00

Ice cream scoops, $2.49 each

TOPPINGS

Whipped topping, 8 oz., $1.29; 16 oz., $1.79

Chocolate syrup, 24 oz., $1.39

Strawberries, 20 oz., $1.99

Maraschino cherries, 25 for $1.19; 50 for $1.89

Chocolate chips, 12 oz., $2.39; 24 oz., $4.29

Sprinkles, 3 oz., $1.49; 9 oz., $2.89

CLEANUP

Plastic tablecloth, 54" by 108", $1.79

Paper towels, 64 sheets for $1.49

Sponge, 5" by 8", $0.99

Small bucket, 11 qt., $5.99

TIPS:

Each $1/2$ gal. of ice cream contains 16 4-oz. servings. (A 4-oz. serving equals one-half cup.)

Each gal. of ice cream contains 32 4-oz. servings.

Serving sizes for toppings listed above:

Whipped topping—8 oz., 28 2-tbsp. servings; 16 oz., 56 2-tbsp. servings

Chocolate syrup—24 oz., 17 2-tbsp. servings

Strawberries—20 oz., 15 2-tbsp. servings

Chocolate chips—12 oz., 12 2-tbsp. servings; 24 oz., 24 2-tbsp. servings

Sprinkles—3 oz., 4 2-tbsp. servings; 9 oz., 12 2-tbsp. servings

(Worksheet 50-3)

Name _____

TALLYING THE COSTS OF A SUNDAE PARTY

Item	Number of Each	Cost Each	Total

Total Cost _____

Divide the total cost by the number of students participating in the party to find the cost per student.

_____ = _____ Cost per Student

312

GOING ON VACATION

Many, if not most, of your students have gone on vacations, but not very many have taken part in planning one. This project gives them the chance to plan a vacation in which they imagine they drive to a major resort.

GOALS: Working in groups of 3 or 4, students will plan a vacation to a well-known resort. Given a specific budget, they will need to calculate their round-trip costs for travel, lodging, food, and, of course, entertainment. At the end of the project, a spokesperson from each group will share the group's vacation plan with the class. *Suggested time*—2 to 3 class periods.

MATH SKILLS TO HIGHLIGHT:

1. Measuring distance
2. Calculating miles per gallon (mpg)
3. Making decisions regarding travel options
4. Rounding numbers
5. Estimating costs for travel, lodging, and visiting a major resort
6. Calculating the overall costs for a vacation

SPECIAL MATERIALS/EQUIPMENT: Calculators; reference books or atlases to estimate distances. *Optional*—Travel or vacation brochures that provide information about specific resorts.

DEVELOPMENT: You have several alternatives in developing this project. You might wish to focus your students on a specific resort, for example, Walt Disney World in Florida, or give them a choice of resorts—Walt Disney World, Disneyland in California, or Busch Gardens/Williamsburg in Virginia—or let them select their own. Giving students several choices will add variety to the project; however, the focus of the project is on resorts that contain theme or amusement parks.

You might also consider sending away for information about specific resorts, which will give you current prices. This can help make the project very realistic. If you decide to do this, be sure to request information well in advance, perhaps six to eight weeks ahead of time.

- Begin this project by explaining to your students that they will be working in groups of 3 or 4 to plan a vacation to a major resort. They are to imagine that their group has won a nationwide contest for the group "Most Likely to Succeed in Math," and the prize is $3,500, which they are to spend on a vacation.

- Tell them the places from which they may choose. They are to plan a round trip by car. They will assume that they will be traveling with a parent chaperone who will handle the driving; the group will pay for this parent's expenses. (If that parent is driving three or four kids on a vacation, he or she deserves to go for free!)

- Hand out copies of Student Guide 51–1, and review it with your students. Emphasize that they are to consider all the costs associated with their vacation. They may stay as long as they can afford to, but they must keep within their budget. This, of course, will depend upon the distance they must travel as well as the lodging, food, and admissions plans they select.

- Hand out copies of Data Sheet 51–2, "The Costs of a Great Vacation." Review it closely with your students. Some will likely have questions. Note that they have plenty of options.

- If you acquired travel or vacation brochures you'd like your students to use in addition to the Data Sheet, hand them out and provide any necessary instructions.

- Distribute copies of Worksheet 51–3, "Calculating Vacation Costs." Students should use this to tally their expenses. Make extra copies available.

- If necessary, review rounding and estimation skills with your students.

- Depending on the destinations your students select, you may wish to schedule a class period (or at least a partial period) in the library so that students may consult atlases for estimates of distances. Students may also have maps in their social studies text they can use. If they do, ask them to bring their texts to class to estimate the distances of their trips. This will eliminate the need for going to the library.

- Remind groups to appoint a spokesperson to share their vacation destinations and plans with the class.

WRAP-UP: Spokespersons share their groups' plans.

EXTENSION: Suggest that students explore plane and train travel costs to their destination. After considering the costs, which is least expensive—car, plane, or train? Which is most practical?

Name _____   Project Due Date _____

GOING ON VACATION

Situation/Problem:

Imagine that your group has won the coveted "Most Likely to Succeed in Math" award. Your prize is $3,500, which is to be applied to a vacation. Your teacher will provide you with the places from which you may choose to go. You will be traveling by car (one of your parents will drive), and you must plan for all the expenses of your trip. You may not exceed your $3,500 prize. Upon completion of the project, a spokesperson will share your vacation plan with the class.

Possible Strategies:

1. If you have a choice of places, decide which one you will visit.
2. Estimate the distance you will travel, and select the type of vehicle you will ride in. Consult Data Sheet 51–2. A compact car gets more miles to the gallon, but you will feel cramped on a long trip. You'll be more comfortable in a minivan, but minivans gobble gas. Based on the distance and gas mileage your vehicle is capable of, estimate your fuel costs. Take your total distance (round trip) and divide by miles per gallon. Multiply the answer by $1.30, which is the cost of a gallon of gasoline. Your answer will be your total costs for gas.

315

3. Assuming you will be able to travel 600 miles per day (60 mph for 10 hours), estimate how long it will take you to arrive at your destination. For example, a 1,200-mile trip would require two days of driving, and you would need to stay one night in a motel.

4. Using Data Sheet 51–2, select what you would like to have on your vacation. Include all lodging, food, ticket prices, etc., and make a rough estimate of your costs. Add to these costs the cost of your gasoline. This should give you an estimate of your overall costs for your entire vacation. If your expenses surpass your $3,500, you must reduce your costs. If your expenses are below your $3,500, you can add some things.

Special Considerations:

- Do not include costs for souvenirs or extras. Individuals are responsible for these expenses.

- Remember that travel and lodging costs must be calculated for a round trip.

- If you have boys and girls in your group, you will need two motel/hotel rooms, one for the boys and one for the girls. This will add to your costs. (Groups of all boys or all girls may stay in one room.)

- You have various choices and options. Study the Data Sheet carefully and select those that you feel will result in an outstanding vacation.

- You may remain on vacation as long as you can afford.

- Remember, you must pay all the expenses of your parent chaperone.

- Use Worksheet 51–3 to calculate your costs. Be sure to write your total costs. For example, if you decide to stay at a resort's Superior Hotel for four days, one room will cost $1,000.

- Appoint a spokesperson to share your plan with the class.

To Be Submitted:

Your worksheet

(Data Sheet 51–2)

Name _____

THE COSTS OF A GREAT VACATION

Following are the costs that you can expect for your vacation. The prices are general, and some assumptions have been made.

TRAVEL COSTS (GAS $1.30 PER GALLON)

A small car gets 35 mpg (miles per gal.)

A family sedan gets 25 mpg.

A minivan gets 18 mpg.

Meals:

$15 per day per person (mostly fast food).

$25 per day per person (a good breakfast, fast food for lunch, a full meal for dinner).

Lodging:

Superior Motel, $79 a room per night (indoor and outdoor pools, restaurant, cable TV, free movies, workout room).

Good Motel, $49 a room per night (outdoor pool, cable TV, restaurant nearby).

Average Motel, $29 a room per night (cable TV).

AT THE RESORT

Lodging:

Superior Hotel, $250 a room per night (huge pool, four restaurants, 24-hour snack shop, health club open to guests, shopping boutiques, arcade.)

Good Hotel, $190 a room per night (mid-sized pool, restaurant, workout room).

Average Hotel, $125 a room per night (small pool, restaurant; 10 minute drive to the resort).

Admission to resorts:

One-day pass $35; two-day pass $65; four-day pass, $115. (With a four-day pass, a fifth day may be purchased for $25.)

Meal Plans:

$35 per person each day of stay (includes lunch and dinner at selected restaurants throughout the resort).

$55 per person each day of stay (includes breakfast, lunch, and dinner at all the restaurants throughout the resort).

Name _____

CALCULATING VACATION COSTS

Destination: _____

Include total costs for each item.

TRAVEL COSTS (ROUND TRIP)

Gasoline: miles of trip/mpg × price of gas

(_____ / _____) × _____ = $ _____

Lodging: number of nights at motel × cost per night × number of rooms

_____ × _____ × _____ = $ _____

Meals: number of days × cost per day × number of persons

_____ × _____ × _____ = $ _____

Subtotal $ _____

RESORT COSTS

Hotel: number of nights × cost per night × number of rooms

_____ × _____ × _____ = $ _____

Admissions: cost × number of persons

_____ × _____ = $ _____

Meals: number of days × cost per day × number of persons

_____ × _____ × _____ = $ _____

Subtotal $ _____

Adding both subtotals together will give you the total cost of your vacation.

_____ + _____ = _____

Subtotal   Subtotal   Total Cost

© 1996 by The Center for Applied Research in Education

Section 6

•••

MATH AND LIFE SKILLS

MAKING A BUDGET

Many students feel money is in endless supply. They buy things they want without considering whether they really need them. Part of the problem is that they have no way of keeping track of how they spend their money. For some students a budget can be helpful. While creating a budget will not guarantee that money will be spent wisely, at least it enables an individual to monitor his or her income and expenses.

GOAL: Working individually, students will create a monthly budget to manage their income and expenses. *Suggested time*—2 class periods.

MATH SKILLS TO HIGHLIGHT:

1. Making a budget
2. Estimating income and expenses
3. Applying the terms *income*, *expenses*, and *surplus*
4. Making wise choices with regards to spending money

SPECIAL MATERIALS/EQUIPMENT: Calculators.

DEVELOPMENT: Discuss the importance of having a budget and how it is useful in managing personal finances. Budgets enable people to see how and where they spend money, helping them to adjust spending habits so that financial goals can be met. You might also discuss the importance of savings, perhaps for a car, college, or for emergencies, and point out that budgets can help people manage their money so that they have some left over to save.

- Begin the project by explaining that students will work alone to create a monthly budget that monitors their income and expenses. If you have students who prefer not to reveal their finances, suggest that they pick fictional, though realistic, amounts to work with. By offering this option, you relieve students of any pressure they might otherwise feel regarding their personal situation with money. They will still benefit from the project, however.

- Distribute copies of Student Guide 52–1, and review it with your students.

- Distribute copies of Data Sheet 52–2, "Tips for Making a Budget." Review it with your students, and point out that the Sheet offers some important budget terms and a step-by-step guide for making a budget.

- Discuss the terms "income," "expenses," and "surplus."

- If necessary, review estimation with your class.

- Although some students might be inclined to underestimate their expenses—to stay within their budget (such kids might make good politicians someday)—caution them that this will only lead to a shortage of funds. Rather, they should overestimate expenses. It's always nice to have a surplus.

- Hand out Worksheet 52–3, "Working on Your Budget." Students should use this Sheet for their budget. Remind them to be sure to list all income and expenses.

WRAP-UP: Collect the worksheets, and discuss any problems or insights students might have had in making their budgets.

EXTENSIONS: Invite a financial planner to class to discuss the importance of budgets and planning for the future. You might also wish to mention that various software programs are designed to help people create budgets and manage their finances. Perhaps you, or some of your students, are familiar with these programs. You may wish to discuss them.

Name _____   Project Due Date _____

MAKING A BUDGET

Situation/Problem:

You are to make a monthly budget that will help you keep track of your income and expenses.

Possible Strategies:

1. Estimate your income by adding all the money you receive during the month.
2. Make a list of *all* the things you spend money on.
3. Estimate your expenses by adding the costs of all the things you buy.
4. Subtract your expenses from your income.

Special Considerations:

- Carefully review Data Sheet 52–2. It provides detailed information about income and expenses.
- If your expenses are more than your income, you are spending too much and must reduce your spending or increase your income. If you have money left over, you have a surplus. You may either save it, or buy some other things you would like.
- Use Worksheet 52–3 to make your budget.

To Be Submitted:

Your worksheet

Name _____

© 1996 by The Center for Applied Research in Education

TIPS FOR MAKING A BUDGET

A budget is an excellent tool for managing your money. A good budget contains your sources of income and your expenses. Budgets may be weekly, monthly, or even yearly. Use Worksheet 52–3 to make a monthly budget, based on the guidelines below.

1. List all sources of your income for the month, and the amount of money you receive from each. Include money you receive from an allowance, part-time job, errands, etc. If a source of income varies, such as a gift, or you are not sure about it, underestimate its amount.

2. Add up your income.

3. List all of your expenses, and the amount you pay for each. Expenses include spending money on things like food (lunch and snacks), clothes, entertainment (movies, video rentals, CDs), sports events and equipment, and car costs. Many people also include savings as an expense. By doing this they are more likely to place money in a savings plan each month.

4. Add up all your expenses.

5. Subtract your total expenses from your total income:

    *   If the difference is zero, your budget is balanced.
    *   If you have money left over, you have a surplus and are to be congratulated. You may put more money to savings, keep it handy for unexpected expenses, or spend it.
    *   If your expenses are greater than your income, you must adjust your budget by spending less or increasing your income.

Name _____

WORKING ON YOUR BUDGET

Fill in your sources of income and their amounts. Fill in your expenses and the amounts. Find the totals, then subtract your expenses from your income.

Sources of Income	(Amt.)	Expenses	(Amt.)

Total: $_____   Total: $_____

$_____ − $_____ = $_____
Income   Expenses

A Floor Plan of My Room

The rooms of teenagers are often messy. Sometimes this is because items are simply thrown all about; in other cases, the furniture in the room is not arranged in a manner that makes best use of the space. A little rearranging can help to make a room more comfortable, keep clutter under control, and make it appear less messy. Rearranging furniture can be a big job, though, especially if the plan is to pull beds, bureaus, desks, and chairs around to see "how they fit best." A better way is to create a floor plan of the room, and try various arrangements on paper before moving anything.

GOAL: Working individually, students will make a floor plan of their room. They will need to measure their room and the length and width of the furniture they have. They will then create a scale drawing of their room, make scale drawings of their furniture, and determine if the furniture in their room can be arranged more effectively. Of course, they may find that the best arrangement is the current one. *Suggested time*—2 class periods; the measuring will be done at home.

MATH SKILLS TO HIGHLIGHT:

1. Taking measurements
2. Making a scale drawing

SPECIAL MATERIALS/EQUIPMENT: Tape measures or yard sticks; rulers; scissors. *Optional—* Calculators.

DEVELOPMENT: Ask students to think of their room. Is it messy? Cluttered? Now ask them to think about how their furniture is arranged, and explain that sometimes rearranging the furniture in a room can make better use of a room's space. This in turn makes the room more attractive or visually appealing.

• Begin this project by explaining that students will work individually to create a floor plan of their room that makes the most effective use of the room's space.

- Distribute copies of Student Guide 53–1, and review it with your students. Make certain that students understand how they are to create a floor plan, particularly finding the dimensions of their room and selecting a scale.

- Hand out copies of Data Sheet 53-2, "How to Measure a Room," and discuss the information. Suggest that all the measurements be made in inches; using inches will make it easier to select a scale.

- Encourage students to draw a sketch of their room first, and include measurements and the approximate locations of doors and windows. Not only will this help them to visualize the overall room, they can also use the sketch to record their room's dimensions. Later, they can take the dimensions from the sketch and transfer them to their scale drawing.

- Explain that students may use either tape measures or yard sticks to measure the dimensions of their room. Perhaps their parents have these supplies, or you may ask your school's technology teacher if he or she can lend you some tape measures.

- Instruct students to measure the length and width of their furniture, and record the measurements on the same sheet as the sketch.

- After they have taken all the measurements and recorded the measurements on the sketch, students should determine a scale. Remind students to consult their Student Guide for instructions on how to determine a scale.

- Hand out two copies of Worksheet 53–3, "A Grid for a Floor Plan," to each student. (One is for a scale drawing, and the other is for drawing the room's furniture.) Have extra copies available for students.

- Instruct students to make a scale drawing of their room on the Worksheet, including all the measurements they recorded on their sketches. Remind students to include the scale on their drawings.

- On another copy of the Worksheet, students are to draw their furniture according to the scale they chose. They should then cut out the figures and place them on the scale drawing of their room. They should try various arrangements of the furniture to see which uses the space of their room the best.

- After finding what they feel is the best arrangement of their furniture, students are to draw their pieces of furniture in place on the scale drawing. (If students find that a new arrangement of furniture utilizes the space of their room better than the present one, they may wish to ask their parents if they can reorganize their room.)

- Students should be prepared to discuss any changes they would make in their current floor plan, or explain why the current floor plan is best.

WRAP-UP: Display the floor plans.

EXTENSION: Students may wish to make scale drawings of other rooms in their home or apartment.

Name _____   Project Due Date _____

A FLOOR PLAN OF MY ROOM

Situation/Problem:

You will make a floor plan of your room, which will include the lengths of the walls, location of the windows and doors, and the arrangement of furniture. Your floor plan may be of your current room, or an example of how you might rearrange your furniture to make better use of your room's space.

Possible Strategies:

1. Make a rough sketch of your room.
2. Measure all the walls of your room accurately.
3. Measure all doors and windows.
4. Measure the length and width of all pieces of furniture.
5. Record all measurements on your sketch.

Special Considerations:

- Consult Data Sheet 53–2 for guidelines on how to measure your room.

- Always measure in inches and double-check all measurements.

- Choose a scale. Consider using $1/4$ inch = 12 inches, or $1/2$ inch = 12 inches. Your scale will depend on the overall size of your room. Choose the scale that works best. To create a scale, follow these suggestions:

  —Note that the side of each square of the grid on Worksheet 53–3 is $1/4$-inch long.

  —If the longer length of your room is greater than 180 inches (15 feet), use the scale 1/4 inch = 12 inches, *or*

  —If the shorter length is greater than 144 inches (12 feet), use the scale $1/4$ inch = 12 inches

  —If neither of these is true, use the scale 1/2 inch = 12 inches

  —If you use the scale of 1/2 inch = 12 inches, remember that every side of two squares on the grid represents 12 inches of your room. A wall 120 inches long would be equal to 20 squares.

  —If you use the scale of $1/4$ inch = 12 inches, remember that every side of the squares on the grid represents 12 inches of your room. A wall 216 inches long would be equal to 18 squares.

- Make a scale drawing of your room on Worksheet 53–3. Label all walls, windows, and doors. Be sure to indicate which way the door swings with a line that represents the width of the door. Your floor plan is now complete.

- Using another copy of Worksheet 53–3, make a scale drawing of each piece of furniture. Use the same scale as you chose for your room. Write the name of each piece of furniture on it so that you don't confuse it with other pieces.

- Cut out each piece of furniture and set it on your floor plan. Arrange the pieces in various ways. You may find a better way to organize the furniture in your room, or you may find that the arrangement you now have is best.

- When you are satisfied you have found the best arrangement, draw the pieces of furniture on your floor plan. You may wish to label your floor plan as "Current" or "Proposed" Arrangement of Furniture.

- Be prepared to discuss your floor plan with the class, and why you feel this one uses your room's space most effectively.

To Be Submitted:

The final copy of your floor plan

Name _____

© 1996 by The Center for Applied Research in Education

HOW TO MEASURE A ROOM

The following suggestions will help you make accurate measurements of your room.

1. Imagine that you are looking down on your room from the ceiling. Make a rough sketch of the floor of your room, and include the approximate positions of the furniture—bed, desk, chairs, etc. This will help you to visualize its contents in their approximate locations.

2. Use a tape measure or yardstick to measure your room. Use inches for all measurements.

3. Measure the length of each wall. Start at the beginning of the left corner and measure to the right corner. Record your measurements on your sketch.

4. To position doors and windows accurately on your floor plan, you must first find their measurements:

   • Start at the left corner of the wall on which the door or window is located, and measure to the left edge of the door or window. Record the distance on your sketch.

   • Measure across the opening of the door or window from edge to edge. Record the distance on your sketch.

   • Measure from the right edge to the right corner, and record the distance on your sketch.

   • *Note:* The sum of these measurements should equal the distance of the entire wall.

5. Mark the position of doors and windows on your sketch, and include measurements. (Remember, you are looking down on your room from above. You can't draw a full window or door. Indicate them by narrow rectangles or double lines.)

6. Show the way any doors swing open with a line that represents the width of the door.

7. Repeat steps 3 through 6 for the remaining walls.

Name _____

A GRID FOR A FLOOR PLAN

THE COSTS OF PETS

Many of your students probably have pets—from dogs and cats to turtles and snakes. Pets offer companionship, enjoyment, and satisfaction. Most also come with hefty costs. While students may love their pets, and even help take care of them, few kids think about the expense of having a pet.

GOAL: Working in pairs or groups of 3, students are to imagine that they are interested in buying a pet. Before they do, however, they are to research the expenses related to that pet, and, along with its purchase price, determine potential costs for veterinarian services, food, cages, toys, etc., for a one-year period. Students are to write a summary report of their findings, and share their findings orally with the class. *Suggested time*—2 to 3 class periods.

MATH SKILLS TO HIGHLIGHT:

1. Researching various cost factors
2. Estimating costs
3. Calculating total costs

SPECIAL MATERIALS/EQUIPMENT: Calculators; reference books on pets. *Optional*—Word processors, computers, and printers for writing the reports.

DEVELOPMENT: Ask your students if any of them have pets. It's likely that many of them do. Ask for volunteers to tell the class about their pets, and direct the discussion to the expenses related to them.

- Begin this project by explaining that students will work in pairs or groups of 3 to determine the costs of keeping a pet. They may select any pet for the project, including one like their own. (No matter which type of pet they choose, they probably have little idea of the expenses involved.)

- Distribute copies of Student Guide 54–1, and review it with your students.

- Hand out copies of Data Sheet 54–2, "Cost Factors to Consider in Choosing a Pet." Review the Sheet with your students, and point out that not all the factors apply to all pets. Note that students should focus on the factors that are relevant to the pet they selected to research.

- Plan on reserving one or two periods in the library for research, depending on the number and kinds of references that are available to students. Prior to starting this project, ask your librarian to reserve books and references on pets.

- Encourage students to conduct additional research on their own, if necessary.

- Remind students to write a summary of their findings, including a list of all costs. If students have access to word processors or computers and printers, encourage them to use the equipment to write their reports. Students should also be prepared to share their findings orally with the class.

WRAP-UP: Students explain which pet they would select, and the costs for keeping that pet. You might also wish to display their summaries.

EXTENSION: Ask students who have pets to estimate the yearly costs of the pet, and then compare these costs with the findings of the class. How close were they? What might account for any differences?

Name _____   Project Due Date _____

THE COSTS OF PETS

Situation/Problem:

Imagine that you are thinking about buying a pet. You and your partner(s) are to determine the costs of having this pet. Select any type of pet you like, then research its purchase price and all the costs necessary to keep it for a year. At the end of the project, you will summarize your findings in a brief report. You will also share your findings orally with the class.

Possible Strategies:

1. Consider the pet you'd like to research. You may choose a common one, such as a dog or a cat, or an exotic one, such as a snake or tropical bird. (Remember, the less common the pet, the harder it might be to find information about it.)

2. Consult reference sources on the pet you chose and estimate the cost for keeping it for a year.

Special Considerations:

- For most pets, the information regarding costs will be presented in ranges or averages. Your final costs, therefore, will most likely be based on estimates.

- Include the purchase price of the pet, as well as all other costs.

- Keep in mind that different pets have different needs. Carefully consider the information presented on Data Sheet 54–2.

- Summarize your findings in a brief report; include an itemized list of costs and a total at the end. If possible, use a word processor or computer to write your report.

- Be prepared to explain your findings to the class.

To Be Submitted:

Your report and costs

Name _____

COST FACTORS TO CONSIDER IN CHOOSING A PET

Pets may be amusing, enjoyable, and satisfying, but they can also be expensive. While not all the factors below apply to all pets, many of them do. Use the ones that apply to the pet you've chosen.

- Initial cost. Some pets can cost hundreds of dollars or more.
- Any fees for a license.
- Food. All pets have to eat.
- Veterinarian fees. Many pets require routine examinations and inoculations.
- Grooming fees. Some pets require regular or periodic grooming. If you do it yourself, at the least you'll need bathing and grooming implements and supplies; if you take the pet to a professional groomer, you'll need your wallet.
- Costs for beds, cages, travel boxes, litter boxes, etc.
- Costs for special items, such as:

  —feed and water bowls

  —collars, leashes, chains

  —brushes, combs

  —toys, scratching posts

  —flea collars or powders

- In the case of fish you'll need an aquarium, air pump, filter, carbon, heater, gravel, light, etc.
- For birds you'll need a cage, swing, and beak sharpener.
- For hamsters you'll need a cage and running wheel.
- For pets such as lizards, salamanders, frogs, or toads, you'll need a terrarium.

SHOPPING BY MAIL

Shopping by mail is big business. Mail-order shopping offers people the convenience of buying merchandise without having to leave their homes. Because the shopper is ordering items by number and description, it is essential that order forms be completed accurately. This project gives students some practice in ordering by mail.

GOAL: Working individually, students will imagine that they have $500 to spend, which they will use to buy items through the mail. After selecting merchandise from mail-order catalogs and salespapers, they will complete an order form and tally their total costs. *Suggested time*—1 to 2 class periods.

MATH SKILLS TO HIGHLIGHT:

1. Estimating costs
2. Completing an order form
3. Calculating total costs

SPECIAL MATERIALS/EQUIPMENT: Calculators; several mail-order catalogs and salespapers, which may be from different companies. You may even use advertising sections found near the back of many magazines. Such sections often offer wide choices in mail-order items.

DEVELOPMENT: To give students different merchandise from which to order, start collecting mail-order catalogs a few weeks prior to starting this project. Most people are bombarded with catalogs offering clothing, electronics, sporting goods, hobby equipment, specialty or novelty items, etc. You may ask your colleagues and students to bring in extra catalogs from home; however, be sure to request only catalogs that are mainstream and in good taste. Don't use any you feel are questionable. Using catalogs will help to make this project more realistic and give students experience in working with a real-life tool. (To ensure the privacy of people, remove any mailing labels from the catalogs before using them.)

- Begin this project by explaining that students will work individually. They will imagine that they have $500 to spend, which they will use to order merchandise by mail. They may not go over their limit.
- Distribute copies of Student Guide 55–1, and review it with your students.
- Distribute copies of Data Sheet 55–2, "Ordering Merchandise by Mail." Review the Sheet with your students.
- Hand out several catalogs and salespapers. (Ideally, try to have one catalog or salespaper for each student in your class.) Encourage students to share the materials so that they have an assortment of products from which to choose.
- Distribute copies of Worksheet 55–3, "Buying by Mail." Review it with your students, and note that all orders are to be written on the Worksheet. The Worksheet is generic enough so that it can be used with various catalogs, and students may combine orders from different ones. Tell your students to fill out as much information as possible about each item they wish to order. They should ignore any order forms in the catalogs. (You might go through the catalogs ahead of time and pull out order forms. This will help to reduce questions about them.) Be sure to have extra Worksheets available.
- Suggest that students keep an estimated tally of the costs of the items they are selecting on scrap paper. This will help them to avoid running over their amount.
- After they have chosen their merchandise, they should fill out the Worksheet and add up their total costs, including shipping and handling charges.

WRAP-UP: Conduct a class discussion about ordering merchandise by mail, focusing on advantages and disadvantages. Ask students to share any problems they encountered with this project as they made their selections and tallied their costs. You may also ask them to relate any personal experiences they have had with mail-order shopping.

EXTENSION: Suggest that students compare the prices of the items they would order through the mail with similar or identical products they could purchase in local stores. Which has the better price? Why might the prices be different? Why might people send away for merchandise they could buy locally?

Name _____   Project Due Date _____

SHOPPING BY MAIL

Situation/Problem:

Imagine that you have $500 to spend. You will look through various mail-order catalogs and select merchandise you would like to order. You will then complete an order form (Worksheet 55–3). You may not go over your limit.

Possible Strategies:

1. Think about some products you might like.

2. Look through several catalogs to find items you wish to buy.

3. As you choose items, estimate your costs by rounding off the price and keeping a running tally. This will help you to remain within your $500 limit.

Special Considerations:

- Ignore catalogs that hold little interest for you, and concentrate on those that contain merchandise you are interested in.

- Refer to Data Sheet 55–2 for information on how to complete order forms.

- Keep a running estimate of your costs on scrap paper. Don't enter any information about your merchandise on Worksheet 55–3 until you are sure what you would like to order.

- Complete as much information about each product as you can on Worksheet 55–3. Assume that you can place an order for any merchandise from any catalog on the Worksheet. You may combine orders from various catalogs and salespapers.

- Add up your total costs on the Worksheet. Include shipping and handling fees.

- Be prepared to discuss any advantages and disadvantages you see in ordering merchandise through the mail.

To Be Submitted:

Your completed worksheet

© 1996 by The Center for Applied Research in Education

Name _____

ORDERING MERCHANDISE BY MAIL

When filling out an order form to buy items through the mail, you must be as accurate as possible and provide all the required information.

BE SURE TO:

- Write your name and address clearly. If the address where the merchandise is to be shipped is different from your home address, make sure this is noted on the order form.

- Include a phone number (if the company requests it) where you can be reached if there is a question about your order.

- Include all the necessary information about the items you are ordering, such as:

   —item number

   —catalog page

   —description of the item

   —color

   —size

   —price for each item

- Double-check all information.

- Add the costs of the items. On most order forms this will be your subtotal. Now add any shipping or handling fees to find your total cost. Be sure your addition is correct.

Note: Most mail-order companies permit customers to phone, fax, or mail in orders. They accept payment by check or credit card.

Name _____

BUYING BY MAIL

Select merchandise from mail-order catalogs and complete the order form below. Remember, you may spend up to $500, including your shipping and handling charges.

Catalog Page	Item #	Description	Color	Size	Qty.	Price ea.	Total
					Subtotal		
					Shipping & Handling		
					Total		

SHIPPING AND HANDLING CHARGES:

Up to $100—$4.95

$100.01–$200.00—$8.95

Over $200.01—$10.95

NUMBERS AROUND TOWN

Most math courses emphasize using mathematics for calculations, measurement, and problem-solving. This is as it should be. However, in our technologically-based society, numbers are also used as indicators to show values, qualities, or conditions. While your students may be familiar with many of these special numbers, they may not fully understand them.

GOAL: Working in pairs or groups of 3, students will research and define various math indicators. Some examples include SPF (Sun Protection Factor), R-value (insulation), and ISBN (International Standard Book Number). *Suggested time*—2 class periods; a partial period to introduce the project, a period in the library for research, and a partial period to wrap it up. Some of the research will probably need to be done outside of class.

MATH SKILL TO HIGHLIGHT:

Understanding the use of numbers as indicators of specific factors

SPECIAL MATERIALS/EQUIPMENT: Dictionaries and general reference books.

DEVELOPMENT: Ask your students if they have ever used sunscreen. Of course, most have. Now ask them if some sunscreens provide more protection than others. How do they know? Someone will probably say that sunscreens come with numbers on their labels. Now ask what the numbers mean. Some students might know, although most will probably say simply that a sunscreen with a number "8" offers more protection than does one that has a number "4." The number on a container of sunscreen is a multiplier for how long a person can be exposed to the sun without burning. For example, if a person starts to burn after 15 minutes of exposure to the sun, that individual, by using a sunscreen lotion with an SPF of 8, can remain in the sun for two hours without fear of burning. (Multiply $1/4$ hour by 8, which equals 2.) Since everyone tans, or burns, at a different rate, the effectiveness of sunscreens varies among individuals.

- Begin this project by explaining to your students that numbers are used in many ways to indicate special qualities or specific factors about products or services. Working with a partner or in groups of 3, students will research some of the ways numbers are used as indicators.

- Hand out copies of Student Guide 56–1, and review it with your students. Note that the number factors they are to research are listed on Worksheet 56–2.

- Distribute copies of Worksheet 56–2, "Math and Indicators." Point out that it is likely students will know of some indicators that are not presented here. This is fine, because the list is by no means complete. Ask them to list any additional indicators on the back of the Worksheet. You may wish to offer a homework pass or similar prize to the student(s) who come(s) up with the most.

- Plan to spend a period in the library for students to get started on their research. Consult with the librarian in advance, and ask her or him to reserve books and magazines that students may use for research. Share the list of indicators on the Worksheet with the librarian so that she or he can locate books that students will find useful in their research. Since it's probable that students won't finish their research in one period, encourage them to continue researching during free periods and at home.

- Following is the answer key for Worksheet 56–2:

  1. *ISBN*—International Standard Book Number. Located near the bottom of the copyright page, the ISBN facilitates ordering by computer.

  2. *No. 2 pencil*—A measure of the hardness of the pencil's lead. The numbers vary from 1 to 4, with 4 being the hardest. A No. 2 pencil is required for use on standardized tests and other computer-scanned forms and documents.

  3. *Byte*—A unit of memory in a computer. It stores one character of text. A character may be a letter, space, or punctuation mark. A kilobyte equals 1,000 bytes, a megabyte equals one million bytes, and a gigabyte equals one billion bytes.

  4. *SPF*—Sun Protection Factor. A multiplier for the length of time a person can withstand exposure to the sun longer than he or she normally would. If you know about how long it would usually take for you to burn, multiply that time by the SPF number to find how long you could remain in the sun using the sunscreen.

  5. *UV*—Index of ultraviolet light. The numbers 1 to 10 (10 being greatest) indicate the amount of exposure to the ultraviolet rays of the sun. High exposure to UV rays have been linked to various disorders, most notably skin cancers. UV rays are the greatest on sunny, summer days.

  6. *Sunburn Index*—An index from 1 to 10 representing the amount of sunshine, which in turn affects sunburn. A sunburn index of 10 means near cloudless conditions with very bright sunshine.

  7. *R-value*—In insulation, a number that represents the insulating material's resistance to heat flow. The higher the R-value, the more effective the insulator.

  8. *Cord*—For firewood, a stack of wood that measures approximately $8 \times 4 \times 4$ feet or $8 \times 8 \times 2$ feet.

9. *Karat*—For gold, a ratio of gold to other metals. 100% gold is 24 karats. Example: A 14-karat gold necklace has 14 parts gold to 10 parts other metals. It is not pure gold.

10. *Carat*—For gemstones, a measure of weight. 1 carat equals $\frac{1}{142}$ of an ounce.

11. *Horsepower*—A unit of power based on the "standard" that a horse could raise a 3,300-pound weight attached to a pulley 10 feet in the air in one minute.

12. *UPC*—Universal Product Code. A series of bars of various widths and a 12-digit computer code found on products. The code can be read by scanners to make check-out lines at stores more efficient.

13. *Windchill Factor*—The temperature of still air that has the same effect on exposed human skin as a specific combination of wind speed and air temperature.

14. *Richter Scale*—A scale developed by Charles Richter that is used to express the amount of energy released at the focus of an earthquake. The scale, which ranges from 1 to 8, with 8 being the strongest, is logarithmic and based on factors of ten. Therefore, an earthquake measuring 2 on the Richter Scale is 10 times more powerful than an earthquake measuring 1. Likewise, a quake measuring 4 is 1,000 times stronger than a quake of 1; and a quake of 8 is 10,000,000 times more powerful than a quake measuring 1.

15. *20/20 Vision*—A measure of visual acuity. 20/20 vision means that a person with "normal" eyesight can read an eye chart when standing 20 feet away from it.

16. *Dow Jones Industrial Average*—The average cost per share of stock from 30 companies chosen by the Board of the New York Stock Exchange. The upward or downward movement of the "Dow Jones" is often a good indicator of general trends of the overall stock market.

17. *GNP*—Gross National Product. The GNP is the total market value of all goods and services produced by a nation during a specific period.

18. *Prime Rate*—The lowest rate of interest on loans offered by commercial banks.

19. *PIN*—Personal Identification Number. A security number chosen by an individual to electronically access bank accounts, automatic teller machines, and similar systems.

20. *Cholesterol Level*—A number that represents the milligrams of cholesterol found in a deciliter of blood. Generally, a cholesterol level over 200 is considered to be high.

WRAP-UP: Discuss the results with the class.

EXTENSION: Have students compile a list of other number indicators. Create a bulletin board of them.

Name _____   Project Due Date _____

NUMBERS AROUND TOWN

Situation/Problem:

You and your partner(s) are to examine the ways numbers are used as indicators. For example, the SPF number on a container of sunscreen indicates the product's effectiveness in preventing sunburn. But what, exactly, does the number on the label mean? Your task is to find out the meanings of the various indicators listed on Worksheet 56–2.

Possible Strategies:

1. Review Worksheet 56–2 and see which terms you know.
2. Divide the tasks of research. You and your partner(s) may check different sources for the indicators.
3. Use a variety of sources, including dictionaries and general reference books.

Special Considerations:

- Define, explain, or describe the indicators thoroughly.
- Be sure to verify your answers through reference sources.
- If the indicator provides a range, include the highest and lowest values.
- If the indicator is derived from a formula, include the formula.
- If the term is an acronym, write what it means.
- If you know of or find out about other indicators, list them and their meanings on the back of Worksheet 56–2.

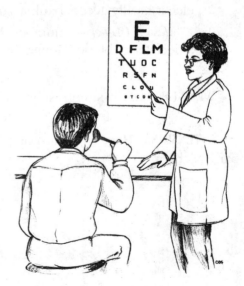

To Be Submitted:

Your sheet that contains the meanings of the math indicators

© 1996 by The Center for Applied Research in Education

(Worksheet 56–2)

Name _____

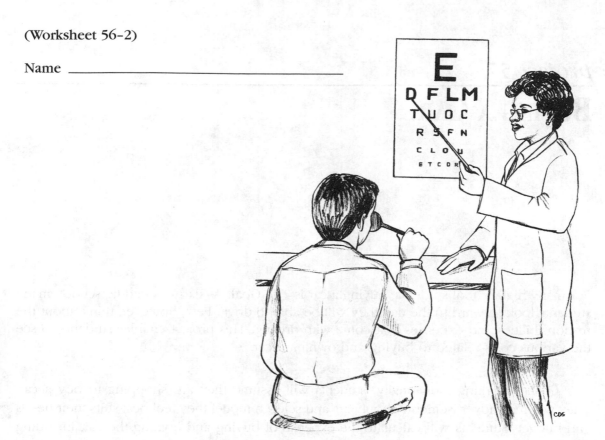

MATH AND INDICATORS

Consult reference sources to find the meanings of the indicators below. Write the meanings on a separate sheet of paper. Also, list any additional indicators you find or know about on the back of this sheet. Be sure you can verify your answers.

1. ISBN
2. No. 2 pencil
3. Byte
   Kilobyte
   Megabyte
   Gigabyte
4. SPF
5. UV
6. Sunburn Index
7. R-value
8. Cord (firewood)
9. Karat

10. Carat
11. Horsepower
12. UPC
13. Windchill Factor
14. Richter Scale
15. 20/20 Vision
16. Dow Jones Industrial Average
17. GNP
18. Prime Rate
19. PIN
20. Cholesterol Level

BUYING A CAR

For many high school students, buying a car is The Goal. As early as middle school, many students look forward to the day they will be able to drive. Few, however, think about the responsibilities and expenses that come with driving. This project enables students to see the various costs related to buying and owning a car.

GOAL: Working individually, students will assume they are shopping to buy a car. They will read advertisements about cars and select a model they feel best suits their needs and budget. Students will calculate the expense of buying and owning the car, including any finance, operating, and maintenance costs. At the end of the project, they will explain their selection and their anticipated costs during a class discussion. *Suggested time*—2 class periods, although students will likely spend time outside of class researching information about cars.

MATH SKILLS TO HIGHLIGHT:

1. Anticipating and estimating costs
2. Tallying various cost factors
3. Understanding the terms *financing, principal, annual percentage rate (APR), finance charge, down payment,* and *monthly payments*
4. Using a formula to find the finance charge on a loan
5. Making decisions based upon cost

SPECIAL MATERIALS/EQUIPMENT: Calculators; the classified and automotive sections of local newspapers. *Optional*—Articles comparing the values of specific cars in such publications as *Consumer Reports, Car and Driver,* and *Road and Track.*

DEVELOPMENT: Ask your students how many of them expect to own a car someday. If you teach high school, perhaps some of your students already do. Of those who don't, most will enthusiastically raise their hands. Now ask if they have ever thought about the overall costs associated with owning and operating a car. Most probably haven't. Aside from the obvious costs such as purchase price, gas, and maybe insurance, most students fail to anticipate the actual costs of car ownership.

- Begin the project by explaining that students will work alone and imagine that they are ready to buy a car. Knowing their financial status (or anticipating what their finances are likely to be), they are to select a car that fits their budget and their needs. A Porsche is out (for most students).

- Explain that students should look through the automotive and classified sections of local newspapers to find a car they realistically can afford. A few days before the project, ask students to bring in those parts of newspapers from home. If you also start collecting materials ahead of time, you should have plenty for the project.

- Publications such as *Consumer Reports, Car and Driver,* and *Road and Track* often contain articles about cars. Students may wish to consult these and similar resources to find information about the cars they are considering. If such publications are not available in your school library, your local library may have them. On-line computer services also usually provide access to such references. If your students utilize on-line services at home, remind them of the costs for time.

- Distribute copies of Student Guide 57–1, and review it with your students. Especially review the steps necessary for finding the approximate finance charge and monthly payments for car loans. You may need to provide your students with some examples.

- Discuss the terms "financing," "principal," "annual percentage rate," "finance charge," "down payment," and "monthly payments."

- Hand out copies of Data Sheet 57–2, "Car Costs." Review it with your students, and point out that the costs listed on the Sheet are estimates and will vary around the country. Students may use the costs on the Data Sheet for this project. If students own cars and are familiar with "real" costs, they should use the actual expenses.

- Hand out copies of Worksheet 57–3, "A Car Buyer's Cost Sheet." Explain that students are to list and tally all of their expenses on the Worksheet.

- Remind students to be prepared to discuss their selection and anticipated costs upon completion of the project.

WRAP-UP: Conduct a class discussion in which students share the information they compiled on their Worksheets.

EXTENSION: Suggest that students compare leasing a car to buying one. What are the advantages of each method? What are the disadvantages? Provide class time for students to discuss their findings.

Name _____   Project Due Date _____

BUYING A CAR

Situation/Problem:

You are to imagine that you are shopping for a car. You are trying to buy a car that meets your needs, but also satisfies your financial status. In selecting your car, you are to calculate your overall anticipated expenses, including the purchase price, finance charge (if any), and operating and maintenance costs. Upon completion of this project, be prepared to explain your choice to the class.

Possible Strategies:

1. Consider the type of car you'd like.
2. Consider your financial condition. Be realistic. Choose a car you feel you can afford.
3. Consult various automotive and classified advertisements in trying to find a car that will satisfy your needs and remain within your budget.

Special Considerations:

- Are you interested in a new or used car? New cars cost more.

- Will you pay cash for your car? Or will you need to obtain a loan? Financing your car (taking a loan) allows you to put down less cash, but you will need to make monthly payments that include interest. Interest will increase the cost you pay for the car. Although banks use sophisticated software to calculate finance charges, you can find the *approximate* finance charge and monthly payments you'd have for a loan by using the following formula:

$$\text{Finance Charge} = \frac{A(N+1)(APR)}{2P}$$

> A = amount of money borrowed (principal)
>
> N = total number of payments
>
> APR = annual percentage rate (interest; for this project use an APR of 9%)
>
> P = number of payments per year

After you find the approximate finance charge, add it to the amount of your loan. This is how much money you will need to pay back. Now divide this total by the number of payments. This answer equals the amount of your monthly payments. To find the amount of your total payments for each year of the loan, simply multiply your monthly payments by 12. (A loan for one year will have 12 payments. A two-year loan has 24, a three-year loan has 36, and a four-year loan has 48. The longer you take a loan, the lower your monthly payments. However, your finance charge will be greater.)

- Carefully review the information and costs on Data Sheet 57–2. Use this information for calculating your operating and maintenance expenses.

- Use Worksheet 57–3 to list and total your costs. Remember to find the yearly cost of operating and maintaining your car.

- Be prepared to discuss your choice of car and anticipated costs with your class after the project is finished.

To Be Submitted:

Your worksheet

(Data Sheet 57–2)

Name _____

CAR COSTS

Following are common expenses in operating and maintaining a car. Include the ones that apply to your car on Worksheet 57–3. Note that the costs are estimates and will vary for different parts of the country.

- Insurance (for a new driver):

    —Small car, $1,800 per year

    —Mid-sized car, $2,200 per year

    —Sports car, $2,800 per year

- Fees for license and registration, $75.

- Gasoline. (Use $1.40 per gal. for estimating your fuel costs.) To find your estimated cost for gas for the year, do the following:

    1. Estimate the total number of miles you expect to drive for the year. You can estimate each week's total miles and multiply by 52.

    2. Divide the total number of miles by the car's rated MPG (miles per gallon). If you don't know the MPG of your car, use these estimates: small car, 35 MPG; mid-sized car, 25 MPG; sports car, 22 MPG.

    3. Multiply this answer by the cost of gasoline.

- Costs for tune-ups and maintenance:

    —Small car, $250 per year

    —Mid-sized car, $450 per year

    —Sports car, $650 per year

- Include any additional costs, such as car phone, stereo, tape player, special seat covers, etc.

Name _____

A CAR BUYER'S COST SHEET

List all of the expenses you expect in purchasing, operating, and maintaining the car of your choice. Operating and maintenance costs should be totaled for the year.

Model and Year of Car _____

Purchase Price _____

OPERATING AND MAINTENANCE COSTS

Description of Expense	Cost
Total Yearly Cost	

WHAT'S ON THE TEST?

Teachers always give students tests. For a twist, this project gives students the chance to give each other tests that they themselves write. Allowing students to write a test that they feel underscores the concepts and skills in a unit is an excellent reinforcement activity.

GOAL: Working in groups of 4 or 5, students will write a test on the current unit of study. They must also provide an answer key and point distribution. *Suggested time*—2 class periods.

MATH SKILLS TO HIGHLIGHT:

Specific skills will vary depending on the unit of study and the skills students select

SPECIAL MATERIALS/EQUIPMENT: Will vary, depending on unit of study. *Optional—* Word processors, computers, and printers for use in writing the tests.

DEVELOPMENT: As you near the end of a unit and announce the upcoming test, ask your students to identify the important concepts and skills they have learned. They should list them individually. Let students keep their lists, and suggest that they add any additional ideas as they think of them. They will refer to their lists for the project.

- Begin the project by explaining that students will work in groups to write a test for the current unit of study. They will also be required to provide a key. Upon completion of the project, you will review the tests and select two that you will administer to the class. You will need two tests so that the groups whose tests you select do not receive their own. Be sure not to divulge whose tests you are using so that students are not tempted to share answers in advance. Emphasize that you reserve the right to add or delete material; however, assure students that the two tests you judge most appropriate will be given to the class.

- Distribute copies of Student Guide 58–1, and review it with your students. Emphasize that each group should divide the tasks and that all members should contribute to the test.

- Point out that the tests must assess all of the concepts and skills covered in the unit, preferably by a variety of questions.

- Note that the groups should include a point distribution for their tests. You may need to explain how students may decide on the value of each question or problem.

- Hand out copies of Data Sheet 58–2, "Elements of a Good Math Test," and review it with your students. The Sheet offers information that will help students design effective tests.

- If students have access to computers, printers, or word processors, encourage them to use the equipment to write their tests. If their software doesn't support writing formulas or numbers (for example, fractions), suggest that they simply write those problems with black pen or a heavy pencil. Of course, students may prefer to write the entire test in that manner. Caution them to write neatly.

- Emphasize the importance of accuracy. Answer keys must be correct.

- Set a deadline for completion of the groups' tests at least two days prior to the testing date. That will give you time to review the tests, make any adjustments (if any are needed in your opinion), and make copies for the class.

- After you collect the tests, be sure to review them carefully and check the answer keys, especially for the two you are planning to use.

WRAP-UP: Students will take the tests created by their classmates.

EXTENSIONS: On the day after the test, ask your students to write their thoughts and comments about the tests they took. Collect the papers and share them with the groups of students who wrote the tests.

Name _____   Project Due Date _____

© 1996 by The Center for Applied Research in Education

WHAT'S ON THE TEST?

Situation/Problem:

Your group will write a test for the unit your class is currently studying. You will focus the questions on the key concepts and skills presented in the unit, and include an answer key and point value for each problem. Upon completion of the project, your teacher will select what he or she feels are the two best tests and administer them to the class. (Two tests will be given so that the groups who designed the tests will not take their own.) Your teacher reserves the right to add or delete material if he or she feels it is necessary.

Possible Strategies:

1. Each member of the group should write a list of what he or she feels are the important concepts and skills covered in the unit. Compare the lists and identify those that all of you feel are the most important.

2. Discuss how to organize the test. What types of problems should it have? How many parts? How long should it be?

3. Divide the tasks of creating the test among group members. Perhaps each member may assume responsibility for a portion of the test.

Special Considerations:

- Think of the various types of problems you've worked on in your study of this unit. The test should reflect those problems and the concepts and skills they contain.

- Think about the math tests you've had in the past. Use them as a guide for designing this test.

- Consult Data Sheet 58–2 for suggestions on creating a test.

- Be sure any directions you provide on your test are clear.

- Leave enough space on the test for students to work out problems.

- Estimate the time students will need to complete the test. Your test shouldn't be so long that students will have trouble finishing it during class. Neither should it be so short that they will complete it in a few minutes.

- Avoid trying to create extremely difficult problems just to "stump" other students. Likewise, avoid making the test too easy. Try sample problems on some of the members of your group.

- If you have access to computers or word processors, you may decide to write your test on the equipment. If your software doesn't allow you to write math symbols or number problems, simply leave a space on the page and write the problem or symbol in with a dark pen. If you wish, you may write your entire test in longhand.

- Remember to include an answer key, and a point distribution.

To Be Submitted:

A copy of your test and answer key

Name _____

© 1996 by The Center for Applied Research in Education

ELEMENTS OF A GOOD MATH TEST

The best tests are those that focus on the important skills and concepts of a unit. Following are suggestions on how to create an effective math test:

- A test should assess what has been taught.

- A test should have different kinds of questions, including:

  —True or false

  —Multiple choice

  —Short answer such as a number, estimate, or term

  —Finding solutions to various kinds of problems

  —Open-ended questions or problems that students must explain, or write a brief description of how they would solve

- A test should provide students with problems that require them to choose one or more of several strategies for finding a solution, including:

  —Guessing and checking

  —Making a table

  —Looking for a pattern

  —Making a list

  —Making a simpler problem

  —Working backward

  —Drawing a diagram

  —Writing an equation

- A test should allow for the use of calculators and such items as rulers, protractors, compasses, etc., depending on the unit of study.

- A test may contain an optional bonus or extra-credit problem that relates to the content but is challenging to most students.

CHECKS AND BALANCES

The importance of keeping a balanced checking account can't be understated. Overdrawn accounts may result in a bad credit rating. For this project, students will have the chance to write checks and maintain a running balance.

GOAL: Working individually, students will be provided with practice checks, a check register, and deposit forms. They will be given a list of expenses and deposits, and will be required to maintain a running balance. *Suggested time—*2 class periods.

MATH SKILLS TO HIGHLIGHT:

1. Tallying costs
2. Maintaining a checkbook balance
3. Understanding debits and credits

SPECIAL MATERIALS/EQUIPMENT: Calculators.

DEVELOPMENT: Discuss the purpose of checking accounts with your class, and explain how they work. You may also wish to note the consequences of not maintaining an accurate checking account.

- Begin the project by telling your students that they will receive materials for a practice checking account, and will work individually to maintain a balance for their account. Emphasize the importance of not spending more money than their account contains; if they do, their checks will "bounce."

- Distribute copies of Student Guide 59–1, and review it with your students. Be certain that students understand what they are to do.

- Hand out copies of Data Sheet 59–2, "Keeping a Balanced Checking Account." Note that the Sheet offers specific steps for writing checks, completing deposit forms, and maintaining a check register. Depending on your class, you may wish to offer some examples before letting students begin the project.

- Hand out copies of Data Sheet 59–3, "Debits and Credits." This Sheet contains various expenses and deposits that students are to use in maintaining their checking accounts. Emphasize that of the various debits, students are to pick six for which they will write checks. They will also need to fill out two deposit forms.

- Distribute two copies of Worksheet 59–4, "Practice Checks," to each student. Since each sheet contains three checks, each student will then have a total of six checks. Instruct your students to number the checks consecutively from 101 to 106, and write their names at the upper left-hand corner of each check. They will use the checks to pay for the expenses contained on Data Sheet 59–3.

- Distribute copies of Worksheet 59–5, "A Check Register and Deposit Forms." Explain that the register is the place an individual keeps a record of the checks he or she writes and the deposits he or she makes to the account.

- If you'd like to expand the project, simply provide students with more copies of Worksheets 59–4 and 59–5. Students may obtain additional "items to buy" from local newspaper advertisements.

WRAP-UP: Have students exchange their Worksheets with a partner who, using a calculator, checks their account, making sure that it is balanced correctly. Collect the Worksheets, and discuss students' impressions of maintaining a checking account. What did they find hard? What did they find relatively easy?

EXTENSION: Invite a representative of a bank to discuss checking accounts, as well as some of the other types of accounts banks offer.

(Student Guide 59-1)

Name _____   Project Due Date _____

CHECKS AND BALANCES

Problem/Situation:

You are to maintain a practice checking account. You will write checks, complete deposit forms, and keep a check register. Upon completion of the project, you will exchange your materials with a partner and will check each other's math. Be prepared to share your thoughts about checking accounts with the class during a discussion.

Possible Strategies:

1. Review Data Sheet 59-3 and pick six items for which you will write checks. Note that your account has a prior balance of $300.

2. As you write your checks, record and subtract the amount of each from your balance in your check register (Worksheet 59-5). This will reduce the chances that you will overdraw your account.

3. As you complete deposit forms, remember to add the sum to your register.

Special Considerations:

- Consult Data Sheet 59-2 to learn how to write checks, fill out deposit forms, and maintain a check register. Be accurate with your math.

- When you receive your practice checks (Worksheet 59-4) and register and deposit forms (Worksheet 59-5), write your name where necessary. Number your checks 101 through 106.

- Remember that checks are subtracted from your balance. These are called *debits*. Deposits are added, and are called *credits*.

To Be Submitted:

Your completed Worksheets

© 1996 by The Center for Applied Research in Education

Name _____

KEEPING A BALANCED CHECKING ACCOUNT

HOW TO WRITE A CHECK:

- Use a pen and write clearly. Don't cross out or change anything on the check.
- Write the date (the day the check is written).
- Write the payee's name (the person to whom the check is written) after "Pay to the order of."
- Write the value of the check next to the dollar sign. Use a decimal point for writing change (for example, $29.99).
- On the line below the payee's name, write the amount of the check in words. Start at the left, at the beginning of the line. Begin with a capital letter and write out the dollar value, then show any change by using the word "and," and the value over 100 (for example, Twenty-nine and $^{99}/_{100}$). If any space to the right remains, draw a line from the words or numbers to the word "dollars" at the extreme right.
- The memo is optional. You may write what the check is for here.
- Sign the check.

HOW TO COMPLETE A CHECK REGISTER:

- Write the check number.
- Write the date of the check.
- Write to whom the check was written.
- Write the purpose of the check.
- Write the amount of the check. Subtract the amount of the check from the balance in your account.
- When recording a deposit, write the date and the amount of the deposit and add it to the balance in your account.

HOW TO FILL OUT A DEPOSIT FORM:

- Write the date.
- Put the amount of money in currency, coins, or checks.
- Write the total.

© 1996 by The Center for Applied Research in Education

Name _____

DEBITS AND CREDITS

Select six debits from the following list and write checks for them. The company, organization, or person to whom you are to write the check is in parentheses. The list is arranged by date, and you must choose the items in order. Also note that some deposits are included for which you must fill out deposit slips. Be sure to maintain a balanced checking account.

* YOU HAVE A PRIOR BALANCE IN YOUR ACCOUNT OF $300.00

April 3.   You buy a new camera, $69.95. (Flash Camera Shop)

April 6.   You buy a new pair of sneakers, $79.95. (High Five Sports)

April 10.   You receive $20 for helping your neighbor clean out his garage. You make a deposit.

April 17.   You pay $48 to have your bike repaired. (Tom's Bike Shop)

April 21.   You buy new in-line skates, $89.99. (The Skate Place)

April 28.   You decide to put the money you have been hoarding from your paper route into your checking account. You make a deposit of $120.

May 2.   Out of cash, you write yourself a check for $40.

May 8.   You pay your mother the $25 you borrowed.

May 16.   You buy your best friend a birthday gift, $29.89. (Highway Gift Shop)

May 20.   You purchase your favorite group's new CD for $19.95. (Great Sound Music Store)

May 28.   Your money for the upcoming class trip is due. You must pay $18. (Your School)

Name _____

PRACTICE CHECKS

_____ 19 _____

PAY TO THE
ORDER OF _____ $ _____

_____ DOLLARS

South River Office
South River, NJ 08882

FOR _____   _____

_____ 19 _____

PAY TO THE
ORDER OF _____ $ _____

_____ DOLLARS

South River Office
South River, NJ 08882

FOR _____   _____

_____ 19 _____

PAY TO THE
ORDER OF _____ $ _____

_____ DOLLARS

South River Office
South River, NJ 08882

FOR _____   _____

Name _____

A CHECK REGISTER AND DEPOSIT FORMS

Check Number	Date	Description of Transaction	Payment Debit	✔	Deposit/ Credit	Balance

DATE _____ 19 ____	DOLLARS	CENTS
CURRENCY		
COIN		
CHECKS List Each Separately 1		
2		
3		
4		
5		
6		
7		
8		
9		
10		
Total		

DATE _____ 19 ____	DOLLARS	CENTS
CURRENCY		
COIN		
CHECKS List Each Separately 1		
2		
3		
4		
5		
6		
7		
8		
9		
10		
Total		

MATH IN MY LIFE—AN ASSESSMENT

At the end of the year, math students who have worked on a variety of projects to supplement their regular curriculums frequently grow in their understanding of and attitudes toward mathematics. They come to see math as not simply a subject taught in school, but as a significant factor in their lives. Because this project assumes that students have had experience working on math projects, it is best assigned near the end of the year.

GOAL: Working individually, students will reflect upon their attitudes and feelings about math, in particular on the class of which they were a part this year. Students will have the opportunity to create a symbol, design, illustration, or model that represents how their ideas about math have changed or grown. *Suggested time*—2 class periods over the course of a week.

MATH SKILLS TO HIGHLIGHT:

Skills will vary depending upon the students' individual responses to the project

SPECIAL MATERIALS/EQUIPMENT: Will vary depending upon the students' needs; however; rulers; scissors; felt-tipped pens; markers; colored pencils; graph paper; poster paper; and similar products should be made available.

DEVELOPMENT: Reflect with your students on some of the projects or mathematical highlights you have shared during the year. You might also briefly review some of the topics you have studied. This will help to focus students' thoughts on the past year.

- Begin the project by telling students they will work individually to assess their attitudes and feelings about math, and especially how they might have changed during this year. Making periodic assessments of one's progress in a specific subject is a good way to keep track of growth. It helps to uncover how much progress has been made and enables a person to adjust his or her goals.

- Distribute copies of Student Guide 60–1, and review it with your students. Note that the Guide offers questions and suggestions that may help students in their self-assessment.

- Encourage students to think of a symbol, design, illustration, model, or some other way—perhaps a poem or song—that will represent how they feel about mathematics, and especially how they have grown in their appreciation and understanding of math. While they may use the materials you can provide in class, suggest that they also use materials they have at home.

- Give students time in class to begin. You may wish to let them brainstorm with friends, but insist that they work alone on their assessments. Depending on their representations, some students may also work at home.

WRAP-UP: Students show and explain their creations to the class. Display their work.

EXTENSION: Conduct a class discussion on the ways students can get the most out of a math class. You'll find that most kids have some good ideas and helpful suggestions.

Name _____   Project Due Date _____

MATH IN MY LIFE—AN ASSESSMENT

Situation/Problem:

You have worked on various topics and math projects this year. Certainly you have grown in your skills and understanding of math. Perhaps your perceptions, impressions, and attitudes about math have also changed. For this project, you are to examine your feelings about math and create a symbol, design, illustration, or model that represents them.

Possible Strategies:

1. Think about this past year in math. On a sheet of paper, list some of the highlights and disappointments.
2. Consider if your attitudes about math have changed. Write your feelings.
3. Think about a way you can represent your feelings.

Special Considerations:

- To get in touch with your thoughts and feelings, ask yourself questions like the following:

    —How relevant is math in my life?

    —What new skills did I learn in math this year?

    —What gave me the most trouble?

    —What would I like to learn more about in math?

    —What kinds of real-life situations can math help me in?

    —What project did I enjoy the most this year?

    —What math skills are my strongest?

    —What will I probably remember most about this year in math?

    —How important would I rate math in my life? Very? Average? A little?

- Be creative in selecting a method to represent your feelings. You may use a symbol of some sort, an illustration, a model, drawing, etc. Perhaps you might like to write a song. Whatever you choose, it should show the importance of math in your life.

- At the end of the project, be ready to show your work and explain your feelings.

To Be Submitted:

Your work